ENDORSEMENTS

"A beautifully written memoir, *Four Before Their Time* illustrates the deep and complex relationship between medical fact and personal faith. We find ourselves wondering what we would do as we witness a gut-wrenching roller coaster of survival and love in a remarkable family."

— MARLA J GOLD, MD
DEAN EMERITA & PROFESSOR OF HEALTH MANAGEMENT AND POLICY
DREXEL UNIVERSITY SCHOOL OF PUBLIC HEALTH

"Tim Spillane's memoir, *Four Before Their Time* is a poignant account of his experience as the grandfather of extremely premature quadruplets, and of how these vulnerable babies manage to survive and thrive against all odds. At times shocking — at one point the family prepares to lose Wyatt, the most fragile of the babies — but always uplifting, Tim's story, by showing the power of family love and faith, can comfort not only readers who have personally experienced the rollercoaster of prematurity, but everyone who's going through a crisis or wondering "why me." It is also a testimony to the sacrifices military families make when duty calls. Anne Spillane, the quadruplets' mother, is also an Army physician. She is deployed to Afghanistan when her four toddlers are still facing considerable challenges. And yet, thanks to grandparents and aunts ready to put their own lives on hold to help, the four children get all the love and attention they need to conquer one obstacle after another, and make life triumph."

— EMMA TRENTI PAROLI, CO-AUTHOR OF *PREEMIES: THE ESSENTIAL GUIDE FOR PARENTS OF PREMATURE BABIES*, SECOND EDITION 2010

"Set against the medical backdrop of the neonatal intensive care unit (NICU), Tim Spillane has shared a powerful and moving story that captures the experience of many families who have had a baby in the NICU. As a father, grandfather and husband, Tim offers a unique window into his family's emotional journey while they supported his daughter's quads — Timmy, Edda, Lily and Wyatt. Relevant for medical professionals and families alike, I believe everyone can relate to this remarkable book."

— CHAVIS A. PATTERSON, PhD
DIRECTOR OF PSYCHOSOCIAL SERVICES, DIVISION OF NEONATOLOGY
THE CHILDREN'S HOSPITAL OF PHILADELPHIA

"*Four Before Their Time* is an amazing and inspiring story... one that brings out the power of faith — the kind of faith that helps us remain hopeful in time of desperation. I had practiced obstetrics for more than 15 years when my daughter was born at 28 weeks weighing less than 2 pounds. Thrown unexpectedly into the world of micro-preemies, my professional logic was overpowered by a mother's emotions and fears. Faith and prayers kept me going. Tim Spillane is a wonderful storyteller and his memoir brings a message of hope, resilience and miracles that I know will lift the faith of many others."

— VINEETA GUPTA, MD, JD, LL.M
GLOBAL ADVOCATE FOR MATERNAL NEWBORN AND CHILD HEALTH

Four Before Their Time

A STORY
OF HOPE,
RESILIENCE
AND
MIRACLES

TIMOTHY SPILLANE

Four Before Their Time: A Story of Hope, Resilience and Miracles.

On the Cover: Edda Grace wearing Daddy's wedding band. Photographer Wendy Staat captured this magical moment and a whole host of other wonderful pictures in the Wilford Hall NICU when the babies were not quite eight weeks old.

Author's Note: This is a true story. It is also a work of memory and thus subject to my own biases, my flawed recollection of some events and the outright omission of others. I have tried to be as accurate as possible, but factual errors doubtless exist. While I was careful in my research, any mistakes in the medical details or the explanations thereof are mine alone. Though the names of some characters have been changed to protect their identities, all are real people.

For information about this title or to order other books and/or electronic media, contact the publisher: SkitterBird, LLC. Information available at www.4b4theirtime.com

ISBN: 978-0-9903523-0-3

Printed in the United States of America
Cover and Interior design: 1106 Design

DEDICATION

In loving memory of my parents, Rita and David Spillane.
You filled my life with hope. You taught me to be resilient.
Your love made believing in miracles possible.

CONTENTS

San Antonio, Texas
Spring 2012

I believe in the power of storytelling. Storytelling is not trivial at all. It is how we make sense of our lives.

Mark Bowden, author, teacher, parent

Lᴛ᧐ᴛᴛʟᴇ ʀᴇᴍᴀɪɴᴇᴅ ᴛᴏ ʀᴇᴍɪɴᴅ ᴍᴇ of the hours I'd spent pacing the long corridor. The whole floor felt nearly haunted, as if the life and warmth had been sucked out of the place and only emptiness was left. The walls were bare now, save for the myriad holes left behind in the dull white sheetrock. An array of framed pictures and plaques once hung here, their arrangement lending color to the dimly lit space, but no more. Now the hallway was mostly dark. The soft glow of the occasional wall sconce did little to dispel the shadows. At the far end, 100 feet from where I stood, a set of double doors were barely visible. Eyeing them, I slid my hands into my front pockets and moved slowly forward. God knew I'd walked the length of the hall enough times. I could probably do it with my eyes closed. I wanted to remember as much as I could. I wanted to make sense of what had happened here. It had been a remarkable time, filled with such joy and so much angst. Something felt different now, though: there was none of the familiar anxiety. Instead, a cold barrenness pervaded.

To the right, doors led to offices, small conference rooms, and storage spaces. I peered briefly through one door. I knew the room well. But the Family Waiting Area was deserted now, the shade drawn, the furniture gone except for a small table with a telephone on it, the receiver off the hook and lying on the floor. To my left, the long wall where the pictures and plaques once hung was interrupted by an opening leading to a second hallway and another set of double doors. I turned toward them. A narrow vertical band of opaque glass in each let light out but did nothing to reveal what lay beyond. A red sign affixed to one door read "Surgical Delivery Rooms." A larger yellow sign on the adjacent door sternly instructed *"STOP — Proper operating room attire required beyond this point. NO Food or Drink. NO Thoroughfare."*

I wrapped my hands around the handles and pulled. I don't know what I expected as I drew the large doors open, but I wasn't prepared for the raw power of the memories that flooded my mind upon seeing the empty suite. Fear gripped me and I felt my face flush, my throat tightening and my eyes fill with tears. In this space, almost exactly two years before, an inconceivable story had begun that would change my life forever. I took a deep breath and slowly let it go. This was also the place where everything could have come to an even more unimaginable end.

Inside the suite were two operating rooms, the wide double doors of each ajar. In front of me, adjacent stainless steel wash sinks were mounted against a wall, and in a crumpled pile beneath them lay a discarded set of surgical scrubs. Still charged with the memories of what had happened here, I crouched down, lifted the two-pocket V-neck scrub top and spread it in the air. It was large enough to fit a man of roughly my size. Imprinted in black ink on one pocket was the inscription: U.S. Government Property — SAMMC. The acronym I knew; it stood for San Antonio Military Medical Center. This was Wilford Hall — the joint military medical command's hospital on the base where my daughter Anne was stationed. I folded the garment against my lap, put it under one arm, straightened up and took a couple steps forward until I stood between the opposing sets of double doors marked Delivery Room #1 and Delivery Room #2. Both were in disarray. Large surgical lights hung from overhead in each of the ORs; apart from them little else indicated that these rooms had once been used for emergency deliveries. Chairs were overturned and covered with blankets the movers had left behind. Most of the drawers and doors of the cabinets and shelving units had been left hanging open. The floors were littered with upended waste baskets, laundry hampers, soda cans and more discarded scrubs. I turned my head from one OR to the other, carefully studying them both, but decided not to enter either.

I knew my daughter had been rushed into one of these rooms for an emergency Caesarean section. In there, her four babies had been cut from her. We had expected them to be born early, but we never thought things would unfold as they had. The babies had been delivered almost four months premature.

Beyond the ORs, a short hall led to another set of double doors with wide panes of clear glass. Through those doors was the hospital's Level III neonatal intensive care unit (NICU). I could see into the large room where Anne's tiny babies had spent their first difficult days and then the weeks and months of the seemingly interminable struggle to survive.

I stepped into the empty room but stopped to look outside. Shades were drawn down on all the windows save one adjacent to the doors. I could see the retail strip shouldering the highway north of the hospital, a sprinkling of commercial buildings and a vast stretch of subdivisions. Beyond them the horizon disappeared into the hazy sunlight of the south central Texas spring. Standing there, I could still feel the visceral stab of both my hope and need, the deep longing for something that two years ago I was never truly sure I would ever have. It was the not-knowing that had been so hard then. I would stand staring through the bank of windows that lined the NICU's north wall, out into a world that my grandchildren might never have the chance to know. And I'd wonder and pray. Often, it was all I could do not to break down and cry. Sometimes I did.

The shadowy, deserted NICU belied any suggestion of how vigorously life itself had once been defended here. Just as it had been in the OR suites and the long corridor outside it, there was little left now to suggest much of anything had ever happened in this place. I supposed the movers had taken most of the equipment. Whatever remained had been upended or left in an abandoned heap on the floor. Wilford Hall was now designated as an ambulatory care center; much of the bustling activity that had formerly filled the hospital was gone. All its trauma wards, the intensive care units and long-term patient care facilities had been transferred across town to the Brooke Army Medical Center. Even the Dermatology Clinic — where Anne still worked three floors below — was slated to be relocated to BAMC. Rumor had it that in another year the grand old hospital that had served the Air Force and later the joint medical needs of the combined military for more than 50 years would be demolished. The finality of that struck me in an odd sort of way. In the desolate room, I sensed that with all that had happened here in the past, some part of those experiences would linger indefinitely. My own memories were still vivid, almost palpable. Even if they demolished Wilford Hall, something here would always live within me.

Thinking photos would make an interesting keepsake one day I pulled a camera from my shirt pocket and began taking pictures of the NICU. I took a shot of the large dry-erase board that hung between the physicians' room and the blood lab. It had once charted patient progress with daily updates, but most of the board had been wiped clean long ago. Only some doctors' names and pager numbers remained. I recognized Astor and Wyeth, Corcoran and Reilly. Each had been involved in the care of Anne's babies.

I turned to snap a picture of the cabinets that were installed in a long line beneath the bank of windows and zoomed in on the numerous electrical outlets and ports that ran the whole length of the same wall. The repeating loop of connections — a grouping of electrical outlets that had powered the life-giving pumps, monitors and other machines paired with ports for medical air, oxygen and vacuum — still laid out the basic parameters of where each of the unit's high-tech isolettes had been set. But with the incubators gone, the room was now mostly empty space. I walked slowly through it, stopping to pick up an officer's patrol cap with dual black captain's bars embroidered onto the camouflaged fabric above its brim. My daughter was a captain. Maybe she could use a spare cover, I thought, and stuck it under my arm with the discarded scrub top I was still carrying.

On a counter cluttered with papers I found a folder. Inside were a number of trifold brochures describing services available to moms in the military, one about breastfeeding and a "Homeward Bound" checklist to help with discharge planning. It must have inadvertently been brought to the NICU from the Labor & Delivery ward on the other end of the hospital's fifth floor. I snickered as I read the opening line on the checklist: "Discharge planning begins at admission. Mother and infant are usually discharged when the infant is 44–48 hours of age." That could hardly apply to any mom whose baby was in the NICU, certainly not in Anne's situation. Another sentence described the birth experience as "one of the most exciting events in your life and a moment that you will cherish and remember always."

I pushed the papers neatly together and fit them back in the folder. I slid the packet under my arm with the captain's hat and the scrubs, telling myself that I would show the postpartum guide to Anne when I met her for lunch later that morning. She would laugh at my having found it in the NICU, and we would joke together about the notion of pregnancy and delivery being a time of unbridled joy. It *was* for most; it just hadn't worked out that way for Anne. Now two years removed from her own child-birth experience, she'd learned that laughter was good medicine. But she also knew that some hurts went much deeper, that some pain was so heavy no amount of lightheartedness could lift it away. Her NICU experience was a gut wrenching, turn-you-inside-out time. She recognized, too, that for some parents, the crucible was even worse.

I took one more memento with me from Wilford Hall that day. I found it next to a door leading into the NICU. It was a bereave-ment card — called a door card, it was a subtle way to alert anyone entering the unit that a death had recently occurred. Hardly larger than a postcard, the front showed a picture of a single leaf afloat in a reflecting image of water and sky. A drop of rain the size of a tear rested on the lone leaf. On the back of the card, there was a poem. Its last stanza read,

> *Just as winter awakens to spring,*
> *Our deepest sorrow harbors the*
> *Seed of hope renewed.*
> *Hope renewed.*

Whether to share something so poignant with Anne was hard for me to decide even after all this time. I didn't want to make her sad. Perhaps catharsis wasn't always necessary. I pressed the card into my back pocket, where I figured I'd probably forget about it, and gathered together my collection of things. I put my camera away and looked around one last time. I did not expect I would ever see the place again.

"Sir?"

The voice startled me. I turned to look back across the long expanse of the NICU floor toward the doors leading from the OR suite but there was no one there.

"Sir?" the voice called out again. "Where are you, sir?"

"Over here by the —" But before I could finish a man appeared from behind a row of tall cabinets. He wore a pressed white shirt and an ID tag hung from a loop around his neck. He had a small, kindly face, dark skin and a black mustache.

He asked how I was doing and then pointed to the camera in my hand. "The pictures you've been taking — will you do me a favor?"

Here it comes, I thought. He was probably part of the hospital's security detail. He would want to know what I was doing on a deserted floor taking pictures. Maybe he would want to see them; he'd probably ask me to delete them all and take no more.

"When you download them — if you see something out of the ordinary — send them to me in an email, would you, please?"

I looked at the man perplexed.

He smiled knowingly, taking a step closer to me. "I mean if you see something abnormal, something that we can't see right now — send that to me. There have been reports of things happening up here."

"Things?" I didn't know if this was some kind of joke or what.

He nodded, raised his hand and pulled it slowly across his chin. "On a couple of occasions, at least." He pointed to the rooms of the adjacent Level II NICU. "When the movers were here they saw a chair roll slowly across the floor in that room. Didn't pay much mind to it until it rolled back the other way all by itself."

I looked over my shoulder to the open door that led to the Level II unit. It was still filled with chairs and piles of moving blankets.

"The movers haven't come back since," he explained. "Another time we had our electricians up here. Doors and drawers started opening and closing for no reason. Things like that. And *those* guys work for me."

"Okay," I said, not sure what else to say.

He handed me his business card. He worked for the hospital's Medical Systems and Communications. He was a systems analyst and project manager. Not exactly the credentials of a loon, I thought.

"You're talking about — something like ghosts?" I asked not quite believing that we were having this conversation.

"Do you know what this place was?"

I told him I did.

"There are some things we just don't know," he said looking around the room as if he might see something that he hadn't seen before.

"My daughter delivered her babies over there," I told him.

He turned to look toward the surgical delivery rooms and then back at me, fixing his eyes on mine. "Everything turn out okay?"

"More right than wrong, I guess," I said and left it at that.

He nodded once more and asked nothing further.

"Are they really going to knock the place down?" I asked after an awkward pause.

He shrugged. "Depends on whether the Department of Defense appropriates for a new building or not. Maybe next year or the year after."

"What about the new NICU? Did they get it up and running at BAMC?"

"Took everything they needed from here with them," he replied.

I thought about that. "It's a totally different feeling here now, isn't it? I mean with the pictures gone from the hallway and everything."

"They took them, too," he said. And then, looking at his wristwatch he said he had to be going. He reminded me to send him my photographs should I see something strange in any of them, repeating that he was serious.

I told him I would.

"Thank you, sir," he said, and just as quickly as he'd appeared, he was gone.

When I met Anne later that morning we sat for a few minutes in her office in the Derm Clinic before going to the hospital's cafeteria for lunch. She was typing patient notes into a computer, her long, thin fingers floating across the keyboard. Army regulations saw to it that she wore the curling waves of her honey-brown hair pulled back tightly into a bun and her slender frame was so lost in her baggy camouflaged fatigues that she struck me as barely half her 32 years. I pulled the scrubs and officer's cap from the bag I was carrying. She took a quick glance at the pile of stuff.

"Once those scrubs leave the base they're stolen property — US Government issue, you know?" She smiled an impish smile. As for the hat, she said, "Thanks, but no thanks."

Figuring she wouldn't want to wear somebody else's cover I suggested she might want to keep it around as a spare if she misplaced her own. "I bet whoever lost this wished they'd had a spare once they realized they'd forgotten this one. You can get in trouble walking out on the base with your head uncovered, right?"

She turned back to the computer screen and, still smiling, said, "I'd get in more trouble for wearing an *Air Force* captain's cover!"

"It's not Army?"

"They do look alike," Anne said, trying not to make me feel quite so dumb. "But the Army has our names stitched onto the back of the caps. The Air Force people that lose their caps, I guess they're just out of luck."

I took my camera from my shirt pocket and turned it on, brought the photos I'd shot earlier onto the screen, and handed it to her. She stopped typing and clicked slowly through the images.

"You went upstairs to the NICU?" she asked after a moment.

"Just killing time while you were busy down here," I said.

"Wow. It's a real mess up there, isn't it?"

"Yeah... And kind of scary in a weird way."

"I haven't been back there in a long time, not since they moved everybody out, anyway. It was scary enough before."

I told her about the man I met in the NICU and the strange things he'd heard, about how he wanted me to send him the photos if we saw something, too.

"I don't see anything," she said, matter of factly.

I told her I hadn't either, and then suggested half-jokingly that maybe the pictures needed to be developed first like old fashioned film. Maybe the images we were looking for would only appear on a negative.

Anne laughed at the absurdity of it. She'd taken a photography class in high school before digital cameras became ubiquitous. She had actually developed film *herself* back then, in a real darkroom.

"Just the same, you have to wonder about it — about the babies, about the ones who died up there, that maybe..." but I let my words trail off without saying more.

We were silent for another minute, Anne studying the camera's NICU images. I started to pull the bereavement card out of my back pocket when she spoke up.

"Do you believe in ghosts, Papa?" she asked, using the affectionate title she'd used ever since we saw the movie "Life Is Beautiful" together when Anne was a teenager. She thought it adorable the way the little boy in the film called to his dad, so that Papa sounded as much a gentle plea as a salutation.

"Ghosts?" I shrugged and said I didn't know for sure. She knew I believed in Jesus and a life after death; she did, too. But ghosts?

"What's that?" she asked, motioning to the card I held in my hand.

"It's — it's something I found upstairs," I answered and handed it to her.

When she looked up after reading it, there were tears in her eyes.

"They're not ghosts," she said shaking her head slowly.

"No?"

"They're angels, Papa" my daughter said. "I know there were angels up there." She looked back at the camera still in her other hand. And then she smiled. "Maybe the angels are just making sure they didn't leave any babies behind."

PART I
Hope

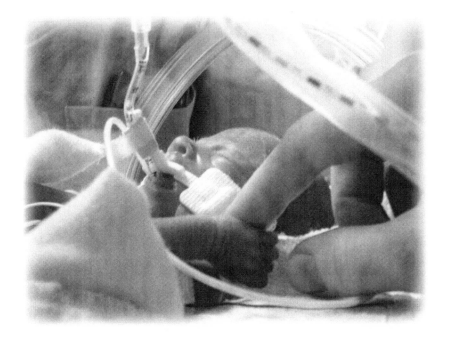

"All the days ordained for me were written in Your book before one of them came to be."
Psalm 139:16

CHAPTER 1

San Antonio, Texas
Spring 2010

From: Donna Spillane

Sent: Thursday, April 08, 2010 3:38 PM

Subject: Babies are here!

Sorry for the mass email.

Anne is in surgery, and babies have just been delivered. Two boys and two girls! We won't know their status for 1-2 hours. Because they are so premature (24 weeks & a few days!) they will need to be intubated and put onto ventilators as well as the other necessary lines started. The Chief of the NICU will get a report to us as soon as the four are "tucked in".

Anne continued to get worse despite her team's best efforts to keep her pregnancy intact. She was in extreme respiratory distress and her kidneys losing function. The OR and NICU staffs were assembled and off she went.

Please pray for all. Anne's condition is pretty serious and she'll be sent to SICU after the surgery is complete. As for the babies, the most critical time will be the first hours as they struggle to adapt to the ventilators.

Tim and Cait are just arriving (their flight was delayed) and Erin is in the air. Both the Army and Air Force Chaplains stayed with me during most of the surgery time; it was great to have their support and not be pacing by myself.

Tim or I will keep you posted as we are able. Thanks for all of your thoughts and prayers. It means so much to Anne. Sorry if this is a disjointed email... I've not been to bed for nearly 36 hours now and am a little off kilter ☺

Ten hours before my wife sent her email and still an hour before dawn, our youngest daughter, Caitlin, and I were en route to Philadelphia International Airport. Our next door neighbor, Ken, had volunteered the night before to help us catch our early morning flight to Texas. Save for some small talk he made to help lighten our mood, we drove mostly in silence. There was nothing to say. No one knew what the next hours or days would hold. When Ken dropped us at the airport, he hugged Cait and shook my hand.

"You know — whatever you guys need — just call me. Anytime. Day or night. Whatever you need."

I thanked him, caught his eyes for a moment, and then turned away. What we needed was beyond what Ken or anyone else could offer. Things were unraveling so quickly in San Antonio. Anne had become desperately sick; she needed to deliver her babies soon or she would die. Outside her womb her babies were unlikely to survive. They were four months too early. The cards were being played out. There was little any of us could do but watch, wait and pray.

When we cleared airport security Cait stopped to wait for me while I fumbled with my license and wallet with one hand and tried to put shoes on with the other.

"Which terminal?" she asked.

I looked up briefly before losing my balance and bumping into the traveler next to me. "'D,' I think. Southwest. To the right. No left. Whatever." I started to mumble something about how I needed to check the departure board.

"Dad?"

"Just give me a second, okay!"

"Dad?"

I pulled my second shoe on. When I straightened up I tried to look past her to the flashing Departures/Arrivals boards. She wouldn't have it, though. She stepped closer until her wide, hazel eyes were right in front of mine. "We're gonna get through this, Papa," she said. "We will."

After 26 years with her I ought to have known Cait would be strong for me when I needed her. That's part of who she is. The youngest of our three children, she had to fight to make her mark in our family. The twins — Erin and Anne — were three years older and seemed light-years beyond her in their accomplishments. They were top-of-the-class students, Ivy leaguers, med school graduates and now officers and doctors in the US Army. Cait hated school and was our wild child as a teenager. Once out of college she blossomed, though. If it had taken her a little longer to grow up than her sisters, she learned some valuable life lessons along the way. She is also some things her older sisters can never quite be. She's funny; they're too serious. People love to be around Cait. She has self confidence that comes easily to people who are happy laughing at themselves. The twins are more often afraid people might be laughing *at* them. And while Cait's sisters are attractive women, if Cait isn't flat-out gorgeous, she's always been adorable. "Cute!" Donna would say about the daughter who caused her endless angst growing up. "Cute is the only thing that kept me from killing that girl."

Once we were at the gate I called Erin hoping to catch her on her way into work. Her days started early at Walter Reed Army Medical Center, so it was no surprise she picked up. Erin told me that she'd already talked with Anne that morning. Her sister hadn't slept well overnight but was feeling a little better. The doctors were working hard to handle the pulmonary edema that was causing her respiratory distress. Anne was still optimistic that she could hold on for a little longer in spite of the mounting problems that were pushing her toward the brink. Caitlin looked up from the McDonald's pancake breakfast she'd been trying to eat. I could see the hope in her eyes.

"Well?" she asked when I was off the phone.

"Anne's feeling better. At least she didn't feel like she was drowning overnight."

"And?"

"Erin says her lab work is getting increasingly worse. She thinks they'll have to deliver today — probably as early as this afternoon."

Caitlin pushed the hotcakes away.

"Erin is only going in to work to get her emergency leave papers signed. She flies out of DC this afternoon. By the time she gets to San Antonio she figures it'll be over."

Cait's shoulders slumped.

"We're gonna get through this together, right?" I said.

Cait sat quietly before straightening up. "There's no turning back?"

"No, honey, I don't think there is."

When we arrived in Houston we found that our connecting flight was delayed. Instead of getting into San Antonio by early afternoon, we wouldn't be getting there until nearly 4 p.m. Neither Caitlin nor I had much of an appetite for lunch. We drank coffee, instead. After an hour of waiting in the terminal, my phone rang. It was Erin calling to tell me that she had been able to talk to her mom briefly at the hospital. They were going to deliver Anne's babies imminently, but she didn't know anything more. Erin said she was about to board her own flight. I wished her a safe journey and we hung up. Cait and I were only 150 miles away from Anne. We may as well have been in another universe.

In spite of blood transfusions and diuretics, by Thursday afternoon Anne's pulmonary edema was returning. Her blood pressure was dangerously high, and her blood work continued to show a low red cell count. There was no real possibility that she could carry her babies until the 28 week mark, though she desperately wanted to. She wasn't surrendering; it wasn't her decision. The department head of the Neonatology unit had been monitoring her lab work. He and another senior neonatologist came into Anne's room in the early afternoon to tell her that it didn't matter if she wanted to try to keep the babies any longer. Her condition had deteriorated too much for that. They were already in the process of assembling the teams that would take her babies from delivery into the NICU. Anne had done all she could for her babies. It would be up to them now.

In an adjoining room, a neonatologist fellow was briefing Anne's husband, Rob, on the procedure. There would be a team for each of the babies. There would be as many as two dozen people on hand — each team would have at least one attending physician and a fellow, as well as residents and nurses. They had run practice drills. They were prepared. They would do everything they could. And then he told Rob the hard truth. No matter what they did it would likely not be enough. The girls had about a one in three chance of surviving; the boys even less. Rob was an engineer. He knew statistics and probabilities. He ran a quick calculation of the odds of all four of them surviving. He later described it as a flip of the coin: heads survival, tails not. Only the odds were not so good. It was as if the coin had two tails for each head and he needed to flip heads four times in a row. I calculated the odds myself. The chances of all four babies coming out of the NICU alive were 1 in 133. But this was no game. None of us were prepared to lose even one of the babies.

Anne was wheeled into the OR as Caitlin and I were finally boarding our plane in Houston. Erin's flight was just getting off the ground. Donna was pacing in Anne's room in Labor & Delivery. Rob had to wait for the anesthesiologist to stabilize Anne before they brought him into the operating room to be with his wife.

Rob is a big man, but his imposing figure is easily offset by his beaming smile and infectious laugh. Not that he had reason to laugh now. Rob would later admit to being terrified as he moved into the room, carefully making his way past the instrument carts, IV poles and monitoring equipment. He was worried that he might bump into something, but he knew the most important thing he could do was to get as close to Anne as possible. When he was he whispered to her reassuringly. He kept his eyes fixed on hers as the surgeon cut her open. He did not watch as his children were pulled from her womb. Anne was not able to see her babies, either; the curtain that blocked her view of her incision also kept her from seeing the babies as the OB doc lifted them, one after another, from her womb. She heard three muffled cries and wondered why she didn't hear four.

When the emergency caesarean section was complete the OB team had Anne moved quickly to the Surgical Intensive Care Unit (SICU) where they could carefully monitor her condition.

Although removing the babies was the cure she needed, the next 12 to 24 hours were still critical for her. She lay alone in her bed in the SICU with no way of knowing the status of her babies. It struck her as ironic that she and her children had all ended up in intensive care. Carrying quadruplets had nearly cost Anne her life; to save her own she'd been forced to leave them with little chance for their own survival. It was unnatural, perverse. How had things gone so wrong? She wondered if she would ever see her babies alive.

When the plane landed in San Antonio I quickly turned on my phone. There was only one message. It was from my brother, Bill, back in Pennsylvania. It read simply: "Go with God."

The origins of the caesarean section might have been of interest to Anne when she was a medical student — Julius Caesar was purported to have been taken from his dying mother's womb — but that Thursday afternoon in early April, she was a pregnant woman in distress. The only historical notion that could be of any remote consequence to Anne as the doctors prepared her for the surgery was that, like Caesar leading his legion into Rome, Anne and her babies would be crossing their own Rubicon. They had reached the point from which there would be no possible return. The harsh reality was that Anne's procedure would be a caesarean in its most basic, primitive sense: the sectioning of the unborn from its dying mother. By the time of her surgery, Anne's body was for all intents and purposes dead to her babies. She could no longer help them though they desperately needed her for their own survival. Continuing to carry them, Anne would only have days or less to live. Her babies would have been entombed within her.

Clinically, Anne's caesarean was successful, but the cost was enormous. Though the operation was the only real hope the babies had left, they lost so much by being so preterm. The physical challenges they faced outside the womb were daunting. For Anne, the challenges would be more emotional. If pregnancy is the bridge that mothers cross to bring their babies into the world, then Anne's section was the road sign that read, "Bridge Out." It was the end of her journey. She had carried her babies across that bridge to a point where she could see the other shore but could take them no further. She would have to leave them there, returning alone without them. Whatever hopes she'd once had of bearing a child, of experiencing the wondrous transition from a woman to a mom, whatever the deep-seated longing to hold the life emerging from within her, all the eager anticipation, the growing excitement, the bubbling-until-you-burst emotions that nearly every mother knows, were lost for Anne that day. Fate had forced her to end her pregnancy far too soon. She might not ever hold even one of her babies.

Later that evening Donna, Cait and I were allowed to see Anne briefly. Before we entered, her nurse reminded us that Anne remained in danger of seizures. The delivery of her babies a few hours before was no guarantee that she was out of the woods. We would not be able to stay for long. Anne smiled bravely through blistered lips when we tip-toed into her room in the SICU. She looked like she'd been in a prizefight; her face was red and puffy, and her hands swollen.

Donna sat carefully on the side of Anne's bed and told her that job number one for this new mom was getting herself better. She said Rob would get to see their babies soon and after meeting again with the NICU staff, he would be able to tell her much more. But for now, Donna said, we would do whatever we could to help Anne get back on her feet.

Cait told Anne she had done a great job and said she couldn't begin to imagine how hard the last 24 hours had been for her. Trying to hold back tears, Cait admitted she had never been so worried in her life.

When it was my turn, I took Anne's hand in mine and told her how proud I was of her. I told her I was sorry and that I should have known to come sooner. I started to tell her that no matter what happened in the coming days I would be there for her. But as I tried to get the words out, seeing my daughter lying there so frail and weak, so spent and exhausted, I began to cry.

"Papa," Anne said, squeezing my hand. She was crying, too, her tears falling from the corners of her eyes, coursing down her cheeks and onto her neck where they disappeared into the strands of her matted hair. "I'm so sorry," she whispered hoarsely. "It wasn't supposed to be like this."

None of us slept very well that night, but after a light breakfast and some anxious chatter over coffee and tea, Erin and Cait and Donna and I crammed into Anne's two-door Mini Cooper and started toward Wilford Hall. In the past when I was visiting, it had always been Anne driving me to spend a day at the hospital with her. At that time, my daughter had been working as a new dermatologist there. Now she was a very sick patient struggling to get better. One floor above their mom's room in the SICU, four tiny babies, barely clinging to life, were being carefully monitored in the neonatal intensive care unit. The only thing we knew as we left for the hospital was that everybody had gotten through the night. We hoped we might visit the babies for the first time before we checked in on Anne a little later in the day.

That second Friday in April, the Texas wildflowers were in full bloom as we turned onto Highway 90. The previous summer, San Antonio had been unusually hot and dry, but from December through early spring the nearly year-long drought had been gradually vanquished by abundant winter rains. The warm, moist weather had produced a spectacular array of wildflowers that filled the fields and embankments along the highway with a kaleidoscope of color. It was a sunny morning and though we'd all been up late the night before, we were unquestionably upbeat. While none of us knew what the next few hours — let alone days or weeks — held for the family, we each knew that we'd dodged a bullet the day before. We were glad for that. My wife and I were new grandparents; our daughters were aunts. And as I let that thought settle in, I smiled. It was my birthday. I'd turned 53 the day after my first grandchildren were born.

Thirty minutes later, I pulled the Mini up to Lackland Air Force Base's main gate and stopped at the checkpoint where two uniformed airmen stood and stared intently at the vehicle. I rolled down the window and handed my driver's license and Erin's identification card to one of the guards. He looked at my license first and then bent a little lower so he could see Donna and Caitlin in the back seat. Lastly, he peered across my chest at Erin sitting in the passenger seat beside me. He looked at her, then at her ID and in a snappy motion lifted his right arm and saluted. "Good morning, Captain," the young airman said. She returned the salute.

Rob met us in the lobby. He smiled briefly but his eyes seemed distant. I told myself the sullen expression he wore was probably the result of his having spent the night sleeping on an armchair in Anne's room. He reported that Anne's condition was improving, but slowly. She was asleep now. He suggested we visit the newborns first, led us to the elevator banks and up to the fifth floor. Once out of the elevator we stepped into a long, wide corridor. At the far end was a set of double doors that led to the NICU. We followed Rob to a sink adjacent to the doors. Above it were instructions for washing your hands and a liquid soap dispenser. Another sign to the right of the sink said that only parents and immediate family members were allowed in the NICU, and that only two people could accompany the parents at a time. When Rob opened the doors he silently motioned to Donna and Erin to follow him. He did not make eye contact with me, and in another moment the three of them disappeared behind the doors. Cait and I stood outside to wait our turn.

"You okay, Dad?"

I nodded, but did not turn to look at Cait. She was standing behind me. "Yeah, I'm okay," I said after another moment. "I guess."

"I'm nervous."

"Me, too," I said and, turning, I put my arm around her shoulder. "We may as well go for a walk," I sighed. "It'll help kill the time."

We walked slowly back up the corridor, past an array of framed pictures and plaques that hung on one wall. There were photographs of tiny babies and smiling toddlers. Most pictures included an inscription; some only a few brief words. I noted the commemoratives and mementos and decided this must be something of a wall of fame. I tried to imagine the parents of babies born too early or seriously ill who walked up and down this hall time and again, for weeks and, in some cases, even months. These were their stories. Maybe this wall was one way they could remember and say thanks.

When we reached the end of the hallway Cait and I stopped to look out the tall picture window beside the elevator alcove. In the distance was Highway 90. I tried to visualize the wildflowers whose brilliant blooms had cheered us during our drive to the hospital. But suddenly I found my memory of them only a hazy image, distant and unreal. The only things real now were right here in this hospital.

We stayed in the alcove for a while, and then began to retrace our steps through the corridor toward the NICU. We walked slowly by the wall of pictures and plaques, and at one point I stopped to read some of the inscriptions.

My eyes were drawn first to the larger plaques, many of them varnished, dark hardwood with engraved or embossed lettering and often a large, juxtaposed photograph of a chubby baby in her mother's arms or a smiling toddler holding his dad's hand. The inscriptions were filled with gratitude and wonder. "Miracles do happen," read one caption about a boy born at 24 weeks who had made it home. Another said, "…your dedication and service allowed our angel to remain with us… you told us to be 'ready for the roller coaster ride of ups and downs' which you helped us through."

Cait had stopped further down the hall, and when she made her way back to me she turned away from the wall, her head down. "I can't do this, Dad," she said, wiping her eyes. "Have you seen some of these? It's so sad."

I hadn't. I was purposefully avoiding the plaques commemorating babies whose only photographs showed gauze-covered eyes and tubes protruding from everywhere. I pushed my hands into my pockets and began to read the inscriptions that I wished weren't there. "To the NICU team… we thank you from the bottom of our hearts for your effort and dedication to caring for our baby girl — now an angel — for 20 beautiful days." The parents of a boy who lived for four weeks wrote, "We appreciate all you've done for our little angel; he'll watch over us until we meet him again." Another plaque quoted scripture: "All the days ordained for me were written in your book before one of them came to be." The verse from the 139th Psalm was shared "in loving memory of Tyler — 21 days."

In time I would come to realize that more than a wall of fame, this was a wall of faith. Behind it was the NICU where the tiniest of lives lay precariously balanced on the razor's edge separating the living from the dead. I would learn that faith was found here both in modern medical technology and in the skilled and caring hands of the people who applied it. And I would find that faith of a different sort was also here for those who sought it, found in that hopeful notion from the Psalms, that the babies who had spent time behind these walls were the children of a loving God long before they ever belonged to any of us. But standing in front of the wall that morning my faith was saddled with fear. Now the babies in the NICU were my daughter's, and I had no way of knowing how things would turn out for them. I looked again at the picture of the boy who had been born at 24 weeks and survived. Miracles do happen. I tried to imagine the day Anne and Rob would hang a plaque on this wall. And I prayed it would tell a tale of miracles, too.

When the door to the NICU swung open a few minutes later, I was startled. My thoughts had wandered from the plaques on the wall to the days, nearly 30 years gone, when my wife had had her own struggles with premature birth. Anne and Erin had been born almost two months early. I remembered how scared we'd been then.

"You should wash up now," Rob said. His eyes were sunken and red. He stepped into the corridor and stood in front of the sink to show us how the foot pedal beneath it operated the faucet. Then he was gone again. The sign said to wash for three minutes. *I should probably wash my whole body. How clean would be clean enough?*

When I finished, Caitlin asked me if I thought they might not allow her in to see the babies. "The sign next to the sink says immediate family," she pointed out.

"You're their aunt, sweetheart."

"That's not immediate family. I need to be a sister or something."

"They let Erin in there."

"She's a doctor."

"Then so are you. You didn't fly all the way out here not to see these little guys."

"I don't know. I'm so nervous, Dad. Do you think they're going to be all right?"

I didn't have to answer. Before I could say anything Erin came through the double doors. Behind her was her mom. Donna was crying. She held the palm of her hand in front of her mouth. My heart sank.

"What is it, honey? What's the matter with the babies?"

CHAPTER 2
Chester County, Pennsylvania
December, 1980

Hᴇʀ ᴛɪɴʏ ʙᴀᴄᴋ ʜᴇᴀᴠᴇᴅ ᴜᴘ in a gentle arc and pressed almost imperceptibly against the palm of my hand with her every breath. I was careful to just touch her, letting only the slightest bit of the weight of my hand rest on the soft cotton shirt she wore. My palm easily covered the whole of her back. When I spread my fingers they reached to the top of her head, and my thumb passed over the elbow of her left arm, which was tucked against her side. Though it never occurred to me to count, she must have been drawing three or four breaths for every one of mine. I had no idea whether that was an appropriate respiratory rate for a newborn or not. That she continued to breathe was the only thing I cared about, and I knew it was altogether out of my hands whether or not she did.

"Lord God give you good rest and peace, and keep you in His care tonight," I said softly. Removing my hand from her back I watched for several moments more — some nights for minutes more — to see for certain that she continued to draw her rapid, little breaths.

Continue to breathe she did; and so, too, her identical twin sister. I don't remember how many nights, weeks, and months passed before I stopped watching Anne and her sister Erin in this peculiar way. I never thought about my own breathing; why couldn't I accept that it would be so mindlessly easy for them, too? I suppose I might have been a bit more sanguine if I had been awake through the nights, first trying to nurse the twins, and then reluctantly resorting to bottle feeding them the high nutrition formula the doctors said Anne, especially, needed. Maybe if it had been me who was up every two hours to feed the tinier Anne, and then back shortly after with her bigger sister who was on a three hour schedule, I wouldn't have had such anxiety about their breathing.

But tucking them in at night and pulling the baby blankets — crocheted by our pastor's wife — around their shoulders, that was my job. I was the sole breadwinner for a family that had suddenly doubled in size. It was important that I get a good night's sleep. Donna mostly agreed with this division of duties; certainly she was grateful, at least, that I didn't wake her and the sleeping babies when I left in the early mornings for work. Besides, this was 1980. Men were less inclined then to wrestle with guilt about not being involved in the matters of diaper changing, bottle washing and burping. In any case, *I* was not so inclined. My duty to the babies was of a different sort.

In those first months when Donna was walking around in a sleep-deprived daze, her blouse by evening half unbuttoned from the constant attempts at breast feeding, her bra an abandoned vestige of that morning's attempt to dress herself, the least I could do was put the girls to bed and let my wife get a jump on the brief uninterrupted hours of sleep she had coming. It was a simple chore, but it was the kind, perhaps, new fathers tend to take too seriously. When you spend so little time each day with your babies — especially if they're your *first* babies — you want to be sure that what little you do, you do well.

I knew almost nothing about parenting or babies. My mother had had lots of children, but as the middle child I wasn't around in time to see the first three, was only two when the fifth was born, and then already five when the first of the final two were delivered. And the last two were girls. By that age, I was away playing with my four brothers; what as boys could we have been expected to do with a baby sister besides drop her? Now, 18 years later, I felt no surer about what to do than I had at five. In fact, I felt about the same: Flee!

But flight was not an option. Duty called, and my mom and dad had taught me well enough to know that it was important to do my best to do my duty. I took to the idea of being the night watchman, the sentry stationed at the walls surrounding the city, the strong father protecting his new daughters. Of course, I had no intention of staying up the whole night — that would go beyond the rational limits of duty. I could, however, make sure the gates of the "walls" were secured and offer by way of the Psalms a prayer boldly uttered each evening as the girls fell asleep in the crib they shared:

> *You will not be afraid of the terror by night,*
> *Of the arrow that flies by day;*
> *Of the pestilence that stalks in darkness,*
> *Or of the destruction that lays waste by noon.*
> *A thousand may fall at your side,*
> *And ten thousand at your right hand;*
> *But it shall not approach you.*
> (PSALM 91: 5-7)

Yet as I looked down on these small babies squirming on their bellies, drawing their legs up tight so they looked like little balls of warm, pink flesh, I could not stop watching them breathe. Their shoulders and backs were in constant motion, heaving up and down with every breath. This then, became what I perceived as my real duty: to make sure they continued to breathe.

I always prayed for Erin first. Maybe it was because she was the oldest (all of two minutes older than Anne) or maybe because she was bigger (outweighing her sister's four and a half pound birth weight by more than a pound). But more likely, it was because Anne seemed the underdog in their battle to make it to one day older. I would pray for Erin, then settle my hand on Anne's tiny back and pray for her. This way I could be sure that before turning out the lights I had seen Anne breathe at least one more time. And if she was breathing, I figured her bigger, stronger sister was, too.

But after watching her rapid, shallow breaths — so much effort for so small a body — I never would get around to my bold prayer of vanquishing the pestilence that stalks by darkness or obliterating the terror that comes by night. Instead, I could only think of a later verse from the same Psalm, *"For He will give His angels charge concerning you..."*

The sobering realization was that there was little I could do for these babies; no way could I assure my daughters another breath. I could only utter my own simple prayer, a quiet but desperate plea: "Lord God give you good rest and peace, and keep you in His care tonight."

Those first anxious nights He did. So I continued to pray those same words with Erin and Anne nearly every night thereafter until almost nineteen years later when we left them alone together at college.

Donna and I were in our early twenties when the twins were born a week before Thanksgiving of 1980. They were six weeks premature but surprisingly healthy and did not stay in the hospital long. While much of what I remember about that time is a blur, what I will never forget is finally taking my wife and our two tiny babies home.

Married less than two years, we were without much in the way of money, and we were a one-car family. It was a pickup truck, which suited my work — I was an apprentice carpenter in my oldest brother's remodeling business — and with Donna taking the train to her job, we thought the truck was all we needed. I hadn't planned on having a family so soon, and we certainly hadn't planned on having twins. The truck would have to suffice as our family vehicle.

My heart pounded while I waited for Donna that early December morning. The pickup idled as its heater struggled to warm the cab. At last, the figures of two nurses and a young woman in a wheelchair appeared through the glass doors of the hospital's entrance. There were winter coats and bundles of blankets and, somewhere in that collection of arms, legs and clothes, two baby girls and their new mom about to come home for the first time.

I helped my wife out of the wheelchair and into the truck and pulled the seatbelt gently around her waist. I remember I was startled to find she'd already lost much of her belly that had been so big just a couple weeks before. She seemed hardly different from the teenage girl I'd met five years earlier: dark brown hair that was long and straight, a wisp of bangs crossing her forehead; silky-smooth skin with freckles sprinkled on the tops of her cheeks and nose; and ever-smiling eyes and pleasing lips.

I stepped aside as first one nurse then the other leaned into the cab to place a baby into Donna's arms. They smiled at me as I gently pushed the door closed. In retrospect, it seems incredible that in early December of 1980 we just drove away from Bryn Mawr Hospital with Donna clutching two premature babies in her arms. But child safety seat laws hadn't yet been enacted nationwide. At the time, most new parents were simply doing what their parents had done with them when they were kids. I'd travelled thousands of miles in the family station wagon with six siblings and nary a seatbelt around any of us. Mom and Dad had their hands full just getting us all in the car. When the last one was finally in, the doors were shut and off we would go. I don't know if my parents even worried about it. I think they just got in there and hoped for the best.

I looked into the cab and then back to the nurses. My mind was racing. Any last words, anything I should know before driving away? They offered nothing more than the cheery smiles on their rosy cheeks. I climbed into the driver's seat. With my own seatbelt in place, I slowly released the clutch. We were going home. I let out a quiet sigh of relief. We were really going home.

I could not know then what our future held. But what I did know was that it hadn't been an easy road getting to that point. What had started so naturally had turned into something entirely different...

When we first married, Donna was barely 100 pounds. At five foot six inches tall, she was not the curvy, voluptuous woman of magazine covers and men's fantasies. But after only a few months of marriage Donna had managed to put on some weight. Married life suited her from the get-go. She loved cooking for me and was a wonderful baker, too. I told her if I was going to indulge in her cakes and pies then so would she. When she said she was worried about getting fat, I told her the weight was ending up in all the right places. But once pregnant she became so ill with morning sickness that it seemed impossible for her to even maintain weight.

The first trimester moved slowly for Donna. She had already suffered one miscarriage. It was only months after we were wed, and though it was very early in her pregnancy the sudden shock of the loss had stung us both. We tried to ignore our apprehension that we might lose this baby, too. Instead, we focused together on finding some way for Donna to keep her food down. And I did whatever I could to see she got some extra rest. The only positive was the realization that every day she spent vomiting was another day she was still carrying our baby.

It wasn't until Donna was in her second trimester that she started to gain weight, and the irony of it was that once she finally began there was no end to it. Pound after pound, the numbers on the bathroom scale started to roll upward. One of her obstetricians decided that she was gaining *too* much weight. I was fit to be tied when I heard it. "Did he even bother to look at you?" I protested. Her belly was huge, but her arms and legs were as petite as the day she conceived. If that doctor was worried about her getting too fat, thinking that she'd been spending her days eating gallons of ice cream and chocolate cake by the layer, then he was an idiot.

"What about twins?" I barked, as if the doctor were standing right there in front of me.

"What?" Donna said. "You don't think —?"

I have to admit, until that moment the idea had never occurred to me. "Well, no, but I don't know. Maybe — shouldn't they at least be considering it?"

With the pounds adding up and her tummy incessantly growing, they finally did. The doctor on the OB team Donna regularly saw told her he had never heard another heartbeat, so he had no reason to suspect twins. He had to admit, however, that she was carrying a big baby for this point in her pregnancy. He decided they would do an ultrasound.

By 1980, the use of ultrasound in obstetrics was two decades old. There had never been any documented safety issues stemming from its use, but no one was able to say for sure at that time whether ultrasounds might yet present any unknown risks to a developing fetus. In any event, their use was far rarer than today. We consented to the procedure with equal parts anticipation and apprehension.

The ultrasound technician wasn't supposed to say anything to Donna, but she managed to discreetly leave the monitor positioned so that Donna could see the pictures on her screen. There was one head, for sure. And there seemed to be too many appendages for just one baby. There was another round object that might have been the baby's bottom, but Donna couldn't be sure.

We later learned that the doctor never heard a second heart-beat because Anne's torso was beneath Erin's. Her head was positioned so tightly against her sister's pelvis that when the doctors felt it they assumed it was Erin's bottom. That other round object in the ultrasound — that was Anne. When I came home from work that evening, Donna tried to be nonchalant about her day. She'd had no way of contacting me then — no cell phones, no email. So she had to keep the news to herself for hours; in turn, she would try to keep it from me for at least a few minutes, just for the fun of it.

"How was your day, honey?" Donna asked when I came in the door, gave her a kiss and grabbed the milk jug from the fridge.

"Good. Yours?"

"Okay."

It was mid-September and still hot outside. I was thirsty from working in the sun all day. Either I had forgotten that her test was scheduled for that day or was drinking milk so fast that it had temporarily frozen my brain.

"Everything going okay at work?" she asked.

I nodded, still chugging from the jug.

"You know I don't like it when you do that. You're going to backwash your food into the milk."

"I haven't even eaten anything," I argued while wiping my chin.

"Well, maybe you should eat something now. Before you know it, you're going to be sharing your food with more people than just me."

I started to bring the milk up to my mouth again.

"Don't do it!" she scolded.

I held the milk for a moment to consider what she'd said. "People?" I asked.

She smiled, her eyes brightening.

"What's that supposed to mean?" I asked, putting the jug to my lips again. And then it hit me. "You got the ultrasound today?" I asked, both excited and embarrassed.

She was smiling wider. She nodded her head.

"People?"

She just beamed. When I still hadn't said anything, she said one word.

"Babies."

She said it as softly as if she'd been holding one at that very moment.

"Babies?"

She nodded. My heart felt like it had climbed into my throat.

"We're having twins!"

It was mind-blowing. I started to laugh. "Two boys?" I asked, throwing my arms around her.

She pulled away from me to fix her eyes on mine. "We're having two babies," she said. "They couldn't tell from the test whether they were boys or girls."

"Right," I replied and pulled her big belly back up against mine.

The exhilaration we shared that evening would last only ten days. Donna went into labor in the 27th week of her pregnancy. She was admitted to the hospital where an immediate drug regimen was administered to slow the progression. The doctors gave her steroid injections over the course of the first 24 hours to help improve the lung function of the babies. But her obstetrician was clear: it would be very difficult for them if the babies were born now. The chances of survival for a single baby at this point in a pregnancy were about one in two; the complications that might follow if it survived could be myriad. For multiples, the odds were even worse. We were in shock. Our joy at the prospect of twins had unraveled so quickly.

Over the course of that first week in the hospital, the contractions slowed and finally stopped. Though her cervix had already begun to dilate the obstetrician felt that Donna would be best served by returning home and going on full bed rest. Thankfully, my parents had recently moved into a new house less than ten minutes from the hospital. Even better, my mom would be home throughout the day with Donna. Maybe not quite miracles, but these small coincidences became like stepping stones helping us find our way. One after another, we moved forward, treading carefully and allowing ourselves to hope.

Unfortunately, the contractions resumed in a couple weeks and it was back to the hospital. In spite of the setback Donna was determined she could ride out this storm. She bolstered her hopes with the knowledge that with each passing day her babies were getting a little stronger. Our families were praying for us and so was everyone in our little community church. And again, the contractions slowed and then stopped. We stepped away from the precipice once more.

Into her 30th week, Donna was able to return to my parents' home. If the babies needed more time to grow, my parents pledged to do anything they could to see that their unborn grandchildren got it. More than a wonderful caregiver and real comfort to my wife, my mom was also there for every emergency, even the most embarrassing ones. When Donna got stuck in the downstairs bathtub it was her mother-in-law who came to her rescue, pulling her up out of the water with both arms and a big "'Heave-ho!" As

Donna stood totally naked in front of a woman she was only just getting to know, Mom gave her the once-over and then laughed, saying, "My, you really are pregnant!"

I think Dad enjoyed having a pregnant woman in the house again. And he was such an optimist. It mattered little to him how bad the news, how stacked against us the odds appeared. "I've been a lucky guy my whole life," he assured us more than once during our dinners together. "My grandchildren will be fine. And so will my daughter-in-law."

His confidence helped because bouncing between the hospital and home and back would be Donna's fate until the babies were finally delivered. We thought that delivery was inevitable in her 31st week when, in the hospital once more, the contractions were more persistent than ever and her cervix dilated to a full five centimeters. But with no rational explanation, things continued to break in Donna's and the babies' favor. She was sent back home again after yet another week in the hospital; that got the twins to their 32nd week. I believe that if determination was enough to win the day, Donna might have carried the twins very nearly to full-term. She has that kind of *stubbornness* about her which, when she gets a hold of something important to her, makes her fight to the bitter end before giving it up. But neither my wife nor her formidable will had figured on the game-changing challenge that would threaten both her and the babies next.

We returned to the hospital for the last time when the contractions resumed the 34th week of Donna's pregnancy. She was nearing the point of complete exhaustion. I was just frustrated. If I'd learned anything at all from the childbirth classes we'd attended, it was that childbirth was supposed to be "normal, natural and healthy." Like every other father-to-be in our class, the bottom line was we wanted everything to go well for our wives. But my hopes for a "normal" childbirth experience were gradually slipping away and with them, my patience, too.

Each time we returned to the hospital, I couldn't help but notice the cyclical rhythm of the hospital's Women's Building: pregnant women came through the doors every day with nervous husbands in tow. Every day nurses brought smiling women in wheelchairs out the same doors, bundled babies in the new mothers' arms, nervous fathers leading the way. It left an empty, lonely feeling inside me, like we were being excluded from what for everyone else was so joyous and so damn routine.

But if Donna felt the same gnawing frustration, she never let on. Instead, she tried to remain focused, but the odds were quickly being stacked against her. She was diagnosed with preeclampsia. Her doctors told her they were wary of possible complications, and if the latest contractions did not stop soon of their own accord, they would have her deliver the twins. She argued with them all, saying that other than being tired she felt no ill effects from her climbing blood pressure. But it was no use. She was asking her doctors to let her walk a dangerous high-wire for the sake of her babies. They wouldn't do it. I think the news finally broke my wife's will. When I helped her out of her hospital bed late in the afternoon of that same day, before I could get her to sit down in the wheelchair to take her to the bathroom, her water broke. That was it. Delivery was imminent, whether we, or the babies, were ready.

What happened from that time forward is hard to say. Donna was fully dilated; the obstetrician was certain she would deliver imminently. He instructed her to push. She did. She grimaced, she cried, screamed, and did whatever she could to endure the pain. But it was to no avail. She went through several intervals of this, the pushing, the deep breathing, and still, the contractions. The doctor would leave from time to time. He had other patients to see, and he thought giving her a break from pushing would help. He was a kindly, middle aged man with a button nose and a smile that pushed his puffy cheeks almost up to his eyes. But he wasn't smiling now. He was becoming exasperated; the troubled look on his face was disconcerting. I don't know if Donna saw it. I think by that time, she could hardly see anything.

The night slid slowly into the early morning of the next day. Still nothing came of all the pushing, the unyielding contractions. Donna seemed practically delirious; exhausted, crying and disoriented. My feeble cheerleading had long since been replaced by silent, desperate prayer. What was normal, healthy or natural about any of this? How any of this could be considered routine was beyond my comprehension.

And then the frenzy began.

I don't know why no one had intervened as Donna's blood pressure rose throughout the day. Now it was going through the roof. The doctor was startled when he returned to our room and saw the numbers on the monitor. He began frantically flipping through papers on Donna's chart, searching for something he couldn't seem to find there. Then he wanted to know when she had last used the bathroom. He was asking the nurse but she didn't know. He turned to Donna. "The bathroom, Donna, when was the last time you went to the bathroom?" When she didn't reply, he pleaded with her. "Have you been urinating?" She only shook her head. "When —? When was the last time?" When she only rolled her head away and wept in reply, he looked to me. My mouth was dry. I opened my mouth for a moment and then felt my lips slowly, helplessly, draw shut. I didn't even know when or if my wife had peed. I didn't know anything.

I sat alone for a long time. I can't remember if I passed the time in the delivery room where they left me or if I wandered to the empty waiting room. They had rushed Donna out of delivery on a gurney, down the hall to the elevators where I could see the doors being held open so they could wheel her in. I watched the doors close behind her. "We'll let you know when you can join your wife," was all they had said.

When a resident obstetrician came he gave me only the necessary details. Donna was stabilized. She was awake. They were ready to begin an emergency caesarean section. She was asking for me.

In the early hours before dawn, the hospital seemed especially cold and antiseptic. The quiet solitude of the night had transformed the building into a forbidding place. It was so eerie, a strange scene in which somehow I had mistakenly become part. I followed the resident, but he wasn't talking. The squeaking of his soft-soled shoes was the only sound interrupting the silence as we made our way. I didn't know how I would react when I got to the operating room. I told myself I would be fine. What difference could it make if I wasn't?

It was a lot to take in. Nurses, an anesthesiologist and the obstetrician were already busy working, and a team from the premature infant care unit was waiting in the back of the room. All of them were wearing scrubs and masks. Donna had been sedated, but they told me she would be awake to see the babies born. When she saw me, she gave me a weak smile.

There followed a few minutes of discussion and instructions being relayed back and forth among the team assembled around Donna. Then a flurry of activity ensued marked by quick and precise motions. Suddenly I was looking inside my wife's belly, the pink, moist flesh, the white tissue and the red droplets of blood. The obstetrician's hands disappeared into her.

"A girl!" he said, lifting the baby high enough so Donna could see.

"Spillane — Baby A," a nurse said as she grabbed the squirming, little thing.

"Erin. Her name is Erin Leigh!" I called after the nurse. I looked back down at Donna. Her half-opened eyes were wet but had such a beautiful gleam in them.

The obstetrician's hands were inside her again.

"Another girl!"

"Spillane — Baby B."

I hesitated and then blurted out, "That's Anne. Anne Patricia Spillane." Turning my eyes back to Donna, I smiled. She was fast asleep.

There was a lot that happened that night that we didn't fully understand. Why had the preeclampsia created such a critical situation for Donna so suddenly? Maybe the obstetrician should have ordered a caesarean section before it became an emergency. We would later discover that Donna had an abnormally small pelvic opening — she never would have delivered the babies vaginally.

So many different things had happened so quickly. But we hadn't put the pieces together. Instead, we counted it a miracle that between the sudden spike in Donna's blood pressure and her kidneys practically shutting down, she hadn't had a seizure. If that had happened, the girls might not have survived.

We were content to leave the arguments over what should have or could have been done better to others. We were happier bickering over smaller things, things like the fact that I had chosen to name our second child Anne. Donna accused me of deciding unilaterally.

"You were asleep," I said.

"You could have waited until the next day."

"I didn't like the idea of calling her Baby B."

"That's what they called her the whole time we were in the hospital."

"Yeah, well, I wasn't going to call her that for even an hour. Besides, we talked about Anne for a second girl's name."

"You wouldn't even acknowledge the possibility of having two girls!"

"If you could have one girl, you might have two," I asserted.

"But you wouldn't even talk about a second girl's name."

"We did. We talked about it in the hospital. You were probably having a contraction or something."

She snorted at this and then sighed. "I just wanted to choose the name with you."

"I like the name Anne."

"I know. She was your mom's aunt."

"She was a sweet woman. Little Anne reminds me of her. Sweet and quiet."

"You hardly even knew your Great Aunt Anne!" Donna protested, but she knew it was a losing battle. It was too late to change her name, anyway.

"Sweet and quiet," I assured her. "You'll see."

It was a lot of work, but having twins was fun. Once the dark cloud surrounding the babies' delivery lifted, there was so much joy for Donna and me. Having twins made us feel special, as if we had done something unique. I suppose we even felt as if we had been chosen to have twins. Certainly lots of other folks made us feel that way. People fawned over the babies when we brought them out. Date night for Donna and me in those first few years was always a trip for ice cream cones at the mall where we'd push Anne and Erin's stroller around the long corridors of store fronts. We were rarely shopping. Mostly we were just showing off like new parents do. And if one baby was cute, two were twice so. Donna sewed many of the outfits for the girls, and she always put them in matching clothes for our nights at the mall. If it's bragging for *me* to say our girls were adorable, suffice it to say that plenty of people told us they were. Our evening outings to the mall always ended with us sitting with our ice cream cones on a bench outside Friendly's. It was our reward for a long week of work. Unless the girls were restless or tired, we took our time and talked. Usually it was just small talk, but sometimes we talked about what the future for our family might be like, how we hoped things would turn out for our girls, and on occasion, we reflected on just how far we had come in such a short span. I told Donna what a great job she had done. She smiled and said, "I just don't know how you could do it with three babies. Can you imagine? And four? Forget it. *That* would be impossible."

A few months after the twins turned three, Donna gave us another daughter. It was the only normal pregnancy Donna would have. Caitlin was born three weeks early — typical for a scheduled caesarean — but still weighed a healthy seven and a half pounds. She was an easy baby and, by gosh, there was only one of her! Unlike Anne and Erin, Cait took to breast feeding fabulously; she never took a bottle. Then after nine months on breast milk she decided she wanted the independence her older sisters enjoyed and started drinking her milk from a cup. Caitlin would be that way for the rest of her life: when she decided to do something she did it; let the chips fall where they may.

That added up to her being a terror as a toddler, which pretty much brought an end to the thought of having more children. Three children in just over three years; four pregnancies, two miscarriages (Donna had miscarried again a year before conceiving Cait), one traumatic delivery; a poster child in Cait for the "terrible twos," and my wife had had it. Enough was enough, she told me. I reminded her that when we were dating she'd said she'd like a big family, maybe six kids. Her response? I had two choices: I could have something done to permanently stem the tide of pregnancies or give up the act of baby-making all together. Women have a way of getting what they want. Cait would be our last child.

If our family planning was evolving so was the world in which we were raising our children. We actually had a car seat for Cait when we brought her home from the hospital. Lots of other things were changing, too. Though laptop computers, the Internet and Facebook, texting, tweeting, and the iPhone were all still years away, technology's reach would soon impact almost every aspect of our lives, and its transformative effects on the practice of medicine would be no less profound. Had Erin and Anne been born even a few weeks sooner, the odds of their surviving 30 years ago would have been slim.

In 1980, there really was no such thing as a *micro-preemie*. But now, Anne's own babies — delivered ten weeks earlier than their mom had been, and the four of them *together* weighing less than their Aunt Erin had when she was born — had a fighting chance for survival. Advances in medicine, especially in Neonatology, had made that possible.

Donna and I still count Erin and Anne's births as miracles and bringing the twins home from the hospital with us an unspeakable joy. But our daughter, Anne, now a woman, a wife and a new mother herself, was facing not just the likely loss of one or more of her own babies; she also knew the prospects of bringing any of them home with her was months or more away. Medical technology had given her babies a chance, but only God could give my daughter hope.

CHAPTER 3

Timmy, Edda, Lily and Wyatt
The first 24 hours

Rob didn't have the luxury I'd had — calling out names to the nurses when Anne and Erin had been born. No one would have listened to him even if he had. Names were the last things the NICU doctors and nurses had in mind in the frenzy that followed Anne's delivery. The babies were simply identified in the order they were born, with the corresponding letters of the alphabet. Timmy, the firstborn, was A; Edda and Lily, each delivered within the next minute, were B and C, and Wyatt, the last to be born, was D. Though they each gasped for breath at birth, wiggled and, except for Timmy, made faint cries as they were lifted from her womb, Anne had almost no way of knowing whether her babies were alive. There was no time for that. Minutes were too precious. In the operating room and in the adjoining neonatal intensive care unit where the babies were immediately taken, the urgency for action took precedence over parents' feelings.

It was little wonder Donna was so upset after seeing the babies for the first time the following morning. Each of them had had to endure a frenzied and frightening welcome into a world they were not remotely ready for and could not possibly begin to comprehend. The tracheal intubations that took place in the first minutes of life were the babies' introduction to the kind of necessary trauma that lay ahead of them now that they'd been removed from the comfort of their mother's womb. The intubation procedure is frightening, an invasive and painful threading of a flexible plastic tube through the mouth and down the throat until it stops mid-trachea. Except in emergency situations, an adult will be administered general anesthesia before undergoing the procedure. That was not an option for Anne and Rob's babies. Instead, firm hands held each baby as still as possible while a respiratory specialist inserted the tube. Positioning was difficult considering the narrow size of the babies' airways. Despite being fraught with risk, the endotracheal tube was the only way to provide the babies the mechanical ventilation they needed to survive. Within only minutes they all had been intubated, each requiring a second attempt to correctly place the tube save Edda who was lucky enough to have it right on the first shot.

Like almost all premature babies born before 28 weeks, Timmy, Edda, Lily and Wyatt would need acute care for respiratory distress syndrome (RDS). Their lungs were not ready to do the work of breathing yet. The drugs administered — corticosteroids given to Anne the day before she delivered and the synthetic surfactant Curosurf right after birth — were designed to promote lung maturation and the build-up of the slippery, protective substance that would help their lungs inflate with air and keep them from collapsing. The surfactant had an almost immediate and positive effect for all four babies: before long, each baby was weaned down to 30% oxygen or less (by volume, room air has 21% oxygen) while still maintaining satisfactory oxygen saturation levels or "O2 sats" as they were commonly called in the NICU.

Next, the NICU teams needed to place several catheters in each of the newborns. The first involved another round of intubation with an orogastric (OG) feeding tube that snakes from the mouth, down the throat and into the stomach. The next two catheters were inserted through their umbilical cords. The open umbilical blood vessels provided ready access for medications, transfusions and the early feeds called total parenteral nutrition. This required the placement of two long, hollow tubes into the vessels. Though not as distressing as some of the other procedures they were already enduring, the insertion of umbilical catheters was still traumatic for the quads and not without risk. Infection was always a concern, and the formation of blood clots along the catheters, or the interruption of blood flow to an organ or limb that could occur, could be life-threatening. But there was no good alternative. The procedures went well for Timmy and the girls. Wyatt had a problem with one of his tubes. Proving himself already feisty, he squirmed so much that after repeated attempts, the doctors resigned themselves to leaving the line barely inserted. They would use it only in an emergency.

Somewhere between intubation and the placement of the babies in their individual isolettes in the NICU, each one was given a more thorough physical exam. Though both Edda's and Lily's exams were curtailed due to their inability to maintain temperature the NICU teams were still able to collect sufficient information for each of the babies. Wyatt was the lightest (1lb 3oz) and the shortest (10-1/2 inches). Though I would report in an email a day after the babies were born that Timmy was the biggest, Lily actually was. She was some 40 grams heavier than her older brother at a whopping 670 grams (which is still less than a pound and a half) and more than an inch longer. Edda, meanwhile, was both light (1lb 4oz) and long (almost 12 inches).

The exam also included an inspection of the babies' skin and, to the limited extent they could, their eyes. Though they had fully developed eyebrows and eyelashes the babies' eyes were fused and wouldn't open for another week or two. They all had pinkish coloring and that was good. But calling their outer layer "skin" was something of a misnomer. Their epidermis was lacking in keratin, the fibrous protein that is the key material in its formation. As a result, premature babies can easily lose heat and water through their skin. They are also at greater risk of infection since germs and bacteria can more easily penetrate their poorly bonded skin; and it is subject to tearing — not uncommon since premature babies have so much tape continually applied and removed. At this point, the fact that each of Anne's babies had skin that was intact was a big plus for them all.

After the initial flurry of post-birth activity died down, the mantra going forward was watching and waiting. Once all the tubes had been placed, the catheters inserted and the monitors connected, Timmy, Edda, Lily and Wyatt were left to rest alone in their isolettes. None of them required sedation to do so.

As the afternoon hours gave way to evening and the first day of their lives turned into night, a quieter parade of activity continued unabated around them. Blood had to be drawn from each of the babies for lab work-ups, and taking even a tiny amount of their blood required quick replacement. Transfusions of packed red blood cells were ordered and administered.

X-rays were taken. They were essential to verify positioning of the various lines and for lung, bowel and abdominal evaluations. Portable radiograph machines were used to take these "babygrams." Timmy's first babygram revealed no abnormalities. The girls' had similar findings though Edda's initial x-ray led to a recommendation to retract one of her umbilical catheters slightly. Wyatt's was more concerning. His first babygram noted the possibility of swelling of his lungs due to fluid accumulation.

Wyatt's condition soon worsened. He began experiencing respiratory problems, and so the x-rays continued for him throughout the afternoon and evening. A babygram taken that night showed his left lung collapsed. The ventilator tube appeared to be too far down. It needed to be adjusted. When that was done the subsequent x-ray showed the tube providing improved aeration to both lungs, but he still had trace indications of excessive fluid build-up in the layers of tissue surrounding his lungs. By midnight, Edda was having her own lung issues. X-rays showed that her lungs weren't getting sufficient aeration as parts of their airspace were filling with fluid. Taken together, the findings meant that she and Wyatt were tottering on the edge of extremely acute respiratory distress.

The first day of the quadruplets' lives rolled slowly over into the second. When all the babies were x-rayed again in the early morning hours of April 9, Timmy and Lily were also having growing respiratory problems. Timmy's lungs were now struggling to keep up, though that was not unexpected. Lily's situation was a little more foreboding. The radiology report noted a small or partial collapse of the right lung that might be the result of an infection. If that was the case, it was a worrisome thing. Though the quads had been treated with a full spectrum of antibiotics and anti-fungal medications, the prospect of severe infection was never far removed in babies with skin that was like tissue paper. And if Lily had an infection, it could be quick and lethal.

But there was good news, too, in the early morning babygrams. Edda's condition had actually improved, if only by a little. Wyatt's was stable; he wasn't getting any worse. Best of all: the babies had lived through their first 12 hours.

The harsh beginnings of Timmy, Edda, Lily and Wyatt's lives were eventually written up in a formal admission report. It summarized each of their conditions at birth and pointed out the need for ongoing observations for *sequelae of prematurity* — medical jargon for the multiple problems that can arise when you're born nearly four months before you're due.

The admission report also managed to reduce the previous week of Anne's life into a terse but illuminating narrative. She had been admitted to the hospital for preterm labor including contractions, increased nausea and diarrhea. She was hypertensive. A diagnosis of preeclampsia followed, then HELLP syndrome and finally pulmonary edema. Her plunging respiratory status led to the delivery of her babies by urgent caesarian section.

The recounting of her physical difficulties was painful enough to read, but what I found especially poignant was how — without actually even saying as much — the report foretold how difficult the emotional aftermath of the delivery would be for Anne.

The admission report identified her as the *sponsor*. That told whoever consulted the document two things. The first was little more than a bookkeeping formality. Because Anne was the parent in the military, for insurance purposes she was deemed the babies' sponsor. The only practical consequence of that was that they would go by the surname "Spillane" rather than "Schlender" for as long as they remained at the Wilford Hall NICU.

The second reference was more jarring.

Though unintentional in its phrasing, referring to her on paper as the babies' "sponsor" was a cold and harsh acknowledgement of Anne's present reality. Her role as mother of the babies was essentially suspended once the babies had been taken from her. The report listed her occupation as a mom and a "Derm resident," but for the time being, when it came to her newborn children she really *had* no other role than to be their insurance sponsor. In fact, whether she lived or died in the SICU seemed to have little to do with how well the babies would do in their first hours and days outside her womb. She could not nurse them. The neonatologists would ask her as soon as she was healthy enough to begin pumping breast milk for the newborns, though it would be some time yet before the babies' digestive systems could begin to process her milk. She could not hold any of them, either. It might be weeks before she did, if at all.

Sadly, one did not have to spend much time around the NICU before realizing that for some moms the first time holding their tiny child was also the last. In those heart wrenching instances, when there was nothing more that could be done, the baby was freed from the tubes and the wires, wrapped in soft blankets, lifted gently out of the isolette and was laid all but motionless upon the breasts of its mother, there to breathe its last in her arms.

The only other information regarding Anne in the report had to do with her prenatal labs, the relevance of her past medical history (nothing was considered particularly significant with regard to her offspring), and the complications that led to the delivery. Preeclampsia, HELLP, and her debilitating respiratory problems — little of that would matter any longer to the NICU docs. Their only concern was by necessity the care of Anne's children. The OB doctor had done well to administer the glucocorticoids to Anne in a timely fashion, and the neonatologists knew that this would give the babies' underdeveloped lungs a fighting chance. Other than that, Anne was someone else's patient going forward.

Once the four babies had been delivered, her relevance to their development was terminated, and Anne's name would all but disappear from her babies' medical charts. There was nothing more — medically — she could do for them now that they were outside her womb. And I knew that nothing was more painful for her than that as she watched her tiny babies struggle to survive in the days and weeks that followed.

I rose early the day after the babies' arrival and wrote a short email to update our friends and family. While I didn't know much at the time — the babies' weights were only my best recollection — I wanted to at least let everyone know that the babies had names. I wasn't even sure yet if all the babies had survived the night. We hadn't heard anything from Rob since leaving him at the hospital with Anne. I told myself that was a good thing. Being optimistic couldn't hurt. Hope, what little we had, was all any of us would have to go on for a long time.

Good morning! As of late last night, Anne was in SICU & doing OK — she was so sick and it will take a little time before she gets back on her feet. But she is now a proud mom. Born April 8 around 3:30PM, were, in the order they were taken from Annie's womb:

Timothy David — 1lb 7oz ('David' is my dad's name and given in memory of Anne's late cousin, Dave)

Edda Grace — 1lb 4oz ('Edda' is Donna's aunt — a sweet, kind woman from Germany)

Lily Joy — 1lb 6oz (What's not to love about a girl named 'Lily?')

Wyatt Lee — 1lb 3oz ('Lee' is Rob's middle name & named for his late grandfather)

All the babies are stable & on ventilators in the NICU. Little Wyatt is in the most trouble as it has been hard getting tubes in him for feeding & meds (he is a feisty little guy and was fighting the nurses!) but they will try again today. They are in good hands there. The neonatal docs were pleased w/the condition of the babies considering their age.

Anyway, we are all together now. Donna is getting some much needed sleep in a real bed as I write this. Rob spent the night in the hospital with Anne (he won't be getting any sleep for a while!).

Just typing out the babies' names made me feel better. They were suddenly, unexpectedly here, *really* here. Timmy, Edda, Lily and Wyatt… I smiled thinking about them and, though I knew that the loss of any one of them could happen any time, I tried to look past that to a time when I'd have a chance to really get to know them.

By the time I finished writing my email, the sun was already warming the early spring air in south central Texas. In another hour the temperature would reach 80 degrees. Donna, Erin and Cait were soon up, and the four of us began anxiously readying ourselves to make the trip to see Anne and her babies. When we left, I turned the bright red Mini Cooper out of my daughter's driveway, wound through the streets of the new subdivision where she and Rob were living, and drove onto Highway 90 where the bluebonnets hung like a garland around its embankments.

In the NICU, Timmy, Edda, Lily and Wyatt were scheduled for their first head ultrasounds (HUS) at 9 AM. A half hour earlier, Wyatt had had another round of babygrams to examine the placement of the line in his groin and verify its proper routing from that point. Wyatt needed it to provide an alternate intravenous access since one of his umbilical lines had never been successfully placed. Here, Wyatt's reputation for feistiness when it came to being stuck, prodded or probed revealed itself again and resulted in the line's placement taking two tries.

Head ultrasounds are a necessity for babies born so prematurely. There is critical concern for these babies developing bleeding in their brains also known as an intraventricular hemorrhage (IVH). The likelihood of IVH is most significant in the first 72 hours of life and then diminishes substantially thereafter. If any of the quadruplets were going to have "brain bleeds," they'd be appearing soon. The procedure was painless for the babies. The real suffering was done by the moms and dads anticipating the results. Rob had been up much of the night before, reading everything he could find about IVH and preemies. What he learned made his stomach churn. When he left Anne early on Friday morning to be briefed by the neonatologists, he did not tell her that they would also soon be giving him the head ultrasound results. She was worried enough as it was. He would get the news first.

The news he received was mixed.

The findings for Edda showed no hemorrhaging. For Timmy and Lily the results were not as good. They both had small brain bleeds confined to the portion of the brain called the germinal matrix. A Grade I hemorrhage confined to this part of the brain was not uncommon for micro-preemies and might not produce serious complications. It would remain a wait-and-see game for the two of them. And the news for Wyatt? For a change, Wyatt caught a break. The findings from his HUS revealed nothing abnormal at all.

I had no idea *why* Donna was crying. She had just come out of the NICU after her first time seeing our grandchildren. Was one of the babies sick or dying? Was it the ultrasounds Rob had told her about? Was she thinking about brain bleeds in Timmy and Lily and the possibility of neurological problems such as cerebral palsy, seizures and intellectual disabilities? Her tears sent a shudder of fear through me. I felt my heart sink.

"What is it, honey? What's the matter with the babies?"

She took a moment to compose herself and then tried to smile.

"They're so small," was all she finally said.

Small? She was crying because the babies were small?

"I knew. Or I thought I knew, but I can't believe how tiny they are. I can't believe a person can be that small and be alive."

I pulled Donna close and hugged her.

"Small's okay," I said. "We can get by with small."

She smiled and wiped the tears from her cheeks.

"You scared me, you know — coming out of there crying."

"Come on, Dad." It was Erin. She was standing at the door next to the NICU's sign-in desk. "Scrub up and come and see your grandbabies!"

I felt awkward, like a young boy being taken for the first time to a big, downtown museum. Only now, it was my daughter leading me. I kept my eyes fixed on the straight, dark brown hair that stopped just above her collar. When she joined the army, she'd cut the wavy hair that had once reached the middle of her back and now kept the curl out of it with a straightening iron. "Just easier when I'm on duty," she'd explained. She was on emergency leave now, wearing "civvies" — flats, pressed slacks and a pastel blouse and not the combat fatigues and heavy boots required when on duty at Walter Reed. Still, I saw that she maintained a military bearing and looked every bit a doctor.

Even with Erin as my guide, I could not shake my apprehension. I didn't know what to do with my hands. I was afraid to touch anything. If I tucked my palms into my pockets they would be dirty when I pulled them out again, wouldn't they? I decided to fold my arms behind my back and trailed behind Erin as she moved further into the room.

It was eerily quiet. I could hear the humming of electric motors and the soft pumping of what I thought must be ventilators. The muffled peal of pages turning drew my attention toward a nurse thumbing through her notebook, tapping her pen lightly on the top of the desk where she sat a few paces from me. Beyond her I could see three figures clad in drab green scrubs hunched over a lab cart. A phone rang somewhere in a room. Somewhere else, a monitor began to beep and a red number was flashing on the corner of a screen. It startled me, but without particular urgency, a nurse stood up from her desk, looked into the isolette adjacent to the flashing screen and then reached up to the monitor's row of buttons to silence the beeping. She sat back down without saying a word.

The steely swish of a curtain being quickly drawn along a metal channel drew my eyes toward the opposite end of the room. I caught only a momentary glimpse of a man and woman before they disappeared behind the curtain. I hadn't even noticed the couple when I'd first entered. A continuous bank of windows spanned the length of the back of the room. Outside, spread like a tablecloth of mottled greens and browns, beneath a canopy of muted blue and stretching toward the distant solitude of the Texas horizon, the world "out there" carried on its business without making so much as a peep. I closed my eyes for a moment and the only sound I heard was that of my own beating heart. When I opened them again I saw in the center of the room affixed to the ceiling tiles a dimly lit sign that read "QUIET **PLEASE**."

Though I would return to the NICU time and again in the weeks and months ahead, my first impression never changed. There was an unmistakable sense of purpose here, not unlike the quiet intensity of a university library, as if the unfinished business of meeting a fast-approaching deadline was being tended to. There was also something serene, almost holy, emanating from within the room itself. Like an ancient cathedral giving furtive sanctuary to the secrets of ages past and the mystery of things yet to come, time seemed suspended in the NICU, the temporal dismissed by the sacred. I found myself afraid, nearly paralyzed from taking a step further, not knowing where to go, fearful of making a misstep. Though Erin was only a few feet from me, I stood still, circumspectly observing, not sure that I wanted — much less was ready — to lay eyes on what I'd come here to see.

I scanned the nursery anxiously, noting with appreciation that someone had made an effort to diminish the intimidating aura of the room, its perimeter lined as it was with row after row of austere looking cabinets and drawers, its ceiling tiles interrupted by tracks of lighting fixtures, expanses of HVAC vents and ductwork, and multiple electrical outlets and cable jacks. Above the cabinets, above the banks of vacuum ports and the connections marked for oxygen and medical air hoses, above the row of interior windows with blinds drawn that separated the Level II NICU from the Level III, above all of that and wherever else there was a bit of space, someone had painted what little wall area was left a creamy coral green and installed a 12 inch tall wallpaper frieze. It was a tropical jungle image, alive with bright and vivid color. Lions roamed across the repeating pattern that also featured playful elephants, rainbow-striped and long-billed birds, and giraffes whose necks reached high into the green fronds of the coconut and palm trees. Someone, at least, wanted to try to make the room feel like a nursery.

Wilford Hall's NICU was not a large unit, not like some in the big city hospitals. Here, there were only 16 care stations where isolettes, cribs or radiant warmers could be placed to provide for the needs of an infant. Floor to ceiling curtains could be drawn around the perimeter to provide privacy. An isolation area for the most critically ill babies was at the far end, next to the doorway that led directly into the NICU from the OR suite. A small table on wheels with a swivel chair was assigned to every station, each attended by a nurse. Comfortable looking, high-back chairs and a few rocking chairs were interspersed around the nursery for parents and visitors. To one side there were doors leading to smaller rooms where the attending physicians, fellows and nurses sometimes congregated. Every square foot of the NICU seemed to have a purpose. Though it was a confining space, it was also uncluttered, carefully organized so that everything necessary was close at hand. No one would have to go far to respond to an emergent situation.

Erin had moved further from me and was standing at the far wall where the exterior windows faced north. The windows closest to her had their blinds drawn halfway; the deep sill in front of them was covered with boxes of gauze, rolls of surgical tape and a dispenser for the kind of blue latex gloves everyone seemed to wear. She stood between two incubators; their bulky bases made of white vinyl mounted on a rolling platform. Printed on the side of one was a picture of a smiling giraffe — the logo for the company that manufactured the specialized type of incubators known commonly as isolettes. At a nearby station, the doctors who'd been congregated around the lab cart were now hovering over an open incubator. The lids on the isolettes on either side of Erin, however, were closed. Both had quilted blankets draped over them. One quilt had bright splashes of color, mostly red and white, across a field of dark blue, and I was struck at first glance that the image was ironically reminiscent of a tiny flag-draped coffin set upon a caisson.

Erin motioned to me to come closer. "Come see Timmy," she whispered.

I moved toward the isolettes. Erin had lifted the corner of one quilt slightly. I saw that the front panel of each isolette had a piece of paper taped to it. The one Erin was gesturing toward had a large A written on the paper in bold black magic marker. The other was marked with a D.

"These are the boys?" I asked. My arms were still folded behind my back, and as I leaned forward, I tightened the fingers of one hand around the wrist of the other to keep my hands from trembling.

"The nurse just got Wyatt to quiet down," Erin said. "But Timmy's been asleep for a while. Come look."

I took a few steps closer so I stood within arm's length of the isolette. An index card was taped near the corner closest to me. It read:

Name: Spillane, "A" (Timmy)
Mother: A. Spillane   **Rm. #:** NICU
Date of Birth: 8 April 2010   **Time:** 1520
Weight: 630 gm   **Length:** 28.5 cm
Head: 21.7 cm   **Chest:** 18 cm

Across the top of the index card, "I'M A BOY!" was printed in a larger font. Next to that were two black ink impressions, one of a foot and the other, the palm and fingers of a hand. Together the prints barely filled one corner of the 3x5" card.

I wasn't sure what I was seeing when I finally leaned forward and peered into the incubator for the first time. The little mattress was covered with a striped white baby blanket no bigger than a dish towel. In the center of it a tiny figure laid prostrate, its torso the shape and color of a not quite ripe tomato, the thin limbs splayed out to each side. The head was no bigger than a lemon and a knit wool cap was pulled down past the ears so I could not even see its face. I saw the rigid, yellow plastic bar that stabilized the ventilator tube just beyond where it exited below the wool cap, but I could not make out a mouth. The first part of the clear plastic tube was small in diameter; within a few inches it split at a "Y" into two much thicker branches each with even bulkier protrusions where they were joined by still another tube and a power cord. Several wire leads — one green, one black, one red and some that were white — and still more tubes were laid around and across the figure in the crib like the tangle of highways and roads that crisscross a map. Two slender filaments of opaque plastic were wrapped together and taped at the torso: these were the umbilical catheters. Another wire was attached to a temperature probe that was placed below the chest with a shiny gold adhesive patch shaped like a little heart. Other leads led to the arms and one foot. A blood pressure cuff was looped around the upper right arm. A pulse oximeter that monitored oxygen saturation levels was secured with surgical tape to one foot; a soft red light formed a hazy glow around the tiny toes. The little figure lay flat astride with knees pointed out in opposite directions and drawn up to the torso; where they joined together a plain white plastic diaper no more than a few inches square was folded, loosely fit around the waist and legs in front and behind. Strips of scotch-tape held the diaper to the skin.

When I looked at Timmy I did not know for sure if what I was looking at was alive. Apart from the reddish-pink of the skin there was little indication of life. Even the skin, translucent and unable to hide the tapestry of veins and arteries just beneath it, was wrinkled like the ill-fitting fabric of a suit worn by an old man. I stepped closer and put my reading glasses on. Still nothing to indicate life, I thought. I leaned over and placed my hand on top of the isolette and pushed the quilt further back. I bent down to get even closer, and that's when I saw his face for the first time.

"Oh, God!" I whispered, my heart pounding. The jarring realization that what I saw was so much more than just a face nearly crushed me. The thought crossed my mind that what I was seeing was the unfinished handiwork of God.

He was as beautiful to behold as he was frightening to see. His eyes, barely protruding below the knit wool cap he wore to keep his head warm, were fused shut; wisps of white-blonde lashes lined his lids where they joined. His nose was just a dollop of flesh, a little pink bump in the center of his face with wide, flat nostrils on either side. Both his cheeks were hidden by broad gauze bandages that secured the plastic stabilizing bar and the ventilator tube. A feeding tube and the vent snaked together into his thin blue lips. A wide strip of white surgical tape held the feeding tube in place, covering all but the very tip of his rounded chin. But for the tube that ran down his esophagus and held his head up and back to keep his throat open, it might not have seemed that he had any neck at all.

The shoulders were rounded knobs, pushed up against the sides of his neck, reaching nearly to the lobes of his ears, giving Timmy the appearance of a turtle trying to pull his head back into his shell. His chest, however, was stout, almost bulbous and his ribs and sternum were well defined, one of the few places on his body where his skin was stretched tight. He had no nipples and as I pondered that, I noticed for the first time the rising of his chest as air was pushed into his lungs. Each rise was followed by a sagging as the lungs expelled the breath, and when they did I watched him with increasing anticipation, anxious for his chest to expand again. He *was* alive, I thought. Even if it was only mechanical ventilation that caused air to course into his body and back out, I found myself exhilarated by each tiny breath, one followed by another.

More than alive, maybe, and as I studied his face I decided he looked like he wanted to stay that way. Call it a new grandfather's wistfulness, but his expression was one of determination, part grimace, but composed; a portrait of steadfastness that said he would try his best to carry on with his part of the bargain.

His fingers were like lithe twigs, thin branches that extended from his tiny palms, slowly stretching open and then closing as if in search of something to grasp and hold. They were long, fine-boned fingers, elegant in a way that reminded me of Anne's, and at the tip of each a miniscule fingernail reflected a glint of light from the fixtures above. I wondered how long before a nurse might have to wrestle delicately with him in order to trim the nails. The thought of it made me smile.

"He's amazing," I said softly to Erin.

She nodded, her eyes still on him.

"I mean, he's so small. I can't believe he's so little but so perfectly formed." I reached forward and lightly touched the clear plastic wall of his isolette. "I'm so happy to meet you, Timmy. You be strong, little guy, and be well. Maybe we can bring your mom in to see you soon."

Timmy twitched as I spoke, a slight shudder of his shoulders, and then he pulled his right arm up toward his face, and with his left he reached straight out. His right hand quivered for a moment and then weakly clasped the tube just below his mouth.

"Wow — do you think he heard me?"

Erin smiled and widened her eyes, lifting her brows to indicate that she didn't really know.

A second later an alarm sounded, a shrill beeping coming from the monitor that was mounted above Timmy's isolette. I instinctively pulled back away, the quilt dropping from my hand as I did, but the alarm stopped as suddenly as it had begun.

I breathed a little easier and took a closer look at the monitor. It was a cardiorespiratory monitor, something like a small television. Across the very top of the screen the date and time was kept, and immediately below three graphics were configured to show the heart's rate and rhythm, the respiratory rate and the O2 saturation levels in the blood. Each graph was a different color: red for the heart, yellow for the lungs and blue for oxygen levels. Using miniature sensors attached to Timmy's skin, each with a lead running from him to the machine, the monitor provided both a snapshot of how he was doing at the moment and a diary of how his day had been. When any one of Timmy's vital signs went above or below the settings prescribed for him, the alarm would sound.

Erin slid her hand under my arm and tugged gently, letting me know that it was time to leave. She motioned with her head to the adjacent station and Wyatt's isolette.

"I don't want to risk waking him," Erin said quietly. "But I think we can sneak a peek if we're careful. Rob said Wyatt was a real pistol this morning."

She led me closer to his isolette and still holding my arm, lifted Wyatt's quilt just a few inches while bending down to peer in. "Can you see?" she asked.

I decided I wasn't going to get too close; that might set another alarm off. I tried to make sense of what I saw, but it was hard to distinguish anything. Wyatt was so overlaid with tubes and hoses and wires that if it wasn't for his quick, jerky motions every few seconds I wouldn't have been able to tell whether there was a baby in the incubator at all.

"Hang in there, Wyatt," I whispered. I continued to stare at the little lump of flesh and the maze of medical paraphernalia surrounding it until Erin replaced the quilt's edge.

Across the way, in the center of the room, two more isolettes were positioned just steps apart from each other. Paper was taped to the end of each, a large letter B written in marker on one and C on the other. Turning away from Wyatt, we tiptoed toward them.

"These are your granddaughters, Dad," Erin said.

There were no quilts covering the girls' isolettes. Instead, the babies lay on their backs, naked save the diapers draped around their waists, awash in a flood of blue light. Specially formed gauze patches covered their eyes, reminding me of the blinders you would see on a race horse; only these were cotton-white and laid flat across their faces, bridging the little fleshy plop of their noses. Though their eyes could not open yet, it was still important that they were shielded from the phototherapy lights — better known as bili lights — used by hospitals to diminish the bilirubin in babies' blood that can cause jaundice. In time, the babies' livers would take over the job. For now, though, most of our visits to the NICU would find at least a couple of the babies bathed in an incandescent hue of blue.

"Say 'happy birthday' to your Papa!" Erin said, turning from one isolette to the other.

"Edda and Lily?" I asked.

"Or Lily and Edda — we're not exactly sure."

I must have looked perplexed.

"Anne knew which baby was where in her womb," Erin began to explain, "but because she was kind of out of it she couldn't be sure if it was Edda or Lily that the OB took out of her belly first. So Mom or I just need to find one of the OR nurses to confirm the position of the first girl they delivered. We're pretty positive that

Edda is Edda and Lily is Lily, though. Not that it matters much, I guess."

"It matters," I whispered, more to myself than to her.

Erin made what looked like a halfhearted attempt to smile. There was uneasiness in the way she stood looking at her new nieces. I wasn't sure what to make of it. Suddenly, she threw her head back, turned toward the rear of the room where the boys were resting and without looking at me, said, "We should go now, Dad. We should go and see Anne."

"What do you think?" I asked before she could push open the NICU doors.

She hesitated and then said, "I don't know, Dad."

"You know a lot. You're a doctor."

"I'm not a neonatologist. I can't say." She turned toward the double doors leading to the corridor. "They're waiting," she said. "We should go."

"Erin?" She looked back at me. I could see she was agitated, but I didn't know why. She wouldn't look directly into my eyes. "The babies — what about them? What do you think?"

"They're all alive. That's enough for right now, isn't it?" Then, abruptly, she turned back toward the doors, walked through them and disappeared.

CHAPTER 4
A family portrait
Snapshots across time

Sent: Friday, April 9, 2010 8:25:05 PM

Subject: day end update

A good day for all. Anne was moved from the SICU to a room back in the maternity floor this afternoon. She's still feeling pretty lousy, but continues to improve. Erin and I were able to get her into a wheelchair and in to see her babies at about 6 pm. She was able to touch each of them!

Wyatt's central line was successfully placed, although he is constantly trying to fight with his tubes and pull them out. He has so much character for such a little guy. Each baby has its own nurse and we were able to talk with each of them which was a real comfort to Anne. Anne's report is that her babies look like chickens! ☺

It's Tim's birthday and I need to run. They're all squawking at me!!!

D.

We didn't have a birthday cake that night, but I do recall that we *did* share a muted but much needed "happy hour" together. Cait found a beer in the refrigerator, and Erin made herself at home, opening a bottle of wine. After I pleaded with my wife to close her laptop — she was trying to upload pictures to include with the email she was about to send — I poured us both a drink, and we all sat down together to toast in celebration.

"To birthdays," I said. "To Timmy, Edda, Lily and Wyatt, and to me. If I never have another one like this one it will be too soon!"

Rob came home only after we were sleeping, and when I awoke early Saturday morning he was already gone. I didn't know if that was a sign of problems with the babies or if Anne's condition had worsened. I could only trust that if something had gone terribly wrong overnight, Rob would have awakened us to let us know. He and Donna had become too close over the last week for him not to tell her something like that. And knowing my wife, I figured she would have sensed if something bad had happened anyway.

I sat in the kitchen while Donna, Erin and Cait slept, looking at the pictures my wife had loaded onto her computer before I'd chased her away from it. Though the folder on her laptop contained only a handful of photographs, I thought it would be bulging soon enough. Still, I knew these first images would always be the most unforgettable.

I saw one of the babies — I had no clue who was who — lying flat on its back, arms bent at the elbows and pulled to its sides. Its legs were drawn up, too, and the fused eyes were squeezed shut so tightly it appeared to be waiting in dread anticipation of the inevitable next test, blood draw or poke. The poor little thing looked so sad and utterly alone. I wondered if she or he was asleep — if it was possible for the babies to rest at all.

Then it was a different baby, also on its back, with one of its hands pulled up beside its cheek and fisted in a tiny ball. The other arm lay out and to the side, its fingers entangled in a web of lead wires. The next photo was of Anne's hand reaching into a crib, the camera capturing her delicately touching one of her children for the first time. Anne's fear that even the slightest touch might harm the tiny baby was plain in the photo.

Rob took photographs, too, and Donna told him he'd better not stop. She wanted to see pictures every day once we were back home. In one of his, he'd taken off his wedding band and slipped it onto a baby's arm. Wedding rings were often used for scale in pictures taken in the NICU because they showed just how small these preemies were. Rob's band did more than just fit over his baby's wrist like a bracelet — it moved easily beyond its elbow to rest on the shoulder. Though I don't know that Rob ever tried, from what I saw, it looked like the babies' legs were skinny enough that his wedding band might have reached all the way to mid-thigh.

But my favorite picture is one I took the day Anne and I visited the babies for the first time together. Her hand is framed by the photo — a hand that to me could only have been Anne's. She always had the most beautiful hands, the long, finely boned fingers, the carefully manicured nails. To me, they embodied all the grace of her womanhood, but here in the photograph, for the first time, her hand also speaks so eloquently to the promise of motherhood. She was reaching into an isolette; her left hand poised gingerly above one of her babies, its face covered by the gauzy bili-shields. The child's chest is plainly visible, but the body below the waist is hidden in a jumble of blankets and a maze of tubes and wires. Its left arm is stretching upward, having found the tip of its mother's middle finger only the moment before the picture was taken. The baby is clasping a mother's hand it is unable to see, and Anne's own thumb and forefinger return the touch.

It's Lily's hand in the photo, and the whole of it is no larger than her mommy's thumbnail. The poignant pose never fails to melt me. Lily would have her mother's beautiful hands and fingers one day, I told Anne that afternoon in the NICU. I hoped one day Lily, Anne and I would laugh and cry when years later we'd look at the old digital photograph together. For now though, I decided I would post the picture as the background on my desktop computer when I returned to Pennsylvania. And I promised myself I would leave it there until Lily had come home. Seeing it day in and day out would help me to keep faith. There was little doubt with four babies in the NICU that hope would wane in the months to come, but I promised myself for Lily's sake and for Anne's that I would never lose faith. Sometimes that's all a dad can do.

Somewhere at home, we have a photo of the old gray mare. She is standing behind the barn; the chestnut foal with a white blaze on its nose that she has only just delivered stands wobbly-kneed by her side.

The twins were not yet ten years old when we got the old mare. Freckles was their first horse. Not much to ride, she was still a fine brood mare, and before Anne and Erin had become teenagers she'd given us a chestnut colt and then a dark brown filly. Seeing chicks and ducklings born and frolicking in the barn-yard each spring was one thing, but watching a foal come into the world was something else. What was more amazing to me, however, was how from this one old mare came much more, and not just horses, but a world — a horse *culture* — that spun without my help and totally beyond my control.

Only Caitlin was spared from the madness. Much like me, she gravitated toward the *good* sports — basketball, track and the like — running and jumping on *your own* legs. Erin and Anne, with their mother in tow, were quickly swept away by the horse-force now loose in our lives. You could drown in the minutiae. The barn filled with blankets, bell boots, bridles and bits, lead lines, lunge lines, liniments and leathers, saddles, snaffles, stirrups and sheets. Inside the house conversations revolved around riding centered, correct confirmation, counter canters, close-contact saddles and full-seat breeches. Even the bathroom reading rack was filled with horse journals, catalogs and magazines. There were Pony Club meetings, rallies and ratings, competitions, events, trials, tests and lessons and more lessons. There were vet visits, blacksmith visits, an occasional house call from the horse dentist and even once an acupuncture specialist for the horses. The horse world had become an intractable part of our lives. How was it that we had survived so long without wormer, fly sprays and pots of beet pulp brewing on the kitchen stove?

Certainly, there was much gained. Anne and Erin learned not just about hard work and responsibility; they also learned self-discipline, how to prioritize their time and organizational skills. They came to appreciate the indispensable value of little things like checklists — because if you arrive at a Pony Club formal inspection without a hairnet, you might just as well have forgotten to wear your breeches. They gained self-esteem and learned humility — what else can a young girl learn from having to thoroughly clean her gelding's sheath? They became more confident as they grew, able to compete individually and with a team. Even I gained some measure of contentment from the horse world we now occupied, knowing that as the twins grew into young women they still liked horses more than boys and that the exhilaration of an open field gallop was the only "high" they sought.

But there was loss, too. There were the disappointments they encountered and setbacks they endured, and for me, the knowledge that tragedies could and would happen. Like any father, I wanted to save my children from hardship and my own heart from being broken.

For them, the cruelest pain was to see their horses suffer. Because Anne rode dressage — a discipline of elegant movements and precise coordination — she required complete soundness in a horse's legs. Erin's cross-country riding demanded a horse with a heart for adventure and more guts than grace. The suffering their horses endured came with bitter irony. Anne's horse became chronically lame, its legs unable to carry her to the competitive level that for years they had worked so diligently toward. And for Erin it was the guts that failed, literally, and twice at that.

First, her sturdy pony who had taught her as a young girl to be bold, was lost to a twisted intestine. Then the veteran thoroughbred who had shown her the cocky confidence the sport required was put down after losing a battle with colic. There were tears, of course, and hollowness where their hopes and dreams had died. What could I say to Anne when her horse, *her* horse because she had put so much of herself into him, was retired to someone else's farm because we couldn't afford to keep a horse that Anne could no longer ride? What comfort could I bring to Erin when *twice* she had to make the return trip from the equine hospital to our barn late in the night with the empty horse trailer rattling behind us?

I felt their sorrow and tried to encourage them through the hardships. I struggled with them in the search for new direction, wrestled with their frustrations in order to find new hope, and sometimes we even found them a new mount. But their horses were not what concerned me.

I kept a diary of sorts in those days, a mental record of the times that fate's shadow slipped closely by. There was Anne's dressage coach — an advanced level rider thrown and knocked unconscious; a teenage girl from our area, killed in a car accident while rushing to a competition in a driving rain; innumerable tales of kicks, bites and falls, bumps and bruises to the girls and their riding friends; but most tragic of all was the loss of Erin's riding coach and mentor, a young man she so admired. He was killed in a riding accident during a cross country competition in the autumn of the twins' senior year of high school.

Little did I know then that the tragedies that had come so near Anne and Erin as teenagers would come closer still — much closer.

It was the last family portrait taken before we all started to leave home. We are gathered around the living room sofa, my brother John and I like bookends on either side of the couch, Mom and the youngest three, Gary, Mary and Laura, are seated between us. Behind them, my older brothers Mike and Bill stand to the right and left of Dad. He is smiling proudly.

My father considered himself the beneficiary of a lifetime of good luck. Mike and I would tell him it was more than luck; he was blessed. But whether it was plain old luck or the favor of God, the good fortune that had surrounded the Spillane family for decades took a turn for the worse in the years following Anne and Rob's wedding in 2006.

With my four brothers and two sisters and me all married, my dad's family had grown to include 24 grandchildren. Mike was already adding great grandchildren to the tally. If my father was a lucky man then his good luck seemed to extend around all of us. My mother survived a frightening bout with breast cancer in middle age; there was never any recurrence. Gary and Bill managed to total two family cars and walk away unscathed. Bill and John very nearly went over a 30 foot waterfall in a kayak on a rain-swollen river. My younger sister Mary and her new husband Charlie were involved in a wintry car accident that very nearly crippled him. I myself fell off a roof at work and crushed my heel, shattered an ankle and fractured a vertebra in my back. People were hurt, people recovered. The fact that my father's good luck had held up for so many for so long was probably nothing short of a miracle.

It was how eloquently my father stated it that I will never forget. We were celebrating his 80th birthday with Mom, my brothers and sisters and our spouses. "I was a lucky man," Dad reminded us as we sat at the restaurant where we had gathered to honor him. He had been lucky to be born to hardworking parents who'd doggedly persevered while they raised their children through the teeth of the Great Depression. He had been a healthy boy; his older brother had not been so fortunate. He died from an ear infection at the age of seven. He had been lucky to be too young to join the Navy until the summer of 1945; older friends who had joined before him never returned home from the war. He had been lucky in love, lucky to find his wife Rita — the right woman at the right time. He had always been in the perfect place when unexpected opportunities opened doors for him in his career. He had been lucky to have good friends throughout his life. And he had been lucky to have children who would grow up to raise children who gave them as much joy as his did him. But that night, we all knew that the reach of his luck had found its limits. He didn't hide from the pain. "A star has fallen from our galaxy," he said at last, holding back his tears. "And I count myself lucky to have known someone as special as my grandson, David."

Dave was my nephew, and my brother John's oldest son. If life's twists and turns are a matter of luck alone, then Dave's luck ran out on a rain-slicked highway a month before Dad reached his 80 year milestone. Dave died a couple weeks shy of his own birthday; he would have been 25. The last time my brother and his wife saw their son was for dinner on Father's Day, only a few days before the accident and a week before Anne and Rob's first wedding anniversary. Anne hadn't seen Dave since the night of her wedding. When she flew home for the funeral I could see the disbelief in her eyes, and I was afraid she would see even worse in mine. The vulnerability I felt that day for the whole Spillane family was a feeling I'd never known before. None of us had. As close as tragedy had come before, it had never touched us directly.

Dave's death shattered the illusion of our peaceful, secure lives. And there was more to come. Two nephews struggled with substance abuse and addiction; a third ended up in jail for robbery. A brother's marriage began falling apart; his wife moved out of the house saying she couldn't live with him anymore. A niece broke off her engagement only weeks before the wedding. A sister's retail business was destroyed in a worsening economy. A niece and her husband lost their house to foreclosure. The constancy we had known for so much of our lives was disappearing. The fountain of our good fortune seemed to have run dry.

I wrestled with this new reality. Some days I was able to convince myself that nothing could change the experience of God in my own life. Other times it wasn't so easy. Though I tried to continually remind myself that He had done so much that was good for me and my family, the future was a darker, more forlorn place to me. But I also began to gradually come to terms with the notion that having faith meant I couldn't pretend to understand His thoughts or anticipate His ways. As irrational as it seemed, I knew I would have to be okay with both knowing and not knowing. I had read Psalm 33 too many times over the years to turn anywhere else to find my way going forward.

> *But the plans of the Lord stand firm forever, the*
> *purposes of His heart through all generations.*
> (PSALM 33: 11)

Whatever His plans were, I would never know them for certain. Whatever fears I had because of the tragedies of the recent past, I committed to making the choice to look for hope again. I decided I could not turn back from faith now, no matter what.

In the months following I began to reach for God anew and to find refuge in His presence. I began in the simplest of ways. I found the first Bible I had bought for myself, the book that I had read over and over as a teenager and young man after I had committed my life to the Lord. It was tattered and worn, the cover gone, pages stained with coffee and who knows what else, the first chapters of *Genesis* torn away, missing altogether. I began again to read and meditate on the verses I had underlined so very carefully with a pen and ruler many years before, the verses that in subsequent readings I had circled and scribbled notes about in the margins. I began to compile those verses on my computer and was determined to put them to use. Each morning, before work, I would paste one verse or passage into an email and add an encouraging comment before sending it to Donna and the girls. Cait was still living at home and would get hers first thing; Erin at Walter Reed and Anne in Texas read theirs when they'd returned home after their long days in the hospitals. Donna would see me later in the day, and sometimes she would say, "Thanks. Today's verse meant a lot."

Sometime between Dave's death and Anne getting pregnant I sent a passage that had always meant so much to me. It's from the Book of Proverbs:

> *Trust in the Lord with all your heart,*
> *And do not lean on your own understanding.*
> *In all your ways acknowledge Him,*
> *And He will make your paths straight.*
> (PROV. 3: 5–6)

Every family is tested and some more than others. Though I had no way of knowing what trials we might yet face, I could do one thing. I took those verses from Proverbs, and like a picture that I could admire every day I hung them in my heart. And come what may, for the sake of my family, I decided I would keep my eyes on them and try to walk forward with faith.

What that faith would look like, I didn't know. "Faith is the assurance of things hoped for, the conviction of things unseen," is what it says in the Book of Hebrews. True though that may be, it's no small help to *actually* see some things that bolster your faith along the way.

Though I remembered to bring a camera when Cait and I hurriedly left for San Antonio, I never bothered to pull it out of my pocket the first few days after Anne's babies were born. In all the frenzy, taking pictures seemed like a distraction. But if I had, I definitely would have wanted to take a snapshot that captured the spellbinding look in Nurse Johnson's eyes.

Anne's condition had been improving throughout the day and by late Friday afternoon she was deemed far enough from danger that she could be released from the SICU. She was still considered critical because her blood pressure remained high, but the resident on call agreed to sign Anne over to the Labor & Delivery ward to finish her recovery. The "negotiated release" of the patient hinged on the fact that Anne and Erin — both being *responsible* doctors themselves, the resident pointed out — had each agreed to monitor Anne's vital signs religiously and to notify her of any abrupt change in Anne's condition. Discharge from the SICU meant that she could visit her babies at last.

She was settled in her new room in time for dinner — "a travesty of the culinary art," Anne called the meal. I considered her criticism of the hospital food further evidence of her improving condition. After Anne had some time to digest, we called the nurse's station. When a young Air Force nurse arrived we asked her if it would be possible to arrange for Anne to go down the hall to the NICU and see her babies. "That'd be Nurse Johnson's call," the young woman explained. "She's the head nurse for the shift. Let me see if I can get her for you."

Nurse Johnson was a short, stout woman with straight black hair pulled back into a bun. Her skin was a rich chocolate with dark creases accenting her lips and eyes, and black, rectangular plastic framed reading glasses rested on the tip of her nose. She was, as she put it, "Just an old, hardworking black woman from rural Georgia. A wife, a mother and a grandmother. That's all. And nothin' more," but she hadn't been back to Georgia for years, she explained. Her husband was retired military — a Master Sergeant in the Air Force who had moved her and her family all over the country and once, and "only once mind you," halfway around the world. His last duty station had been here in south Texas, and when he retired they'd decided to stay in the San Antonio area because there was plenty of work for a nurse like her, and they both liked the climate and the easy-going manner of the people. "Good, godly people," was how she referred to them. And besides, most of her children and grandchildren were scattered around the country. Not much reason to return to Georgia, she said.

She also saw no reason why this new mom in her care — with a little extra attention — couldn't go to the NICU for a visit.

In short order, Nurse Johnson found a wheelchair with an oxygen tank strapped to its side — Anne was still on oxygen from the surgery — and brought it along with a blanket and some other odds and ends to Anne's room. She helped Anne gingerly move from her bed to sit down in the wheelchair. She carefully positioned the IV pole that would accompany Anne on the trip and then told her, "You take your time now, honey. Your baby isn't going anywhere just yet."

"Babies!" Donna said, and everyone laughed.

"Babies? My, my!" Nurse Johnson said and pushed Anne toward the door.

Rob had gone on ahead of the rest of us to warn the NICU staff that "Mom" was coming. As we exited the Labor & Delivery ward I asked Nurse Johnson if I could push my daughter the rest of the way. I explained that two of my daughters were doctors and my wife was an EMT. She stopped pushing when I said that, puckered her lips as she pondered it and then agreed. "I'll wander down in a bit to check on y'all," she said. "You give your baby love from Nurse Johnson," she called to Anne as we moved out of the ward.

"Babies," my wife said softly.

I pushed Anne down the long corridor, past the tributes and commemorative plaques, toward the double doors that led into the NICU suite. Rob was coming out the doors by the time we reached the sink next to them. He was wearing this glum look he gets, and it was a sure sign that something was troubling him.

"What is it?" Erin asked, recognizing his expression.

"Well, it's — you know — the sign posted says that — um, we might not all —"

Erin cut him off. "Just speak, Robert!"

It was NICU policy that only two parents and two grandparents or two parents and two of the baby's siblings could come in at one time. He pointed to a sign explaining as much posted to the side of the sink. "And they reiterated it at the desk inside," he said.

"Cait and I have already been in there together," Erin said. "You don't have to be a sibling of a baby to get in there."

"I know, I know."

"Anne has four babies!" Donna practically shouted. "That should mean she can have two people with her and you at *each* crib!"

"I know!" The rule *was* stupid. But Rob was trying to tread softly. No sense making enemies with the NICU staff — not with babies that were likely going to be long-term residents in the facility. I understood his dilemma.

"Let Erin take Anne in first," I suggested. "She's a doctor and nobody is going to be able to tell her to leave."

"I'll see if I can't bring your mom in with me after a few minutes," Rob agreed.

Cait and I would be left outside to fend for ourselves again. When I looked at Cait to see if she minded, she only shrugged.

After Anne and Erin finished washing their hands Rob pulled open both double doors and Erin pushed the wheelchair with her sister inside. I could see them turn toward the entrance to the Level III NICU, and before the doors could close behind them, Rob quickly stuck his head back out and told Donna to wash her hands and come wait inside. She did, leaving Cait and me alone with our thoughts and the NICU's Wall of Faith once more. Cait said matter-of-factly, "That's bullshit, Dad. That's a ridiculous rule."

We both laughed.

Then she said, "I'm not looking at any of the stuff on that wall again. You know I can't do that, right?"

I told her I understood.

We waited together as one minute became five, five became fifteen, and fifteen became thirty. Finally, Erin pushed open one of the double doors and rolled the wheelchair through.

"This is a real pain in there," she said. "Can you guys take it back to the ward? Anne's doing okay on her feet. Mom and I will walk her back to the room later. You okay, Dad, Cait?"

But neither Cait nor I had the chance to say anything before Erin was gone again.

Cait sat down in the discarded wheelchair. "I'm exhausted, Dad," she said. "And it's your birthday."

"I know, Cait."

We waited some more and then I decided to kill time by returning the wheelchair.

"Don't look!" I said as I pushed Cait and the chair back down the corridor, past the Wall of Faith and its pictures both happy and sad.

She covered her eyes with her hands. "I'm so worried for Anne's babies."

"I know, honey."

At the other end of the hall, a dark figure appeared and began walking with resolute strides toward us. It was Nurse Johnson.

"She wants her wheelchair back," Cait said as she sprang up out of the seat.

"How's momma making out?" she asked in her slow, southern drawl when she reached us.

"All right. She's doing okay, I think."

"That's good," Nurse Johnson said, "but where're you folks taking her wheelchair? She's gonna need her chariot, right?"

"She says she'll be fine — the walk might do her some good," I said.

"Okay." She nodded. "And the baby — oh, that's right, you said it was *babies?* How the young'uns doing? A boy and a girl?"

"Boys and girls!"

"Two boys and two girls, actually," Caitlin added.

Nurse Johnson's eyes grew wide. She began rubbing her chin between her forefinger and thumb. "Four babies — quadruplets?" she asked after a moment.

Cait and I nodded.

"That slight, sweet little girl?" she asked.

"Yes Ma'am," I answered.

"Lord-y be!" Nurse Johnson said, and reaching in front of me, grabbed the handles of the wheelchair to push it herself. But then she hesitated. "I don't know much of anything about your daughter, sir," she said, looking at me and then Caitlin and back again with sharp eyes. "But those babies — those children are favored by God!" Her stare became mesmerizing. "You hear me now," she repeated herself, "those babies are favored by God."

And then just like that, she turned her back to Cait and me and headed toward Labor & Delivery with the wheelchair and its tall oxygen tank in front of her.

Cait looked at me with astonishment in her eyes. "Did you hear what I did?"

I nodded. I had, indeed. If I had never heard a prophet utter a single word up until that moment, I was sure that just then I had.

Cait and I stood looking at each other. I don't think either of us knew whether to continue down the hall or head back to the NICU. But then the double doors at the end of the corridor behind us opened and Rob appeared; he was holding one of the doors open with his right arm and kicking at the other with his left foot. Then Anne appeared, her mom and sister on either side of her, each holding an elbow to support her. Anne was clutching the IV pole.

"Sorry we took so long," Donna called to us.

I said nothing. Favored by God? Those were the only words I'd heard.

Maybe what Erin said the first time I saw the babies was right: I should have been thankful that Anne's children were even alive. They were so small, so fragile and vulnerable that their grip on life seemed wholly untenable. And apart from recent advances in the specialized care of the tiniest of babies, Timmy, Edda, Lily and Wyatt would have had next to no chance in life at all.

Anne and Erin had spent nearly two weeks in the NICU in 1980, but so much about the care of premature babies has changed since then. I still remember holding Anne and her sister, one in each arm, the first week after they'd come home. They were like little dolls. I was afraid that if I took my eyes off them, one or the other would slip through the crook in my arm, but also terrified that if I squeezed too hard while holding them I would crush the life out of their tiny bodies. Now nearly 30 years later, the combined weight of the four babies Anne delivered did not exceed the threshold for the medical definition of *one* low birth weight baby. At a total weight of 5lb 5oz, they missed that mark by 3oz.

The term neonatology didn't even exist when my wife and I were babies in the 1950s. And less than a century prior to that, physicians frankly gave little or no thought to the notion of infant mortality. Ironically, I would only learn after Anne's own babies were born that the beginnings of neonatology were not so different than Anne and Erin's own first experiences practicing "medicine" when they were young girls.

Donna and I raised our family in a small house overlooking a stream and a few boggy acres. The high ground was gradually filled with the twins' horses, a barn and associated paraphernalia. We reserved the lowland for duck houses, chicken coops and the makeshift infirmaries the girls would occasionally erect. In time, our twin daughters became seasoned practitioners of what our family vet referred to with a wink as "chicken medicine" — the mostly futile attempts at nurturing back to health the maimed ducklings, injured chicks, and lost fledglings they often encountered around our little farm. Precious few of their patients survived, but the ones that did made their efforts feel more than worthwhile. And while it would be a long time before they were doctors *for real*, Anne and Erin's early experience in medicine would help shape the kind of physicians they would one day become.

I have to wonder if it also helped them appreciate the fact that the roots of neonatology grew not from the ivory towers of academia, but from a chicken incubator display in a zoo in Paris, France, in the late 1800s.

It was while studying the eggs and hatchlings in the zoo's incubator that the French obstetrician, Stephan Tarnier, was inspired to use a similar device to help the infants who often succumbed to hypothermia in the maternity wards where he worked. Tarnier's invention wasn't such a novel idea — mothers had been using laundry baskets, blankets and bottles filled with warm water for far longer — but what was significant was the statistical data he compiled suggesting the incubators really did make a difference.

Soon, Tarnier's incubators were in hospitals throughout Paris and a system of hospital-based care for the sickest babies was established in maternity wards. Following in Tarnier's footsteps, another Parisian obstetrician, Pierre-Constant Budin, began to include mothers in the care of their sick infants, to encourage breastfeeding and to assist the mothers and their babies after they were discharged from the hospital. Budin's work became the foundation on which modern newborn medicine was built.

The end of World War II brought rapid change. Soon after, specialized nurseries called newborn intensive care units (NBICU) were developed and the terms "Neonatologist" and "Neonatology" were used for the first time. By the end of the twentieth century, new and improving technologies for temperature regulation, ventilatory management, and fluid and nutrition delivery combined to push the threshold for premature infant viability to a point that was unimaginable only a few decades before. Babies as small as one pound and those with gestational ages as early as 23 weeks were surviving more often. These were the babies so tiny they were called "micro-preemies."

Despite all the advances in the care of preemies, babies still had to make the transition to life outside the womb — and in many ways they were still on their own. In that sense, some things hadn't changed at all. Once delivered, a baby's lungs have to begin to breathe air. Without its mother to depend on, the way a baby's cardiac and pulmonary circulation systems worked would have to change. The baby would have to take food, digest it and excrete the waste. The kidneys would have to eliminate waste, as well, and begin to balance fluids and chemicals in the body. The baby's liver would have to get in gear, too, and its immunologic systems would need to come online. Most babies, even many preemies, did these things automatically. The very premature baby, however, could hardly do anything by itself yet; and some things it simply could not do at all.

Today, while nearly 90% of babies in the United States are born at full term — generally healthy, most likely chubby and hopefully happy — more than half a million are born premature. Fortunately, very few of those babies are born younger than 28 weeks and even fewer are born weighing less than two pounds. Timmy, Edda, Lily and Wyatt just happened to be four of them.

How small were they? Once, while drinking my morning coffee I wondered what it might have been like to hold Wyatt right after he was born. Curious, I put my mug on Donna's kitchen scale. Sip by sip I worked the cup down toward the weight I was looking for. Having finished the first half of my coffee, I took one more mouthful and set it back on the scale. The screen read 540 grams exactly. I picked the mug up — its stout shape a fair approximation of the size of Wyatt's torso — and let it rest in the palm of my hand. That was all there was to him at birth. Wyatt Lee Schlender… Barely 1 pound, 3 ounces, or the weight of half a mug of coffee.

CHAPTER 5

New York City
May, 1999

THERE ARE NO PHOTOGRAPHS from that weekend, not even one from this special evening. I don't mind, however. The pictures in my memory are as clear as day. Anne is the sweet and quiet girl I promised Donna she would be, but she is more than that now. Tonight, she is downright beautiful. It is as if both Anne and Erin have been transformed and until this moment, I hadn't noticed. All the childhood warts and the awkwardness of adolescence have fallen away so that what appear before me are no longer my little girls, but two daughters now very much in the blossom of womanhood. Call it a father's vain indulgence, but they are knockouts, plain and simple. And I am floored.

It was the second of two nights we three spent in New York City. It was a rainy May weekend in the girls' senior year of high school. Neither Anne nor Erin had dated much, so the notion of finding just some guy to take them to their senior prom wasn't appealing. But if the prom didn't matter much to them, it didn't mean they couldn't appreciate new dresses, stiletto heels and a handsome escort to show them around town for a night. They figured they would be as happy exchanging the traditional high school gala for an afternoon of clothes shopping with their mom and a weekend of painting the town red with their dad. And even if having your father fill in as the handsome escort left something to be desired, spending a whirlwind weekend in the Big Apple sure beat a night in a high school gym filled with balloons and boys in ill-fitting tuxedos.

In New York, as Erin and Anne took turns taking their showers, blow drying and doing each other's hair, I snuck in a short nap. When I awoke, I glimpsed Anne and Erin standing in front of the mirror in their new dresses. I smiled impishly to myself at the thought of Donna and Caitlin at home probably bringing the horses out of the muddy fields and into our barn for the night.

Like my father, who never brought me to New York City as a boy without somehow including a subway ride as part of the trip, I had picked a restaurant far enough away from our hotel to warrant our own excursion on the underground trains. It was there, as we stood on the platform waiting for the low rumble and rushing wind of an approaching train, that I saw my two daughters as I had never before. Their long frames filled the evening dresses they wore, and the effect was beautiful. Their gleaming heels, the elegant shawls wrapped around their bare shoulders, the sparkle of the necklaces they wore, the soft curls of their flowing hair — there was a grace and femininity in my girls that was delightfully new to me. I stepped slowly back so I could see them better. They were craning their necks, leaning ever so slightly over the sunken tracks, peering into the dark tunnel from which a single bright light would soon appear. When it did, they turned together with smiles on their faces, but not finding me there, they were momentarily startled.

"Papa!" Anne called out. There was an affectionate scold in her voice when her eyes found mine. "Come on, Papa! The train is coming!"

It was a long subway ride from the Upper West Side all the way down Broadway to Lower Manhattan. When we exited the subway at Cortland St. we followed the corridors through the concourse to a wide bank of towering escalators that climbed out of the bowels of the World Trade Center into a central ground level plaza. From there we walked toward the North Tower and before entering, we each leaned back to try and see the top of the building before it disappeared into the mist and darkness of the night.

We took the elevator to the 107th floor and the Windows on the World restaurant. I had been there once before with Donna. I remembered how awesome the view had been that night. Through floor to ceiling windows in the lounge, Donna and I had seen the Hudson and East Rivers joining below us, the Statue of Liberty and Ellis Island, and in the distance, the twinkling lights on the suspension cables of the Verrazano-Narrows Bridge. It was spectacular. But when Erin and Anne and I stopped in the bar for a Tanqueray martini straight-up and two Shirley Temples for the ladies, we could only see rivulets of rain coursing down the long panes of glass.

Whatever disappointment I felt due to the weather began to dissipate when the maître d' seated us at what appeared to be the best table in the restaurant. Perhaps he sensed a father's angst, or maybe he was as stunned as I was by how pretty the girls looked. Maybe we were just lucky. In any case, he deferentially guided us to a table with a commanding view of the dining room in a spot where the rest of the patrons couldn't help but notice the lucky guy with a beautiful woman on each arm. We felt regal.

It was wonderful. I ate an appetizer of raw oysters on ice and had a second martini. The girls declined my recommendation of the Terrine of Foie Gras for two, but braved the Carpaccio of house-cured beef and melon salad. The waiter gave them entrée-sized portions of the asparagus ravioli with fresh wild morel mushrooms. I had the obligatory "Statue of Liberty" rack of lamb with stuffed grape leaves. At some point during dinner I noticed the rain had stopped and the skies were beginning to gradually clear. By the time we were enjoying the chocolate and raspberry terrine with fresh berries, parts of uptown New York were visible and then, as though on cue, just before we rose to leave our table, the Empire State building appeared from beyond a shroud of clouds, its lights illuminating the gleaming tower in all its grandeur. It was an intoxicating nightcap to an incredible evening.

That dinner in Manhattan was more than a substitute for their prom. It was also a celebration of Erin and Anne's acceptance, a few months before, into the college they had only dreamed of attending. I take credit for having forced them to apply. Fathers can have that kind of power over their daughters, if they choose to exercise it. They both told me it wouldn't matter if they applied; they would never get accepted anyway. I told them they would never know if they didn't try. They told me they wouldn't even visit the school. I told them it might plant the seeds of hope in them if we did, so we went.

Like our weekend in New York City, our exploration of Cornell University began in the rain. They said it was a bad sign. I said it wasn't a hard rain, and we would walk the campus to see what we might discover. We trekked from one side of the sprawling campus to the other. Nestled in the hills surrounding the Finger Lakes of New York State, the campus is perched high above its surroundings, and with its Classical architecture and ubiquitous gothic arches, in the rainy mist of that afternoon it appeared almost a kingdom in the clouds. As we walked, I sensed the seeds of hope and possibility begin to grow in the twins — and in me, too.

The last stop on our tour was a suspension footbridge tucked into a remote corner on the north end of the campus; I'm not even sure how we found it. But I'd seen it on the campus map and I felt a familiar need to cross it. Bridges are built for an obvious purpose, but in crossing them, I'd always felt they and the waters they span were wonderful metaphors for our lives. In them, we find symbols for our sojourning nature and for the passage of time, for our desire for connectedness and the allure of the *other side.*

As we started to cross, the bridge began to subtly sway in response to our movements, making the structure seem alive. The sinewy, elegant pattern of the suspending cables allowed them to flex with every step we took, so that by the time we reached the middle of the span we could feel the whole bridge undulating in a series of slow and gently rolling waves. We stopped there and as the motion subsided, we looked over one side and then the other. Down and to the west was the southern shore of Lake Cayuga. To the east, the waters that rushed from Beebe Lake toward Cayuga's shore had carved the great gorge over which the bridge was suspended. And below us, divergent torrents of water coursed toward one another and merged together into a boiling white cauldron of foam and froth.

The girls and I had been laughing out loud at the unexpected delight of crossing the bouncing footbridge, but now as the three of us stood peering down from it, we had each become quiet. It was very nearly dusk, and time to be heading home. But we lingered, fearing to lose the hope I think we all felt. Leaving the bridge meant leaving Cornell on that other shore, part of a realm just beyond our grasp. We made no move to depart. Instead, the girls threw pennies down into the water a hundred or more feet below hoping to hit their imagined target: a crucible of boiling waters formed by the convergence of rocky ledges directly beneath the bridge's span.

"You throw one, Dad," Anne said. They were having no luck hitting the mark.

I could not escape the girls' eyes that were now riveted to mine, or the pregnant weight of that moment. I dug my hand into my pocket and pulled out what coins I had. A single quarter lay prominently among the nickels, dimes and pennies. I let the rest of the change pour back into my pocket and then, in one rather absurd yet poignant gesture, closed my fist around the quarter, stretched my hand toward my daughters and asked them to place their hands over mine.

"This is it," I said, "like a fleece before the Lord. Let this be a sign. Our hopes go with this quarter." And I threw the coin into the air, and with it, a symbol of their destiny to the wind.

Though the act was literally meaningless, our eyes widened as the quarter cut a path downward. Our hearts pounded so that I thought the bridge might begin its bouncing anew. In the next instant, the spell was broken. The clock of our lives resumed as we felt the seconds nearly audibly ticking away once more. Reluctantly, we left the suspension footbridge and returned to our car. No one spoke. We were unwilling to speak, I think, lest we upset the precarious balance of fate. We smiled instead. We smiled at the beautiful picture of that quarter vanishing into the heart of the glistening crucible. We had hit the target.

Anne met Rob in her junior year at Cornell. Back then he was just the mystery guy who lived upstairs in the dilapidated old home next to *The Chapter House* bar on Stewart Avenue, where Anne and Erin rented an apartment. Though the boarding house was in a run-down part of Ithaca, it was where the off-campus students fought one another for the right to rent rooms and apartments. There simply weren't enough rooms near the campus — and even fewer close to a good local hangout — to accommodate the students who wanted to live in town. That was what made this "guy upstairs" so mysterious. His name was posted for months on the door to the room he'd rented but no one had ever seen him. What kind of guy would rent a room in such a sought-after location and then just not show up?

Ithaca is a cold, snowy place in winter, and outdoor recreation opportunities diminish significantly during the season's short days and long, dark nights. In the coldest weather, the girl's only exercise was walking up and down the steep hills that hugged the perimeter of the Cornell campus on the way to class. At night, to try and get their blood moving, Anne and Erin would occasionally stroll over to the *Chapter House* for a pint of Guinness draught and a game or two on the foosball tables. The activity was conducive to the kind of easy, mostly meaningless conversation that helped pass the frigid and seemingly interminable winter.

The subject of the mystery guy upstairs was the topic one particular winter night. While the twins worked the colorful wooden players on the foosball table — their eyes following the ball so intently that they could scarcely steal a moment to look at one another — Anne suggested that maybe their absentee neighbor worked nights. "Not a chance," Erin said, "too quiet around here. We would have heard him for sure. Guys are noisy like that."

"Well, what about his name? What do you make of that?" Anne asked.

Erin hesitated as she tried to remember what the name she'd seen on his door was.

"I don't know," she finally said. "Bob, Rob, Robert — what difference does it make?"

"No, I mean his last name."

"His last name?"

"Did you see the spelling?" Anne asked. "How do you think you pronounce that?"

"What? You've got a photographic memory or something? All I remember is Rob or Bob or whatever, and a last name that starts with S."

Anne spelled the name for her sister. "S-c-h-l-e-n-d-e-r."

"You *are* nuts. What are you doing memorizing how to spell the name of a guy you've never even met?"

"When we were wandering around to see who was moving in upstairs, I saw his name and I wasn't sure how to pronounce it. It just kind of stuck in my mind, I guess."

"Spell it again."

She did, and then asked, "Is it Shhh-lender? Or Scklender — you know, like the 's-c-h' in 'school'?"

Erin thought about it for a minute. She continued looking down intently at the game that flew on uninterrupted. "Never trust somebody whose last name begins with four consonants," she finally answered, shaking her head.

"That's 'never trust somebody who has a first name for a last name,'" Anne corrected. "You know — James Thomas or Thomas James. Names like that."

"You run into those types all the time. How many people do you know with a last name that begins with four letters and not one's a vowel?"

"I can't even think of a *word* that begins with four consonants," she decided.

"Exactly my point," Erin added.

"Just the same," Anne persisted, "how would you say his name?"

"Whatever. Pronounce it however you think. I still wouldn't trust the guy."

"Yeah," Anne finally conceded. "If he ever shows up."

Rob "The Mystery Guy Upstairs" Schlender did finally show up, though not until a few weeks into March. Anne had noticed him in the building but hadn't been able to get a good look at his face yet. *What kind of person doesn't show up on campus until the semester's half over?*, she wondered. With her curiosity killing her, I found out later, Anne conscripted Erin to help corner the poor guy one day before he could make his way upstairs to his one room apartment. The first thing they noticed was his size. The twins were both almost 5'8" tall and Rob towered over them; he was at least eight inches taller than they were. But he had big eyes that sparkled when he smiled, high, ruddy cheeks that gave him a pleasant, jovial face and a broad chin. His brownish hair was short, and with his receding hairline and wire-rimmed glasses, he seemed older to the girls than he actually was. He was broad, too, with large hands, a thick neck and wide shoulders that sloped just a bit. They immediately deemed him attractive, though he did not strike them as particularly athletic. But he was plenty tall and that was important. Besides, there were too many girls in the house as it was. Upon introducing themselves they told him they were glad to have him as a housemate.

Over the course of the following weeks, Anne and Erin would learn that Rob was from Washington State and lived north of Seattle. He was an undergrad at the University of Washington and had come to Cornell to help build a satellite, but offered little more detail than that. He was one of those people who studied electrical engineering/computer science/mathematics and was unbelievably bright, but not quite articulate enough to explain to others just what he was up to. Something to do with a satellite was good enough for Erin and Anne. Rob wasn't sure how long he would be at Cornell; he hadn't even known exactly when he would start on the project, either. He rented the room months early just to be safe. And his name? He pronounced it "Shhh-lender."

The twins and Rob quickly became good friends. When spring finally came the three of them would meet in the afternoons once or twice a week to go for a run, and when Anne and Erin got to know him a little better they'd have him down for dinner. He couldn't be bothered cooking for himself, or didn't know how, so he really appreciated something as simple as a home-cooked spaghetti dinner. And he liked Anne and Erin's cat, too, which was something of a litmus test for the twins when it came to guys. In time, they decided he was okay.

Rob stayed in Ithaca that summer to continue his work on the satellite project. The girls remained, too, working on internships to pad their resumes for their medical school applications and because the Finger Lakes region was beautiful during the warm summer months. The three of them often swam in one of the nearby gorges or walked across campus together for ice cream in the cool evenings

While the outings helped sweeten the friendship between Anne and Erin and Rob, I think the beginning of Anne and Rob's romantic relationship actually had more to do with a newspaper than the swimming or ice cream. One night after dinner at the girls' place, Rob noticed a copy of *The Wall Street Journal* on the sofa. He asked them what they were doing reading the *Journal*. Not too many students read that paper in his experience, and he was impressed. They told him the subscription was a perk the twins had gotten when they enrolled in a study course to prepare for the MCATs, which they had recently taken. Rob was astounded, not so much by the fact that Anne and Erin were reading the paper, but by the fact that they seemed nonchalant about getting it daily.

"Do you know how much it costs for a subscription?" he asked.

"Do you know how much that prep course cost?" Erin replied. Besides, she added, the publisher probably figures it's great marketing, putting it into potential medical students' hands now so they'll get used to it and be happy to pay for it once they became doctors. A good point, Rob agreed.

"Do you think when you're through with the day's paper you could let me read it?" he asked. "I'll pick up the old copies every couple days, if you don't mind."

"Sure," said Anne. "I'll drop them off in front of your door in the mornings before I leave."

True to her word, Anne would tiptoe up the stairs and leave the old paper in front of his door. Rob often worked well into the night on the satellite project, and she didn't want to wake him. But he must have retrieved each paper, because every morning when she went up the old copy she'd left the day before was gone.

One morning, she was surprised to find a bouquet of flowers outside his door. The card simply read "Anne."

"Look, Erin," she said. "Rob put flowers out for us to thank us for those copies of *The Wall Street Journal*."

Erin looked at the card and then back at Anne without saying anything.

"That was really nice of him, don't you think?"

"Are you just that much of an idiot?" Erin asked.

"What do you mean?" And then she caught her sister's drift. "You don't think —?"

But she didn't need to say anything more.

A marriage proposal was overdue. Anne certainly thought so. Erin said that was just the way Rob was. She'd taken to teasing him, good-naturedly, comparing him to Eeyore, the sad-sack donkey from *Winnie-the-Pooh*. But it'd been a long time since I'd read A.A. Milne's stories about Christopher Robin and his friends.

"You know, how Rob gets himself all twisted in knots when it comes to making decisions. Instead of doing something, he starts with his stammering: 'Well, uh, well, I uh, well you know it's like, um, you see the problem is…' He overthinks everything, second guesses any decision and the whole thing ends up getting him as moody as Eeyore. It's like he can't help himself. You have to wonder if the guy will ever come around to asking Anne to marry him."

I'd been wondering that for some time, too, and so when Erin gave me a copy of *Winnie-the-Pooh* and said, "See for yourself," I decided I would. Reading a children's book to glean insight into a potential son-in-law's character was bordering on the absurd, but I figured fathers sometimes had to stretch the rational limits as part of their due diligence. And I had to laugh as I read the first page of Chapter IV: "In Which Eeyore Loses a Tail and Pooh Finds One."

> The old grey donkey, Eeyore, stood by himself in a thistly corner of the forest, his front feet well apart, his head on one side, and thought about things. Sometimes he thought sadly to himself, "Why?" and sometimes he thought "Wherefore?" and sometimes he thought, "Inasmuch as which?" — and sometimes he didn't quite know what he *was* thinking about. So, when Winnie-the-Pooh came stumping along, Eeyore was very glad to be able to stop thinking for a little, in order to say "How do you do?" in a gloomy manner to him.
>
> "And how are you?" said Winnie-the-Pooh.
>
> Eeyore shook his head from side to side.
>
> "Not very how," he said. "I don't seem to have felt at all how for a long time."
>
> "Dear, dear," said Pooh, "I'm very sorry about that."

For sure, Erin's depiction of Rob was a playful caricature; it was fun *and* her right to needle the guy. He was, after all, going to *someday* steal her twin sister and best friend in the world from her. But in an odd way it was a revealing jibe. Like that old donkey, Rob could lose himself in a prickly thicket of endless questions. If a procrastinator is a person unwilling to act on his decisions, Rob was the kind of a person who is unwilling to make a decision on which to act in the first place. Even simple choices could bog the poor guy down as he wondered "why," "wherefore" and "inasmuch which?"

Once, I asked him for his help picking out a universal remote for our new big screen TV, thinking he could also give me some keen insight into desktop computers. "Donna and I are running out to an electronics store to get some things for our office," I said. "Would you mind going with us? I'd appreciate your advice."

I thought this would be a simple task for someone as technically inclined as Rob. I was wrong. He wanted, first, to go online and research universal remotes, computers and who knows what else. It was more of the same at the store. I left him in an aisle after ten minutes pondering remotes to do my own shopping. In short order I returned with a new desktop computer, a monitor, a keyboard and a printer. Donna met us with a small television she was buying for the kitchen counter and a few other gadgets she needed for the office. Rob was standing in the aisle with a different remote in each hand.

"Ready to go, Rob?"

I thought I startled him. Rob's mouth dropped open as he looked at me and then over to Donna and then back to me. His blank expression told me he'd been absorbed in his thinking, but it quickly changed to something like disbelief.

"You're just going to, um, what about — did you even — I mean you're not just going to buy all this stuff?"

He grabbed one of the boxes in my cart, turned it over, and then looked back at Donna's shopping. He started to laugh — a wry, sardonic guffaw that just erupted from his insides. Blushing, he shut his mouth then, fearing, I suppose, that he'd insulted us. I told him it was stuff that we needed for the office. The price was right and it was brand name electronics. No big deal.

"Don't you think you should, uh, you know — I mean, it would be a good idea to maybe consider what else is available."

"Decide which remote you want, Rob," I said. "It's time to go."

Rob was quiet on the ride back. When we got home he programmed the remote, got the new computer set up and when he was finished, ate a late lunch at the kitchen table and read the newspaper. I left him alone. It wasn't until later that evening when I uncorked a Pinot Noir and told him how much I appreciated his help that he loosened up.

"But I didn't do anything."

"You set everything up," I said. "That would drive me insane."

"You're welcome, but I have to tell you, you guys are something." He laughed, clinking glasses with Donna and then me. "That was pretty impressive the way you just bought all that stuff. I could never do that. I have a hard time pulling the trigger."

"It's only stuff, Rob. We're not talking life-changing decisions here. What's the worst that would happen? Shoot myself in the foot, maybe."

"But that's the point isn't it — not to shoot yourself in the foot?"

"*That's* the point?"

"Well, sure. You can't undo something you've already done."

"Injuries heal," I replied. "Getting paralyzed over every decision that comes along — that's a permanent disability."

Rob just nodded.

I supposed he got my meaning, but I suspected the next time I asked him to make a decision he would still shake his head from side to side, pondering like Eyeore, "why," "wherefore" and "inasmuch which?"

Just the same, I liked Rob. He was fun to be around. He took my sarcastic needling in stride, my criticisms with a healthy grain of salt and he was pretty good at returning the salvos, too. But what I liked best was that when I got to him, he would sometimes give up and laugh. He could laugh at himself. I couldn't recall Eeyore, the gloomy old grey donkey, ever doing that.

Rob did eventually ask Anne to marry him. After leaving those flowers for her outside his apartment, he went about the challenging task of trying to date a girl who was almost never apart from her identical twin sister. It would have driven many men out of their minds. But he was persistent, patient and probably recognized from the get-go that he had a good thing in Anne. He would have to learn to live with the fact that Erin would always be close to Anne in a way he never could be. He was smart enough to recognize that and sanguine enough to accept it. It was another point in his favor.

Their relationship blossomed over the course of that first summer together in Ithaca. But in autumn, Rob had to return to the University of Washington to complete his degree. I told Anne not to fret, because if he was the right guy, the time and distance between them would draw them closer together. It had done as much, after all, for Donna and me. We had spent the better part of three years apart when we were dating, while I got my degree at Colorado College and Donna worked back in Pennsylvania. We'd made due with handwritten letters and payphones. They had cell phones and email, I reminded Anne. True love never fails, right?

After they both graduated, it was more of the same. They each embarked on their respective post-graduate paths: Anne and, of course, Erin went to Baltimore to study medicine at the University of Maryland. Rob returned east to study robotics and electrical engineering at Carnegie Mellon in Pittsburgh. At least the young couple was in the same time zone again.

Rob would visit Anne at the apartment she and Erin shared in downtown Baltimore once a month, taking the late night Greyhound on Friday nights. He slept on the bus, carried the desktop computer he had made (which was as big as a suitcase) with him in the wee hours of Saturday morning through the dark streets of inner city Baltimore to the twins' apartment, only to sleep on an air mattress on the floor in their living room for a night or two, and then take the late night bus back to his apartment in Pittsburgh. It was plain to see he loved Anne; he doted on her, and was always polite and courteous, treating her with absolute respect. He seemed the right kind of guy to me.

Rob finished his Master's thesis and left Carnegie Mellon in the spring of 2005. He took a job with Northrop Grumman in Baltimore, working to develop a robotic mail-sorting device, and rented an apartment a block from Anne and Erin. He and Anne had been dating for three years by then. She was 25 years old; he a year older. Everybody knew they were going to get married. It was only a matter of when.

When turned out to be summer of 2006, just days before Donna and I celebrated our 27th anniversary. Anne wanted to return to Ithaca, and so we arranged to have the ceremony in Sage Chapel in the middle of Cornell's campus. The reception would be just across the way at the University's hotel plaza.

It was one of the best days of my life. All the worry and hard work that had gone into preparing for the ceremony and reception (done mostly by Donna) and my anxiety over the exorbitant cost of the whole affair was replaced by feelings of bittersweet joy and aching hope as the day wore on. Until that afternoon, when I walked with Anne down the aisle, I had never experienced such a melding of happiness and loss. I would miss my little girl keenly. But she was a woman now, elegant and so poised that I was stunned by her beauty. I was so proud to be her dad.

We have a framed photograph in our home of Anne standing between her sisters right after the ceremony. They are together in an alcove outside the chapel, the dark salmon and vermilion of the façade's elaborate brickwork framing the bright skin of their shoulders and the cool sea foam green of Erin and Caitlin's bridesmaid's dresses. Anne's gown is entirely hidden by the large bouquet of pink and white roses she is holding, so only her bare upper arms and shoulders, long neck and smiling face are exposed. She looked like Eve.

I don't remember if I cried. After I took her hand and put it into Rob's at the altar, I did what no father ever wants to do: I turned my back on my daughter and walked away. Anne's life would be fully part of another man's now; she would live under his roof, share his dreams and become with her husband a new family, no longer really mine. As I looked at her, her white gown washed vanilla in the soft chapel lighting, the veil and train draped like gossamer across her back, down to the floor, I saw her once more as that baby girl in the soft, white cotton shirt lying on her belly in the crib. I wanted to reach out to her one more time, place the palm of my hand across the tiny back that gently arched with every breath she took and pray my simple plea for her again, "Lord God give you good rest and peace, and keep you in His care tonight." I hoped so much that He would. And I knew then, more than ever before, that I myself could not.

For all the beauty of the day, Anne had come close to not marrying Rob. I found this out years later, when circumstances made the reasons for their almost breaking it off seem nearly prescient.

"I told him it was a deal-breaker," she said. We were sitting together on the guest bed in their home in San Antonio. Almost four months earlier, Anne had delivered Timmy, Edda, Lily and Wyatt. This would have been around their due date if they'd been born full term. Maybe Rob had been right, she wondered. Maybe none of this would have ever happened if she'd listened to him.

The deal-breaker had been the issue of starting a family, and it had become a thorny one. Rob didn't want to commit to having children. It wasn't that he didn't want children — he thought kids were great; he contributed to various kids' charities practically from his first paycheck — but his tendency to overanalyze made the prospect disquieting. He had questions and there weren't any answers. What if things went wrong? Wasn't it irresponsible to take the risk if you thought you knew something could happen? Felt it would happen? There were enough children in this world without adequate food, without sufficient shelter, with unmet health needs. Maybe they should consider adoption. But Anne told him she wanted to be a mother; she knew she wanted children of her own. She was adamant. She would not marry him if he wouldn't have children with her.

Her voice softened as she told me the rest of the story, "He didn't want to bring kids into this world without being sure he could provide them a good life. He didn't know for sure that he could."

"He was worried about finances?" I said. "That's borderline ridiculous. You're a doctor. He's a really bright guy. You're going to make plenty of money — so what was the real problem?"

"He does worry about money. Maybe for him there can never be enough. I guess what his dad went through in his construction business has something to do with that — business doing well one year and then going bust the next. Moving his family all over the place to find work — that would be hard on a kid growing up."

I knew about construction. I worked for my brother's construction business for ten years before going into it on my own. Cycles of boom and bust — on top of the world one year, staving off bankruptcy the next — were the nature of the industry. "Well, if I've heard him say, 'You never know when the bottom might fall out' once, I've heard him say it a hundred times," I said. "Still, he doesn't seem to worry so much about money — not that he lets on to me, anyway. Besides, you said he was okay with the idea of adopting. It's not like it's any cheaper to raise an adopted child."

"I know. Money wasn't really the whole issue."

I was groping for understanding. "He wasn't too worried about supporting kids if they were adopted? But he couldn't support his own? How does that make any sense?"

Anne was suddenly focused on her hands, which were spread out over her knees.

"So, what was the problem?"

She kept watching her hands. "Do you believe in destiny, Dad?"

"Is that a loaded question?"

Anne didn't say anything.

"I think some things happen that we can't control, yeah," I said.

"That's what I think, too," she agreed, and then added, "You know that I believe I'm going to die in a plane crash. I just know it. It's my destiny."

I wasn't sure how to respond. It wasn't exactly where I was expecting the conversation to go. "I hope that doesn't happen for a while, anyway," I said and forced a laugh.

"Sure, but sometimes you just know things."

I thought about that before saying: "Your Uncle Bill thinks he's going to be eaten by a shark someday. Just knows it. That's his destiny, he says."

"Stop making fun of me."

"I'm serious," I said. "Did you ever see the original *Jaws*? It was all the rage when we were teenagers. That opening scene where the guy and his girl drop their clothes on the beach at night and go swimming in the ocean together? Pretty erotic scene for a teenage boy to watch, until she gets torn apart by the shark."

"Is that really true about Uncle Bill?"

"I know for a fact that he doesn't swim in the ocean at night anymore."

Anne was smiling now.

"So, you're going down in a plane?" I asked.

She nodded and gave a little nervous laugh.

"And Rob?"

"Maybe. Maybe all of us."

"Don't say that."

She shrugged.

"Well, if you do, let Mom and me know so we can go with you. And Cait and Erin, too. We almost left Cait behind once already, remember?"

Anne nodded. That was an experience she likely would never forget.

We'd taken Anne and Erin to Ireland during a college spring break. There was something wrong with our jet's landing gear as we approached Shannon Airport. We flew circles above the airport (*Draining down the fuel?* I remember thinking) for an hour, while everyone on board watched the manic emergency preparations on the tarmac below. The flight crew led us in a choreographed chant, "Brace-brace-brace!" as the jet began its final descent. The twins and Donna were seated in the row behind me, and they were trying their best not to give in to the hysteria. I tried to comfort myself by acknowledging that, at least, we would all perish together. Whatever consolation I might have found in the thought disappeared when I realized Caitlin was not on the trip with us! In another minute it was over. To everybody's tremendous relief nothing happened; the landing apparatus worked properly and we landed safely.

"Maybe you already beat your destiny," I suggested to Anne.

"I don't think so, Papa."

I sighed and then rubbed my hands across my chin.

"And Rob?"

Anne's expression was suddenly serious.

"We're talking about his destiny here, aren't we?" I said.

There were tears in Anne's eyes.

"He thought it just wasn't in the cards for him to have normal children. I told him he was being absurd."

"He couldn't know that. Nobody can."

"If we adopted a child, you know — well, you know what you're getting. If I got pregnant, everything would be completely out of his control. I don't think he was comfortable with that. He didn't want to make a wrong decision with something as important as our kids."

"There is no right or wrong when it comes to decisions like that," I said.

"Rob just thought it would be risky to have children. He told me that he felt like he really knew something bad would happen. Not that he wouldn't care for them or love them. But if you really thought you were going to have a child that would suffer…"

After a pause, Anne asked, "If you knew that something would have been seriously wrong, you wouldn't have tried to have us, would you?"

I felt my throat tighten. It's not a question any father wants to contemplate. "He really believed if he had kids they were destined to suffer?"

"I don't know," she said, her attention back on her hands resting on her legs. "I don't know what he really thought. Maybe he was just afraid. I was too caught up in thinking about having a baby that I don't think I even heard a thing he was saying."

"You weren't wrong for wanting to have children, honey."

Her shoulders slumped so that her long, curly hair hung limply in front of her face.

"You didn't do anything wrong," I said. "Neither did Rob." I reached for her hands and pulled them up toward my chest.

"I don't know," she whispered. "Look at what I've done. Sometimes I think I should have listened to him."

But there's no changing the past.

By early winter of 2009, Donna figured Anne and Rob had been married long enough; it was time somebody got around to giving her a baby to coddle and love. Wasn't it reasonable for our only married daughter to think about starting a family of her own? I don't know if it was grandchildren my wife had a pining for or just her need to hold a baby in her arms again. She loved newborn things — puppies, foals, ducklings and chicks — and we'd had plenty of them over the years while our own children were growing up, but that was in the past. If she didn't have a grandbaby to hold soon, she warned, she would have to start raising animals again.

In fact, Anne wasn't just thinking about starting a family; she and Rob had been trying to conceive for several months. We just didn't know it. Anne assumed that getting pregnant would be a snap, and what fun it would be to surprise Mom with a phone call from Texas one evening to say, "Get ready for a grandbaby. I'm pregnant!" The only surprise, though, was how difficult it was turning out to be.

With a quiet house and more time to spare, Donna returned to doing the hand work she loved so much. Not that she was lacking for things to do; she still worked with me, taking care of much of the administrative minutia that consumes time in a small business. She also began volunteering with the local ambulance corps, learning to first drive the rescue rigs and then getting her emergency technician certifications so she could provide hands-on care. In some ways, it seemed everything she did had something to do with her hands. She used to sew a lot when our daughters were very young, making dresses and outfits for Christmas and other special occasions. Now with evenings pretty much to ourselves, Donna and I would often sit together during the winter months in the family room with a fire going in the little gas-burning stove and watch the news or just talk. But now, instead of sewing as she had done for years, my wife began to knit.

Knitting turned out to be something Donna had more than a knack for; she was gifted. I don't know how she did it — can you actually learn to do a cable cast-on, a buttonhole stitch or a three-needle bind-off by watching a YouTube video? However she learned, it didn't take her long to get the knit-one purl-two thing down and by the time she mastered turning a heel for a pair of socks, she was obsessed. Almost overnight, she'd filled the house with a kaleidoscope of color: exotic hand-dyed wools, furry alpaca skeins and an array of beautiful natural fiber yarns. There were kits and cases and sets of single and double point, circular, wooden and even bamboo knitting needles in practically every room. And she always had multiple projects going at once: a lacey merino scarf for Erin draped over the arm of the leather chair in the family room; half-finished pairs of crazy-colored *Noro Kureyon* socks for Cait and Anne lying in a basket next to her living room chair; the pattern for a Maltese Fisherman's hat for me spread on a table. More than anything else, though, she loved knitting for babies.

At this point in our lives, we knew plenty of babies recently born or on the way, and Donna was committed to knitting something for every one of them. She knitted darling little socks so small I could use them for thumb warmers; mitten-sets with thumbs so miniscule that I couldn't even get a pinky in them; adorable pastel blue and pink hats to keep little cherubs warm; and more beautiful than anything, the sweaters she lovingly crafted. When Anne and Erin's best friend from high school had a baby boy, Donna made a matching sweater and hat set for the little guy for his first winter. She got a photo and a note from his mother early that summer, not long after the baby boy had been born:

> *Mrs. Spillane,*
>
>   *I know it's not quite the time of year for sweaters & hats, nor does Arlo quite have the right body size, but I couldn't wait until winter to try them on! Thanks again for the gorgeous gifts. They make me smile and think of you often.*
>
>   *Love, Katie*

Katie had also scribbled a note from little Arlo himself around the edge of the photo that pictured him wearing the still-too-big sweater and hat in the middle of June: "Your hat is so soft I can feel the love in every stitch." Though such gratitude was more than enough reward for my wife, what Donna really wanted, more than anything else, was to be knitting for grandbabies of her own. And so she decided she would.

After six months of trying futilely to conceive, Anne was beginning to worry that maybe something was wrong. She thought that she wasn't ovulating consistently; she wasn't even sure that she was ovulating at all. Since she talked with Donna nearly daily, she decided to give up on surprising us with news that she was going to have a baby. As she told Donna, she was concerned that she might not be able to become pregnant at all.

Donna counseled patience. Both Anne and Erin had been taking oral contraceptives since they were teens due to irregularities in their menstrual cycles. Anne had only stopped taking hers six months earlier, Donna pointed out, and she probably needed to give her body a chance to adapt. Fertility could be a funny thing, she said.

There wasn't anything practical that I could do for Anne, so I decided I would do what I could. I would pray. And I would pray specifically. I began to put a request before the Lord that Anne would be pregnant by Thanksgiving of that year. Donna went one step further: she would take short breaks from her various and sundry knitting projects and start working on something for a grandchild of her own. It would be like an act of faith.

It was also something Donna found soothing; knitting was a comforting way to pass the time. The cost of a skein of exotic yarn was a small price to pay for that, I decided. She started bringing her satchel of knitting paraphernalia almost everywhere we went. She knitted in the car when we drove to visit Erin in Washington, D.C. She carried the needles and yarn on the flights we took to visit Anne and Rob in Texas. By late fall of that year, with more sweaters made for more babies than I could keep track of, my wife pulled what she had been knitting for her first grandchild out from under the chair in our family room to show it to me. It was a baby's blanket, a beautiful pastel green. I told her how lovely it was and asked when she had finished it. "It's not finished yet," she said and holding it up across her shoulders, she explained how much larger it would be when she applied the border.

"Are you knitting a beach blanket for the baby or what?" I asked. It seemed awfully large for one tiny newborn.

"I thought that if I just kept at it, that before I finished, Anne would be pregnant. It's a kind of faith blanket, I guess."

"I know how you feel. I've been praying, too."

"I don't want to stop, you know what I mean?" she asked, hugging the blanket to her chest.

"I do, I know," I said. "But if you keep this faith blanket thing up for very much longer you're going to have knitted a blanket big enough to cover who knows how many babies."

She just laughed, pulled her reading glasses down to the bridge of her nose and started working on the blanket's border.

CHAPTER 6

San Antonio
Fall 2009

By September 2009, Anne had been trying to get pregnant for over a year. She was well into her Dermatology residency, and if she didn't conceive soon she might end up giving birth near the end of that residency with her graduation and certification exams on the horizon. After that, she and Rob would head to their newly assigned active duty station on an Army base.

This timeline presented two problems. First, if they *did* have a baby much later than planned, what would happen if Anne were deployed? The Army frequently deployed new dermatologists to Afghanistan and Iraq to serve as general medical officers to help free up the surgeons, orthopedic doctors and other trauma specialists already stationed there. Could Rob handle a newborn all by himself? What if the baby wasn't weaned when the orders came in? Anne knew she wouldn't be the first Army mom in that situation, but still she didn't want to leave her baby just as they were beginning to bond and then not see her again for a year or more. She would miss so much.

As Anne and Rob weighed whether it was even worth trying to get pregnant for much longer, they also had to grapple
with the second problem. Tim, a resident in Anne's department
who'd spent the first part of his career as a family practice doctor,
asked Anne if she had considered infertility treatments. Neither
she nor Rob had given the idea a lot of thought. They weren't
sure what their options were, and the cost of IVF, which wasn't
covered by military insurance, seemed prohibitive. If that turned
out to be their only option, maybe children just weren't in the
cards. But Tim told her that he had seen a number of women
have some success with the fertility medication clomiphene
citrate, commonly called Clomid. The Clomid Challenge Test,
he explained, evaluated a woman's pituitary hormone levels and
was a useful indicator of what types of fertility interventions
might work. The catch was that CCT and the other infertility
treatments offered by the Army were only available at major
military medical centers. Anne was currently at one, but the
other major med centers were few and far between, and there
was no way of knowing where Anne would be stationed after
her residency. If she wanted to take advantage of the infertility
protocols available in the Army, now was the time. Anne and
Rob had a decision to make.

Our Thanksgiving was small that year. Erin drove up from
Washington, D.C., and Caitlin was already home. It would just be
the four of us. Anne and Rob decided to stay in San Antonio and
celebrate Thanksgiving with another resident from the Derm Clinic
and his wife. We all missed them that day, except maybe Donna,
who fielded a couple dozen calls over the course of the day. Poor
Anne was in a panic, fearing her turkey would be undercooked,
the twice-baked potatoes burned and her pie crust just plain awful.

"I think she's going to come undone," Donna said when the phone rang yet again. Erin said her sister was just nervous. "Well, she's going to give *me* a nervous breakdown," Donna replied, picking up the phone.

The last call from Anne, later that night, was to thank her mom for being so helpful and patient.

"Next time, have a glass or two of wine when you're cooking. That way it won't matter as much if you ruin the meal," Donna joked. Erin chimed in to say she doubted Anne had drunk any wine at all.

"Considering how many times she called today," I said, "I can believe it."

We sat in the living room after our own turkey dinner. For the sake of conversation, we started talking about plans for the holidays. Erin was hopeful that she would be able to get enough leave to spend Christmas and New Year's with Anne and Rob.

"I really hope you can get the time off," Donna said. She was sitting in the overstuffed armchair, knitting. "It'll be so nice for you and your sister to spend some time together."

Erin said she was pretty sure she would get the leave she needed.

"I wish they were coming here," said Cait.

"I wish we were all going *there*." Donna put her knitting down and reached into the large satchel set on the floor beside her chair. "That was the plan, anyway — that Anne would be six months pregnant or so by now and we'd all be going out there and helping her set up a nursery over Christmas. That would have been so nice."

Cait and I nodded. Erin was looking at her phone.

"What're you working on, Mom?" she asked without lifting her eyes.

Donna pulled a knitted blanket up and held it open. Erin looked up.

"That's beautiful, Mom! Who's it for?"

"It's for Annie's baby. Well, it will be."

Erin smiled.

"It's a faith blanket. That's what I'm calling it anyway."

"Amen," I said.

"I guess you're figuring she's having a big baby?" Cait laughed.

"I know I kind of went overboard," Donna admitted.

"Maybe she'll have twins like you did, right?" Erin said. "And who knows — maybe she'll even have a baby by next Christmas."

Donna reached out and handed the blanket to Erin, who put her phone down and held the blanket up to admire before passing it to Cait.

"You guys wouldn't know it," I said, "but I was praying that Anne would be pregnant by this Thanksgiving. I really thought she would be."

No one said anything.

"Just seemed like 'ask and you shall receive' is what Jesus said."

"And you've been giving me a hard time about the size of my blanket?" Donna asked playfully.

"You're right!" I said. "I've been busting on you about that faith blanket. I just thought it'd be great for Anne to be pregnant by this Thanksgiving. With the holiday season, I just got it in my mind a few months ago to ask God to do something about it. I thought He might."

"Good for you, Dad — don't give up," Cait said, smiling.

Erin didn't say anything. She'd picked up her phone and was staring at the screen again. It looked to me like she was grinning.

I slept in the next day, and when I walked into the office with a cup of coffee, Erin was sitting in front of a computer. "What're you doing up?" I teased. "You should be getting your beauty sleep when you can."

Erin smiled without looking up. She was typing away on the keyboard.

"That's not work, I hope. Black Friday, today — no working; shopping only."

"Yeah, right," Erin said. We made it a part of the family credo never to go shopping the day after Thanksgiving. She admitted, however, that she was *looking* at Christmas gifts online.

"Well, just don't buy anything," I said grinning and turned to look out the window in front of my desk. There was still frost on the ground in the shadows. Where the sunlight hit the lawn, rising steam and wet grass glistened in the bright sunshine.

"Anne's pregnant, Dad."

I'd obviously misheard Erin. "That would be great, wouldn't it?" I replied without looking at her.

She grabbed my hand and repeated, "Anne's pregnant."

I assumed it was wishful thinking until I saw the expression on her face.

"She told me a week ago once she was sure herself. She didn't want to tell anybody — except for Rob — for a couple weeks in case, you know, something went wrong."

I was stunned. "But everything's OK?"

"I think so. She thought it would be a nice surprise for you and Mom if she didn't tell you until Christmas morning. But after last night I called her to tell her how disappointed you were that your prayer didn't get answered. She was so touched that you were praying for her like that."

I felt tears in my eyes.

"But she still doesn't want to tell Mom until Christmas," Erin added.

"Your mother will kill us all if she finds out we know. She's been working on that darn blanket forever. Besides, Anne's going to need her mother, don't you think?"

Erin nodded and reached for her phone. "I'll call Anne. She probably needs a wake-up call anyway."

"She should be the one to tell Mom," I agreed.

Erin pressed the speed dial. "This is going to be awesome, isn't it, Dad?"

In mid-October Anne and Rob had decided to go through with the Clomid Challenge. Previous tests had showed Anne with no uterine or fallopian abnormalities. The Clomid test was the logical next step.

It's uncommon for women taking the challenge to get pregnant; that's not the point of the test at all. But in Anne's case, the "challenge" was the cure. Lab results indicated that she did, indeed, ovulate during the test, and by the way, had also conceived. She and Rob were stunned. Doctors had told Anne not to get her hopes up — there was less than a 10% chance that she would conceive during the test. But there they were, just a few weeks later, with a date of conception pegged at October 31.

Donna was overjoyed. At long last, she could start knitting for her own grandchildren. "A baby!" she would exclaim each evening when we sat together in the family room, and she picked up her needles and gathered the yarn. "Our little Annie is going to have a baby." She would repeat it then, as if doing so would cement the reality of what just days before hadn't seemed remotely possible.

Anne was six weeks pregnant when Donna and I got the news. By that point, the fertilized egg she carried had already put down "roots" in Anne's uterus, had determined whether it was a boy or girl and had been busy dividing cells into two groups that would form the baby and its placenta. Its heart was already beating; little buds had formed that would grow into arms and legs, and this tiny new life, though not quite a sixteenth of an inch long, had begun to develop eyes and ears and a small opening for a mouth.

Donna was falling in love. It was an amazing thing, I thought, watching such a strong bond begin between her and a child she wouldn't see for another eight months. Still, we knew we needed to focus on Anne, who was already battling morning sickness and nerves. Her upcoming ultrasound was making her anxious. What if there were abnormalities or a problem with the baby? What if she was carrying twins? Donna offered what support and encouragement she could, but doing so via telephone wasn't the same as being there. She couldn't stand that we were so far away, and I knew how she felt.

Rob was reluctant to accompany Anne to the ultrasound. I think he was even more worried than his wife was, but Anne insisted, and he went. As it turned out, what the ultrasound showed was something probably best experienced firsthand. It was the longest of long shots — about three chances out of a thousand, we would later learn. Rob told us that the doctor at the ultrasound simply said, "Jackpot!" Anne was pregnant, all right — very pregnant. "I'm counting four," the doctor told them. "And I've counted twice." Everything else seemed normal — though if the doctor actually said that, I doubt that either Anne or Rob heard anything after "four".

It was Erin who called us with the news. I think Anne was as speechless as she was near hysterical, and Erin said her sister wanted a day or two to let things settle before she talked with us.

"Babies," Donna said the evening we got the call from Erin. "We're going to have grandbabies."

"Lots of them," I agreed.

Donna was sitting in her chair in the family room with her various projects piled around her, but she wasn't knitting. Instead of needles, she held a tumbler filled with scotch and soda and ice. We were celebrating.

"Here's to you, Grandmom!" I said, raising my own tumbler of vodka.

"Babies — four babies." Donna shook her head.

"Ask and you shall receive," I said. It seemed strange that only a week earlier, I had thought that my prayer for Anne had gone unanswered. I laughed, wondering which was more humorous — that I didn't know then what Anne knew or that at the same time, Anne didn't know what God knew.

"You're going to have to put your drink down and start knitting."

"Four babies," Donna said again.

"Four baby sweaters, four baby hats and four pairs of baby booties. You've got some work to do."

She took a long sip from her glass and set it on the table between us. And then she leaned over, lifted the satchel filled with skeins of yarn, and began working them with her fingers. "Boys or girls?" she asked.

"Better go with a neutral color," I said. "That way you can't go wrong."

"That's no fun," Donna protested.

"Well then, blue, green, purple and pink."

"Unless she has four boys or four girls."

"What are the odds of that?

"Odds?" said Donna. "You're going to talk about odds now?"

She had a point. "Look," I said, "You're just going to have to knit two sets of everything. Pinks and blues."

She sighed.

"This is your own doing, you know." I said.

"What are you talking about?"

"The blanket."

She was unsure what I meant.

"*That* blanket," I repeated, and pointed to where it lay neatly folded at the foot of her chair. "The faith blanket you've been working on. I told you it was too big."

Anne called her mom a couple days after the ultrasound. We'd soon learn that carrying quadruplets was going to take a significant toll on Anne both physically and emotionally. For now, Anne had other things on her mind.

"She's embarrassed," Donna told me. "And she feels stupid."

"Stupid — she said that?" I could empathize with embarrassment thanks to distasteful sagas such as "Octo-mom" and *John and Kate Plus Eight*. Perhaps there was something of a stigma attached to having so many babies at once, but I didn't understand why Anne felt stupid.

"She feels like she rushed into fertility treatment too fast."

"One dose of some drug and she feels like she was rushing things? It's not like she had some IVF doctor pump her full of eggs."

"She's a doctor. She says she should have understood the risks associated with Clomid therapy."

"Is that what she's calling her pregnancy — a risk? She's not carrying babies; she's carrying a liability?"

"Don't be mean. I don't think you understand."

"Apparently I don't."

"She feels like she was rash in her decision and too selfish, like she wanted a child too much. And she feels like she let Rob down."

"How's that?"

"When the doctor explained the chance of multiples, she said she'd love twins, and she convinced herself that even triplets would be manageable, but she dismissed every other scenario. Rob was wary about taking the chance. As long as there was a possibility of higher order multiples, he thought it too risky. Anne insisted."

"Higher order multiples? So instead of babies it's a math problem?"

"Why are you being so difficult?" Donna asked.

I paused. She was right. "I'm sorry. It's just that this is what she wanted — what we all wanted, what we were hoping for, praying for. Isn't it?"

"It's really overwhelming for Annie. You're going to have to give her some space."

"It's not supposed to be like this," I said, more to myself than to my wife. What I'd wanted for Anne was the simple joy of expecting a baby and the anticipation of a newborn. Already, this was anything but simple.

"Where do things go from here?" I asked.

"Don't jump on me for saying it, but Annie's is a high-risk pregnancy."

"Not exactly the miracle we were hoping for."

"We're going to do everything we can for her."

"Is Anne going to be okay?"

"She needs to eat, but she can barely keep anything down," Donna said. "She's so sick. When I try to encourage her to eat she gets mad at me."

"She doesn't mean it."

"I know. She's just having a really hard time right now."

"Well, she *is* pregnant. And pregnant times four," I suggested, trying to put things into perspective.

"It's more than that," Donna explained. "She feels like she did something wrong, like she made a mistake. And she's struggling with guilt because of that."

"This is all a mistake?"

"Don't start," Donna scolded.

I forced myself to stop talking. Looking in Donna's eyes I could see it wasn't my wife talking anymore, but Anne's mother. She was defending her child and would push me out of the way to do it. I knew then that Donna had steeled herself for whatever was to come. This was not about me or her or what we wanted. It wasn't about grandchildren. It was all Anne. I would have to get over myself. Donna wasn't finished. "You're not going to want to hear what I'm about to tell you."

I waited.

"Annie knows she might not be able to carry the babies for long. There's a real risk she'll lose them all over the next few weeks."

"Miscarriage?"

Donna nodded. "I think it's likely. Anne knows the risks." Then she paused and I could see she was searching for the right words. "I think right now Anne thinks it best that… that right now she'd rather lose them."

My heart sunk.

"She doesn't want us to tell anyone she's pregnant. No one in your family, and not any of our close friends, either. She said she would feel better if no one knew."

"So what do we do now?"

"We give her room."

The first weeks of December crawled by for me. Every time Anne called I was afraid it was to say she had miscarried. It had happened so quickly in Donna's first pregnancy. She had hardly been pregnant at all, and then just like that, our baby was gone. There was nothing I could do for Donna then, and there was nothing I could do for Anne now.

Things weren't any easier for Anne. Nine weeks into pregnancy, she was coping with mood swings and persistent nausea, and maybe even feeling equally powerless. But progress was being made. Though the quads would grow more slowly than a singleton, each was by this point about the size of a small green olive. Anne could hear their hearts beating on the fetal Doppler now, and each of her children had little feet with tiny toes beginning to appear and faces complete with eyes and ears and the tip of a nose. A tongue was forming in each mouth, and webbed fingers and a thumb were growing on every hand. Bones and cartilage were developing. And though she would not feel it yet, in another few days Anne's babies would begin to move inside her womb.

With every new week, the likelihood of miscarriage diminished. And the passing time slowly eased Anne's anxiety. Things started to brighten considerably for me, too, when Anne called to proudly tell me she had gained a few pounds.

"That's such great news, Annie!"

"Now I weigh as much as I did before getting pregnant," she said and laughed.

"Well, it's a start!"

She asked about Christmas — had I strung the lights outside and put the life-sized plywood cut-out of Santa up on the roof yet? When I said I had, she gently scolded me. "You didn't climb up there by yourself, did you?"

"Cait helped, sort of."

"You should get one of the guys who work for you to do that."

"Bah humbug," I said. "What fun would that be?"

"You can't keep doing that yourself forever. I'm not going to say you're getting too old, but you *are* going to be a Grand Papa." She paused. "Someday."

"Someday soon, I hope."

My words hung in the air until Anne finally said, "I prayed so hard for a baby, Papa."

"We all did, honey."

"But I don't understand."

"Understand what, Anne?"

"Now when I pray, I ask God, 'Why did You give me more babies than I can possibly keep?'"

I was just coming to terms with medical jargon like higher order multiples and high-risk pregnancy when I was thrown for another loop. I'd never heard the term before: *Selective reduction of multi-fetal gestations.*

Military health insurance did not cover the procedure, but the topic was still broached with Anne and Rob. Anne's doctors made clear reduction was not a necessity, nor was it their place to make a recommendation for or against it — it was simply their obligation to describe all options available to Anne. The best window for reducing her pregnancy was rapidly approaching. Whatever the best course of action for Anne and Rob was, they needed to make a decision soon.

I was furious when Donna told me. "Selective reduction — that's abortion, isn't it? Is *that* what they're telling Anne to do?"

"Nobody's telling her to do anything."

"Then what are we talking about this for?" How had the joy of pregnancy become a grisly choice that potentially pitted one sibling against another and a mother against her own children?

"You're going to have to give Anne and Rob room here."

"Anne is finally close to being out of the woods when it comes to miscarrying, and instead of being relieved we're talking about abortion?"

"It's not our decision. Some doctors say it's not really abortion anyway."

"Then what do they call it?"

"Abortion empties the uterus. I think that's the distinction they make. This is supposed to preserve the pregnancy, not end it."

I wasn't buying it and I knew Donna didn't either.

"So we're back to talking about pregnancy instead of babies? Talk about splitting hairs!"

For Anne and Rob, however, that kind of distinction was a moot point. I knew Anne would not want an abortion, and yet there were clearly sound medical reasons for a woman to consider selective reduction when higher order multiples were involved. The risks to the babies were significant. Trying to carry them all could also doom them all. The risk to her health could be substantial, too. As a doctor, Anne knew all this. As a mom, her heart would have to guide her decision.

Rob, I guessed, would look at things formulaically. He would read as much about the procedure as he could, consider the data, analyze the risks to determine the likelihood of an undesired outcome, and then consider the professional advice. As cold as that sounds, I knew Rob better than that. For him it would come down to what Anne wanted.

"How do you make a decision like that?" Anne asked me. She just wanted to put the whole thing behind her. It was a few days before Christmas and Erin would be flying to San Antonio to spend the holiday with her and Rob. She didn't want to spend the few days she and her sister would have together dwelling on her decision.

"I think you're making the right choice," I told her.

"I don't want to play God," she said.

"Nobody does."

"Papa? On Christmas Eve, when you're with your mom and dad and your brothers and sisters and their families, you tell them for me, won't you? Tell them your crazy daughter has gone and gotten herself pregnant with quadruplets."

I told Anne I would be proud to. And though I did not say so, I was more than relieved — I was ecstatic. I told the family the news that Christmas Eve. My brother Mike was the first to speak and all he said was "Seriously?" I told him I was. What followed was a cacophony of cheers, laughter and toasts.

Word spread rapidly beyond our family as we knew it would. Responses ranged from lighthearted and cheery — "Hi Tim, how is your daughter doing with the multiple babies? I think I heard quadruplets. I'm not even sure I know how to spell that!" — to the simply stunned — "Wow! Hard to wrap your head around a minivan right out of the gates!"

To stay connected with people who wanted to be kept in the loop I started to send out an occasional email to family and friends. I sent out the first of what became known as the "updates" only a couple days after New Year's.

Hello there — I promised to keep sending out an update every now & then about Anne & the "gang" to those of you who asked, so here is the first one. Anne is now 12 weeks or so into her pregnancy; so she's almost through the first trimester. Yesterday, Anne had another ultrasound and all appeared fine. Three of the babies happened to be awake and "swimming about" so that was neat for Anne to see! I think the babies are too young to be able to tell whether they are boys or girls yet, and as I'm still not sure if Anne & Rob want to know or just be surprised, it may be sometime before any of us know.

There is still the question of Anne needing to have her cervix stitched or something like that but, being a guy, that doesn't completely register with me. In any event, if/when I get more news about that, I'll pass it on as best I can.

So, there you have it: All is well right now! The goal is to have Anne carry the "gang" until about week 30 or so. That would make a due date around mid-May.

Thanks much for your prayers and support. Our God is good!

This was probably the first time I'd given serious thought to a timeline for Anne's pregnancy. We were hopeful, but I recognized, grudgingly, that between the moment I first learned my daughter was pregnant and Christmastime things had changed. All bets on how the pregnancy would progress were off. For now, at week 12 of their gestation, the babies were about two inches long. Their heads were taking up about half the length of their bodies. The fingers and toes that had previously been webbed had separated. Genitals were taking shape, and the babies' kidneys were beginning to produce urine. They were about to enter the phase in their development when their organs and tissues would grow rapidly. The hope going forward was that there would be no stopping them.

But, of course, Anne's four babies would never reach full term. That much was a given. There were too many of them and her thin body was not well-suited to carry them for 40 weeks. She was in a race against time. If she could carry them for 32 weeks, they would be small and fragile, but they would have more than a fighting chance of surviving and leading normal, healthy lives.

Rob, who was devouring every medical journal article he could get his hands on, was holding out for 34 weeks. He knew that every day in the womb was worth two outside of it, and he was desperate to give his children the best outcome possible. Donna was willing to accept 30 weeks, in part because she knew how hard the coming months would be on her daughter, and in part because she knew the babies would have crossed the most crucial bridge in their development by then. Curious, I asked my wife how early a child could be born and still survive. Twenty-four weeks, she told me. Some survive younger, but you don't want to go there. With multiples, it's anyone's guess. We'll pray for 30 weeks, she said, but we'll take 28.

Anne wasn't thinking in terms of weeks, however. She was just living from one day to the next. There was almost nothing I could do for her other than encourage her to have faith. I made it a point to keep sending her daily scripture passages.

It was early in the morning in mid-January when I typed a passage from the Gospel of Mark into an email. At 5:35 AM, I pushed send and, in an instant, the Word of God shot across the

Internet to my wife and our daughters. I had no idea whether what I was doing was making any real difference, but I tried to be faithful in it. That morning I was thinking of Anne.

Hey there! Lots of the stories repeat from gospel to gospel. Earlier, in Matthew's Gospel, the disciples had asked Jesus why they had been unable to help a sick child and cast out the demon that tormented him. "Because of the littleness of your faith," Jesus replied. Here now in the Gospel of Mark is the beginning of that same story, with the boy's father pleading with Jesus to help his son if He can...

And Jesus said to Him, "If you can! All things are possible to him who believes." Immediately the boy's father cried out and began saying, "I do believe, help me in my unbelief." ...And after crying out and throwing [the boy] into terrible convulsions, it came out; and the boy became so much like a corpse that most of them said, "He is dead!" But Jesus took him by the hand and raised him; and he got up. [Mark 9: 23-26]

Enjoy a life of the possibilities that are yours through faith!

It took a few days, but Anne did respond to that morning's Bible verses.

Papa,

"If you can! All things are possible to him who believes." I need to paste this on my mirror and repeat it to myself every day! How inspiring and comforting. Again, papa, thank you for your daily scriptures. I don't always comment, but I always read them and particularly like your encouraging thoughts.

I certainly need to depend on someone other than myself over the next few months — and forever! — so thank you for helping me get there in my faith.

Con mucho amor,

Ana

Not too long after I sent that email, I left for Texas with a clear directive from my wife: get Anne to eat more. A lot more. Donna had just returned from San Antonio — it was the first time either of us had seen Anne since she'd become pregnant — and she was concerned about Anne's weight. She needed to gain more. A lot more. I promised to do what I could.

I'd already told Anne we would do three things when I got there: we'd go minivan shopping; we'd figure out if any room in their house could be converted into a nursery big enough to fit four cribs; and we'd make it a point to do something fun together.

Anne bounded out of her bright red Mini Cooper when she arrived at the airport and shouted, "Papa!" After stopping abruptly to reach back into the little car — I could see her eyes suddenly widen and her small mouth form the "o" for "oops!" — she re-emerged, grasping the Army beret she'd left on the dashboard, trying to frantically position the thing over her hair while rushing toward me. She halted at the last instant, stood at attention and then threw her arms around me. Holding her felt different than any time before.

"You look great, Captain Doctor," I said, using the expression I'd coined because I could never quite figure out the correct salutation for my two daughters who were both Army captains and medical doctors. I held her at arm's length and apologized for squishing the babies that had been sandwiched between us.

Laughing, she told me not to mind *them* — some jostling would only serve to toughen them up and, don't you know, they hadn't exactly been making life very easy for her, either.

"Come on," she said excitedly, "I'll show you the little guys in the car."

In the Mini, Anne lifted the jacket top of her combat fatigues — even stateside, soldiers wear them as a sign of solidarity with the troops in Iraq and Afghanistan — revealing a plump bump of a belly beneath her Army-issue T-shirt. I asked if I could touch her tummy.

"Give me your hand, Papa," she said, and when I did she set the palm of my hand on the top of her stomach.

"Oh my gosh — I can't believe it. Four babies in there?"

"I don't know what to say," she said.

"This is so cool!" I said, smiling widely. "Just don't tell Mom. When she was pregnant with you and Erin I almost never touched her belly. I don't know why. It freaked me out or something. But this is so awesome!"

She jumped when an airport traffic officer blew his whistle, motioning for her to move.

"Let's go home," she said. "I'm so glad you're here."

We went minivan shopping the next morning. Anne and Rob settled on a Honda Odyssey. Color didn't matter to Anne; she only insisted the car have seat warmers up front. When I suggested that they order exactly what they wanted, Rob demurred. I think he was afraid that putting a minivan in your driveway before you've brought even one baby home from the hospital was jumping the gun. I didn't protest.

Rob agreed that the front room, which he and Anne were currently using as an office, would suffice for the nursery. The cased opening would need to be fit with French doors, but there was little more than that to be done. I called some area contractors to get quotes, but Rob said there was no rush. I agreed it could wait until spring.

With half of my agenda already accomplished, I turned my attention to Anne's diet. In spite of the fact that she was entering her second trimester — the most comfortable and enjoyable stage of pregnancy, one maternity guide called it — Anne was still nauseous and vomiting. I also thought the challenge of having to take in so many calories every day was weighing on her. This wasn't the familiar and fun "eating for two" mantra; Anne felt an overwhelming sense of guilt that she could never meet her responsibility to eat for five. She could barely eat for one. Not much of an eater in the first place, Anne couldn't make herself eat what she didn't want, and she didn't want much. Where were the wonderful cravings, she wanted to know, for chocolate ice cream or pickles? Most food made her want to puke.

I mulled this over. In the guest bathroom, a small plaque hung on the wall beside the toilet. It read "If God brought you to it — God will get you through it." Anne thought someone might have given it to them for a house-warming gift, but since she never used that bathroom, she'd forgotten it was there. I told her that wherever it came from, she ought to consider its message a timely reminder to keep faith and to take things one step at a time. Forget about gaining 60 or 80 pounds and about eating heaping quantities at every meal. "Think instead," I said, "about gaining one pound today."

To help her get started I drove her to Jamba Juice. We ordered two super-sized chocolate smoothies with double strawberries, sat down in a corner booth and went to work. Have one of these every evening on your way home from the Dermatology Clinic, I suggested. The little things add up. Nothing good gets done overnight. Then I told her a little axiom I'd made up for her while flying to San Antonio: "Block by block, brick by brick, we're building babies." When you think of me after I've gone home, I said, think about putting another brick in the wall for me. One block at a time; one brick on top of another — that's how the biggest projects get done.

When we returned to the house, Anne went off to take a nap, giving Rob and me a chance to talk about a decision more serious than minivans or French doors. It was one Anne and Rob would have to make soon, and it was a big one with considerable consequences both for the near term and for years to come.

"To be honest, I don't know what to do," Rob said.

Donna had told me that Anne and Rob were considering moving Anne's prenatal care outside the military. Rob had found a clinic in Phoenix that specialized in the care of mothers pregnant with multiples and had an excellent track record of helping moms extend those difficult pregnancies.

"The data looks solid," Rob said. "The clinic has extensive experience with super twins."

"Super twins?" I asked, smiling. "I like the sound of that a lot more than a multi-fetal gestation."

Rob laughed but then was back on topic.

"I've already talked with the director of the clinic. He seems pretty astute and is real straight-forward about their approach."

"They do something different there?"

"They use magnesium sulfate to help prolong the pregnancy."

"So?"

"They use it in extremely high doses."

"Is that dangerous?" I asked.

"He says it isn't. Magnesium sulfate is used to treat mothers with preeclampsia all the time, but from some of what I've read high dosing as part of a drug regimen for mothers without that diagnosis is pretty controversial."

"What do Anne's doctors think?"

"They disagree with the method and think that the research supporting it is baseless. They say it is an unnecessary risk and will not use it for Anne."

"That's pretty cut-and-dried."

"But it really isn't."

I wasn't convinced. "I thought you and Anne said the NICU here is awesome. Why would you want to go someplace else, a thousand miles from your home?"

"It's not the NICU," Rob said. "It's about limiting the amount of time the babies will have to spend in intensive care." He explained that if Anne could carry her babies for as long as 34 weeks they might be out of the intensive care nursery in as little as three weeks. Every week outside the womb prior to that extended the babies' time in the hospital and increased the likelihood of complications associated with extremely low birth weight. The average delivery for quadruplets is 31 weeks, he pointed out. That was already perilously close to inviting serious trouble for the babies. Every additional day in the womb meant precious time for lung development and each ounce gained meant less risk of the neurological disorders such as cerebral palsy that were so common among very low weight babies. "I just want to give my kids every possible opportunity for a healthy life," he said, sighing.

"Sounds like you've done your research."

"But I just don't know that magnesium sulfate is a wonder drug for pregnancies like Anne's."

"What if it's not?"

"That's what I wanted to find out from the staff here. There's only something like 400 sets of quads born in the country each year. That's not a lot. Not every hospital is going to have the experience to handle this kind of pregnancy. The clinic in Phoenix does. So I asked the OBs here about their track record."

"And?"

"They evaded my question and kept insisting that magnesium sulfate was not the way to go. When I asked them how long the mothers of quads in their care in the past had carried their babies, they balked. Because they're hiding something? I don't know. When I pushed a bit they got defensive."

"Well, that's not very helpful. Maybe they're worried about patient privacy laws," I suggested.

"Maybe."

"What if you do decide to take Anne's care to Phoenix? Will your Army insurance even allow that?"

"I don't know. That's the next hoop I have to jump through."

We sat in silence until Rob grimaced and said, "I just can't get this wrong. Anne's already been through so much. This is the least I can do."

There was even less I could do, but I told Rob I could play devil's advocate. There were certainly legitimate concerns about the cost, logistics and emotional impact of transferring Anne's care to Phoenix. Even if Anne's military health insurance would cover the care in Phoenix, there would be no compensation for travel, housing or living expenses. And in spite of this facilities' reputation for providing superior care to mothers carrying higher order multiples, no one could guarantee a good outcome. If the babies were born very early in Phoenix in spite of everyone's best efforts, what then? Anne would only have six weeks of maternity leave regardless. If she used several of those weeks on bed rest at their maternity ward, which was likely, what if the babies had to remain in the Phoenix NICU? Would Anne have to commute almost a thousand miles and back on weekends once her leave was used up? How would they get the babies home? What if only one baby was very sick? Would Rob be left living at the NICU in Phoenix while Anne tried to manage with triplets in San Antonio? And what about Anne? Was it really going to benefit her to leave her home and friends, and the support she was already receiving from her fellow residents in the Derm program? It just wasn't possible to predict how all these things would work out. None of us could know, I told my son-in-law.

"You know me better than that," he said. "You know I'm an engineer."

I did. As an engineer, Rob was accustomed to the concept of risk assessment, where every decision is made in favor of minimizing the possibilities for poor outcomes. But I also knew that in this situation, he recognized that risks were unavoidable. Knowing as much was tearing at him. There was too much at stake not to make the right decision. But how could he know what that was? I certainly couldn't tell him. I could only offer him my advice.

"Don't try to see too far down the road," I said. "Focus on the positive. I know you'll make the best decision you possibly can. But no matter what happens, never blame yourself for your choices. There's no right or wrong here, so just do the best you can." The last thing I told him was that, for now, the most important thing he and Anne could do was not put too much pressure on themselves.

On Sunday, Anne and I drove to Government Canyon State Natural Area, a short drive from her home. The park is part in savannah brush lands and part on the Balcones Escarpment whose steep, entrenched canyons mark the eastern edge of the Edwards Plateau and the Texas Hill Country. I was taking her for a hike. "It might be a while before we get to do something like this together again," I said as we left her car and headed up into the back country trails that climbed into the carved face of the escarpment.

After checking the park's map I led Anne onto the Overlook Trail that climbed to a point where I hoped we'd get a good view of the winding Government Canyon Creek far below. Taking Anne on a hike that included a mile and a half of gradually ascending trails was something of a calculated risk. When I told Donna about it later she practically clobbered me. Was I just that stupid, she wanted to know? Any kind of excessive physical activity could trigger premature labor. I hadn't known that, and anyway I didn't really believe labor could actually begin when Anne's belly wasn't much bigger than a small melon.

I hadn't hiked with Anne since she and Erin were on an internship together at the Jackson Laboratory outside Acadia National Park in Maine. We'd hiked up the park's steep Beehive Trail that scaled the high granite ledges of a massive rock reaching more than 500 feet above Sand Beach on the southeastern edge of Mount Desert Island. "There were some sections of that hike that left me wondering whether you were trying to kill your old man," I said as we walked and reminisced about hikes we'd been on before.

She laughed, remembering how after she and her sister had made the arduous trek themselves the week before, they'd agreed to bring me back with them and test my mettle there. "Consider it payback," Anne said, "for all the times you tried to kill us as girls on those icy mountain trials."

She meant the winter hiking trips we'd taken in Pennsylvania's World's End State Park when the twins weren't even teenagers and Caitlin not yet ten. My favorite route was the High Rock Trail that traversed the steep canyon walls rising above the Loyalsock Creek, crossed a large fallen tree that spanned a cascading waterfall, and then climbed still higher until the trail reached a rocky knob overlooking the creek some 400 feet below. The first time we did that hike we came at it from the west end of the trail where a large red sign was posted warning of slippery wintertime conditions and the serious injury or even death that awaited those who did not employ extreme caution on the trail. I told the girls not to mind, assuring them they would do fine so long as they used a firm, straight branch for a walking stick and always kept it toward the downward slope.

"What were you thinking?" Anne asked. She continued to playfully chastise me, recounting the terror she and her sisters experienced back then as I'd prodded the girls, one after another, to cross the trunk that served as a bridge over the falls that plunged down the rocky ravine below.

"I was holding your hand," I said in self-defense.

"So that if you slipped and fell you'd take me with you, too?"

"It was the only way to get to the top. I wanted you to see the view from there."

I reminded Anne how when we'd gotten to the overlook, we'd stand as close to its ledge as we dared and look down in wonder at the Loyalsock winding like a steel-gray snake through the narrow, brown and black, icicle-laden canyon walls.

"It *was* beautiful," said Anne.

The trail that Anne and I were now on was no Beehive or High Rock Trail, but we hadn't come looking for a challenge. It took a little longer to reach the overlook than I anticipated, but the Texas winter weather was crisp and cool, and the sun was bright and warm. And though the view wasn't very impressive, the sunlight reflecting off the water in the places where the creek broke clear from the thicket of brush along the canyon floor was a pretty sight.

We stood together for a few long minutes, looking across part of what had been the Texas cattlemen's life in an earlier era. Before we turned to leave, I hoisted Anne up on a small limestone outcropping and took her picture. She was wearing a black cowboy hat, her brown hair hanging in long curls that reached in front of one shoulder while disappearing behind the other. Her jacket was tied around her waist, her legs were crossed and the green cargo pants she wore stopped short of the shoes that were still streaked with black mud from the trail. Such a beautiful woman, I thought, and to me such a young girl. You'd have no idea she was pregnant with quadruplets in the photo. It was the last picture I'd take of Anne where I'd think of her more as a daughter than as a mother.

Before leaving, I pointed to a hiker following the flat-lying trail that hugged the creek and told Anne that would be her soon. "No more hiking in the hills for you," I said. "Not for a while, anyway. From now on you'll get your exercise walking the sidewalks around your neighborhood."

She smiled. "What's the fun in that?"

"It's only a temporary inconvenience," I suggested, and then added, "Before you know it, we'll be back up here with enough little hikers to make your own scout troop."

"That'd be great, wouldn't it? Me and my babies and their Papa hiking together."

We walked lazily back down from the overlook, following the same path, but still looking carefully at the flora and fauna for things we might have missed. Soon we were talking about her, about the pregnancy, about how she was doing — how she was *really* doing.

"I'm worried," she said. "I worry that I won't be able to carry the babies long enough."

"You're already in your second trimester," I countered.

"It's not losing the pregnancy I worry about," she said, walking carefully. "Not anymore. I'm afraid I won't be able to stay pregnant long enough. So much can go wrong if I don't."

I asked her about the clinic in Phoenix.

"I don't know. I like it here. I trust the doctors who are caring for me. But it's got Rob in a bunch, that's for sure."

"He just wants to do the right thing for you and your babies."

"I know. But how do you make those kinds of decisions? How can you ever know for sure what's the right thing to do? He keeps asking me what I want, but I don't know what's right."

I thought about that and then suggested there might be a good reason Anne and Rob were paired together in this.

"How's that, Papa?"

"Rob's an engineer, a 'head guy,'" I said. "You? You're more like me; we operate from the heart."

She lifted her eyes and looked into mine.

"I think it's a good balance," I continued. "Together you'll do what's right for you and your babies."

"I hope so, Papa. I hope you're right."

As we came out of the woodland's shade into the sunlit savannah grasses, we paused to drink from our water bottles. "You know your Uncle Mike is a song writer, don't you?"

"No, I don't think I knew that."

"Maybe not so much anymore, but he wrote some really good songs when we were younger. I find myself still singing one even now. I'd sing it for you, but I sing about as poorly as you do."

Anne laughed. "So, tell me about it instead."

I told her the lyrics came from the Psalmist's own plea to God:

From the end of the earth will I cry unto Thee,
When my heart is overwhelmed:
Lead me to the rock that is higher than I.
(PSALM 61:2)

"I need that rock, Papa," she said, looking like she might cry. "There's so much pressure to do the right thing."

By the time we reached the car, Anne had explained to me the cervical cerclage she was likely going to need, what having her cervix stitched actually entailed and how that had become something of a point of contention in her care. "My doctors want me to have the procedure done sooner rather than later. They want me to agree to have it done right away."

"Okay," I said. "Is that a problem?"

"The doctor in Phoenix disagrees. He says a cerclage is no guarantee that a high risk pregnancy will last longer and there are risks in doing it at all. There's always the possibility of infection and in some cases the procedure has actually induced preterm labor. He says there are more holistic ways to prolong a pregnancy."

"What do you think?"

"You know Rob is all about the data," she said. "He hasn't found enough good research to show which women, if any, actually benefited from a cerclage. Just saying that having a cerclage seemed to work well is not cutting it with him. He tends to agree with the Phoenix clinic. Why take an unnecessary risk?"

"And what do *you* think?"

"I'm a doctor and I don't have any idea. The guy at the Phoenix clinic isn't overseeing my care, at least not yet, so I feel like I should trust my doctors here."

I knew she was a good doctor; she wanted to be a good patient, too.

In the car, I asked Anne if I could lay my hand on her tummy and pray for her and the babies. I didn't know what else to do. I couldn't make the tough decisions for her and Rob; I didn't know the right answers, either. While we prayed, what I saw in my daughter's eyes broke my heart. Instead of an expectant mother embarking on an exhilarating journey, Anne was entangled in a stressful reality flush with grim prospects.

"Thanks for praying, Dad," she said wiping away a tear. "Thanks for coming out here to see me."

"You're going to get through this," I said.

"You think so?"

I nodded, my hand still resting on the bump of her belly. "You know God's got a better view from His vantage point. But I think before He lets you see more you're going to have to trust Him and cross the logs over the waterfalls to get to that rock."

"What if I fall?"

I lifted my hand from her tummy and grabbed hers. "Then you'll take me with you."

"Maybe falling would be easier," she said.

"You know what, Annie?"

"What, Papa?"

"It's time to start becoming a mom."

She pulled her hand back a bit, not quite sure what I meant.

"Put aside the worries and the anxiety about what the right decisions are. This is who God has called you to be. Your babies need *you* now. You are the only home your babies have right now; there is no other place in the world ready for them yet. Nobody else can help them — not Rob, not your mom or me, not any doctor anywhere. You're all the hope they have and everything they need." I put my hand back on her tummy and said, "These little guys are depending on you not to lose heart, so stay hopeful for them, Annie."

She put her hands on top of mine, on top of the bump of her belly, but said nothing.

"If you do, you'll fill their tiny hearts with hope. I know it," I said, and hoping as I did that what I was saying was true. Hope was really all the chance her babies had.

Donna and I might as well have just thrown a kiss to each other as we passed in the Southwest terminal in Philly. At least, that's the way it felt. I'd only been home a few days before my wife was already on her way back to San Antonio. Anne had reluctantly decided to go ahead with the cervical cerclage. She and Rob were still unsure about transferring Anne's care outside the military, but for now they agreed there was less risk in having the cerclage than facing the chance of regretting that they hadn't later. It would be an uncomfortable procedure involving a speculum and stitches, and Donna wanted to be there for her daughter. Plus if something unexpected happened, Anne would want her mother there to help get her through it.

On January 20, I sent out my second email update. I told everyone about minivan shopping, the decision to convert Anne's office into the nursery and the joy of our father-daughter hike. I attached the picture I'd taken of Anne that day and concluded by letting everyone know what was on the road ahead.

> Donna has already told some of you that Anne is having a procedure on Friday to have her cervix stitched in a preventive measure to limit the possibility of pre-term labor and so forth. It is something of a painful procedure (spinal epidural and all that) so Donna is flying out tomorrow morning to be with Anne for the procedure and recovery. The good news is that yesterday's ultrasound showed everything being OK and now that Anne is through 14 weeks we are hoping for 18 more weeks of clear sailing to get to the doctors' goal of a 32 week term.

Eighteen weeks seemed an eternity away as I wrote the email. Hoping for "clear sailing" was like suggesting that Christopher Columbus was more concerned with the weather than he was about discovering a new route to India. We didn't have any idea what lay beyond the horizon for Anne and her babies. The recent ultrasound results, at least, renewed our hope and let us believe the best.

At 14 weeks, the four babies' faces were becoming more human every day. Vocal cords were beginning to grow, and though the ultrasound wouldn't reveal anything yet, their genitals were sufficiently developed to distinguish the girls from the boys. Each was nearly three inches long and weighed more than an ounce. They were even exercising already, practicing inhaling and exhaling and moving their tiny hands.

I was wrong to tell my daughter that hope alone would be enough. In the weeks and months ahead, who knew how far away the shore would seem or how difficult the struggles to get there? Hope alone might not suffice, and Anne would need to find a reservoir of resilience. And when she did — as her dad I was sure she would — could she possibly find enough resilience in herself to share it with her babies, too?

Though we didn't know it yet, they would need it even more than she would.

O Lord God, would they ever.

PART II
Resilience

"Upon Thee I was cast from birth;
Thou hast been my God from my mother's womb."
Psalm 22:10

CHAPTER 7
The first days of life (DOL)

Our euphoria was evaporating. The adrenaline gone. We tried to hold on, but the image of a morning abloom with bluebonnets and yellow primrose was slipping away. We were grateful that the babies had survived their second night, but the grim reality of their plight was finally hitting us. Timmy, Edda, Lily and Wyatt were fighting for life minute by minute, one long, hard hour after another. Though no one acknowledged as much, we were all watching the clock. Somehow we'd learned that micro-preemies who die often do so in their first 48 hours. The medical charts called Saturday "Day of Life: 3" (DOL 3), but Anne's babies had not yet been alive 40 hours.

By the time Donna, Erin, Cait and I were on our way back to Wilford Hall that morning, the babies were all having respiratory difficulties. That was not unexpected for such early preemies. Wyatt's situation, however, was becoming dire. He was slowly losing the fight, his lungs tiring and nearly giving out. That was no real surprise, either. I think we all knew if any of the babies died, Wyatt would be the first. He was so small, his lungs so weak. The odds were stacked highest against him. Though many micro-preemies survive the challenges they face, others never have a chance. The plaques outside the NICU had foretold as much. Some, as one inscription read, were simply "born before their time into this breathing world."

When we got to the hospital, Rob was sitting with Anne. They were quietly discussing something. Anne's eyes looked glazed; she barely noticed us entering. Rob stood and as he did, Anne turned her attention to us and tried to smile. But her eyes went quickly back to her husband's. He looked like he was awaiting a response.

"I don't know," she whispered.

"They are going to need to know, if it comes to that."

Anne looked down and shrugged.

"I want you to come with me," Rob continued. "We need to make these decisions together. And you understand this stuff better than I do."

Anne slumped, silent.

"What is it?" Donna asked, sitting down next to Anne on the bed. She put her arm around Anne's shoulders and looked up at Rob. "Who is it? What's the matter? Is it Wyatt?"

The room was quiet until Erin, who was standing behind Rob, said, "Mom, you go with Rob. I'll bring Anne down with me after a bit." As she spoke she put her hands on her brother-in-law's shoulders and rubbed them. "Rob?"

He hesitated and then nodded without looking back.

Donna hugged Anne, stood up, and looked at me briefly. "There's a cafeteria in the basement," she said. "Why don't you see if you can get Anne a cup of hot tea and a donut?"

Wyatt went from bad to worse. I don't know exactly what happened. I got the story in bits and pieces over the course of that afternoon and as I did, I tried to imagine what it would've been like being in the NICU then…

At first glance things seem normal in the neonatal unit. Rob and Donna are watching Edda and Lily, their backs to the boys' isolettes. A monitor's alarm sounds. The two of them try to act unfazed, staying focused on the girls who are enjoying another bath in the blue glow of the bili lights. The alarm stops. A nurse is looking at the monitor mounted near Wyatt. She is studying the baby boy and the screen simultaneously. Suddenly, she is gone. Almost immediately, the alarm sounds again. In an instant, two nurses and a physician rush to Wyatt's side. There is a flurry of activity. The monitor keeps up its awful beeping.

Realizing something is wrong, Donna turns to find Anne, but as she does Rob grabs her arm and holds her firm by his side. One of Wyatt's lungs has collapsed. The child is going into acute respiratory failure. There is no way in the moment, however, that either of them has any way of knowing that. They don't know what is happening. The NICU staff comes perilously close to losing Wyatt during the course of the next hour. Rob tells me afterwards that it is a lump-in-the throat time, watching and not knowing. Donna, trying to hold back tears, recalled it as the worst feeling, wondering if you were witnessing the end of the little child's life, completely and utterly helpless to do anything about it.

At one point the attending physician pulls Rob aside to say he feels Wyatt should be put on high frequency oscillatory ventilation. Using HFOV could result in less injury to Wyatt's lungs than the higher pressures of the conventional ventilator. Though the oscillating vent is a rescue treatment he believes is necessary, the doctor takes time to tell Rob the associated risks. Wyatt might not tolerate it. He was already in such an irritated state that his nurses had been laying bean bags across his tiny arms so he would stop tearing at his indwelling lines. HFOV might push him over the edge. High airway pressures from the treatment might lead to dangerously low blood pressure and shock. It could also lead to hemorrhages in the fluid-containing spaces in the brain known as the cerebral ventricles. The short-term benefit to the lungs might be outweighed by the permanent harm done to the brain.

Earlier in the day Rob had been briefed by a resident that it might come to this. He had tried to explain it to Anne, but she didn't want to think about it. Not sure what to do, Rob consents to the HFOV therapy. "Do what you have to do," he tells the attending. "I have to go with what you tell me is best." The risks to Wyatt later in his life won't matter if he doesn't survive the day.

Within minutes another machine, a contraption of hoses and dials and LED monitors, is stationed next to Wyatt's isolette. The respiratory tech secures a small mask over Wyatt's still-intubated mouth. It almost covers his entire face. For the next hour the staff hovers around, watching the tiny baby boy who is now completely motionless save for the wiggling of his chest. At some point, Anne and Erin arrive. The activity continues unabated, a controlled mayhem that is both a spectacle to behold and a nightmare to witness. Had a nurse not slid a rocking chair toward Erin's arms at just the right moment, Anne might have collapsed onto the floor.

There is no immediate improvement in Wyatt's lung condition. He remains in profound respiratory distress. But the whirring electric motor of the HFOV inflating Wyatt's lungs with multiple small breaths of air every second is buying him time. He is in extremely critical condition — though stabilizing — and that will have to be good enough for the time being. Nothing more can be done for Wyatt now. As hard as it is, Rob and Anne cannot focus solely on him. They have three other babies living on a razor's edge.

Saturday morning's chest x-rays for Timmy and the girls showed little change. Lily's vent tube needed to be repositioned. This would become an almost routine problem for all four babies. Because they were so tiny even small movements could push the tube too deep or pull it up too far. In either case, the end result is inefficient aeration of their lungs, often referred to as "decompensating on the vent." Edda's x-rays showed her left lung improving a bit, her right lung not so much. Timmy was still struggling to breathe but not in particular danger. They each appeared poised to make it to the 48 hour mark.

By the time Cait and I returned from the hospital cafeteria with drinks and donuts, Anne and Erin were gone. We sat by ourselves and waited for at least an hour and a half, with no way of knowing what was happening in the NICU.

Rob and Donna were the first to return. They were so deep in conversation they did not even acknowledge us. When the twins came a few minutes later they were both stone-faced and silent. I could see that Anne had been crying. But when I caught her eye she forced a small smile as if to assure me everything was okay. Caitlin handed Anne the tea we'd brought — by now completely cold — but instead of taking a sip she set it on the nightstand, pulled her legs up under the blanket, laid her head against the pillow and turned away from us. I was just about to ask Anne if everything was okay, when Donna silently mouthed, "She's just tired."

That afternoon was the first glimpse of how, in our own ways, we would struggle to cope with the overwhelming stress of the days and weeks ahead. If Anne was trying to escape her frightening reality by burying her head in the sand, her mother and husband seemed intent on doing the opposite.

While Anne slept, Donna and Rob took turns explaining the morning's events. They were both oddly upbeat, as though they were part of a peculiar fantasy that had robbed them of any sense of how close to losing Wyatt we'd come. I was dismayed. Were they oblivious to the critical nature of Wyatt's situation? Hadn't they just explained to me how quickly, how easily it could've all come apart? Erin obviously wasn't. She watched her mother and brother-in-law with incredulity as they spoke about the high tech

HFOV machine and the precision with which the NICU staff had operated. She finally turned away from them and their storytelling to stare out of Anne's window into the haze and heat of the Texas afternoon.

In time I would understand that it was more than just a coping mechanism. What my wife found that morning in the NICU was something that bolstered her belief that a rising tide of desperation could be turned back by a beachhead of commitment. Donna knew as an EMT what it was like to be in the back of an ambulance with a victim who was coding, to rush into an emergency room to transfer a critical patient to the care of a team of doctors and nurses. What she saw Saturday morning in the NICU — what I think she was trying to explain to Erin, Cait and me — when Wyatt's condition suddenly worsened was what she always admired in the people she'd worked with in emergency medicine: a no-nonsense, get-it-done, do-it-right, right NOW mentality; a fortitude that, faced with certain failure, would not accept it. She knew Wyatt was in trouble. She was not choosing to delude herself. What she witnessed that morning in the NICU scared her, but it also reassured her that he was receiving the best care humanly possible.

Rob's response was similar. The difference was that he seemed inspired by what people do when the situation requires a response that *exceeds* what humans can do alone: they turn to technology and its machines. As an engineer, Rob saw problems as riddles begging for solutions. Intellectual curiosity begot innovation and that was what made real human progress possible. He lost me when he began to describe how the HFOV worked, but what it meant to Rob personally was that such technology was the driving force behind the marked decrease in the mortality rates for children born as young as his own. Mechanical ventilators — imperfect though the technology was — had saved countless preemies' lives. The new machine propped by Wyatt's bed that morning not only improved Wyatt's chances of survival, but it also improved his dad's outlook. It helped him find optimism in a situation sorely lacking it.

Erin's take on the morning's affair, however, was something altogether different. She was decidedly somber; what she saw gave her little to be optimistic about. She was a pragmatist. Her medical training left little room for the impossible. More so than her mother, Erin had seen the disciplined precision of surgical teams at work, that kind of do-whatever-it-takes and let-the-odds-be-damned mentality that sometimes did bring back the all-but-dead. Like Rob, she appreciated the medical devices and new technologies that made the once impossible nearly routine. But she had also seen the unintended consequences of the heroic endeavors undertaken by doctors and their machines.

Yes, she had seen soldiers returned from Iraq and Afghanistan at Walter Reed. It was a marvel, she said, that so many had fared so well after suffering the kinds of wounds that in wars past would have left them dead on the battlefield. Though most considered themselves *fortunate* she had also seen those who no one would consider so: the soldiers left deaf, blind and horribly disfigured by burns and blasts, the triple amputees and quadriplegics, the soldiers emasculated physically and others emotionally. She had seen their families' burdens, too. The young wife just married to a man who now would never recognize her again; the parents who could hardly bear to see their daughter, whose crippled body was little more than a shell in which she was entombed. Some things, Erin felt, were just not meant to be.

Erin feared Wyatt's trouble went too deep. No matter what Rob and Donna wanted to believe, not even all the king's horses and all the king's men would likely be able to put this tiny baby back together again. It might end up being the same for Timmy, Edda and Lily, too. Now her only concern was for her twin sister. She would not trade her sister's life for the lives of four babies born too young for this world. It just didn't make any sense. She only wanted to protect Anne from as much suffering as she could. But there was little hope of that.

We'd all chuckled the night before when Anne told us her babies reminded her of chickens. But the poignant, painful reality of what my daughter was alluding to was not that her newborn children were as cute as the fuzzy little chicks she'd seen frolicking in our barnyard in years gone by. The truth was that she'd been sobered, shocked, by what she saw in her first visits to the NICU. She'd been stunned — nearly repulsed — much in the same way when for the first time as a young girl she'd watched her mom carefully lift a squawking hen from her nest to reveal the just-hatching creatures. Anne would never forget the surprising sight of the featherless, fleshy-red and wet things, their thin, fragile bodies a squirmy, ugly and wholly unrecognizable form to her. Seeing her own babies in the much the same condition she could only ask herself, what had she done? She was struggling to connect with her babies. She did not know if she wanted them to live or die. She was only sure she did not want them to suffer.

Late Saturday, Donna and Erin helped Anne get a sponge bath, wash her hair and put on some makeup. Rob returned to the NICU and took Cait with him. Chest x-rays continued for Wyatt throughout the afternoon. There was some good news: the condition that had led to the collapse of one lung had dissipated and his breathing was improving. Wyatt had returned to the point where it was back to watching and waiting.

Rob was exhausted by evening, but with Wyatt still in a precarious state and his wife emotionally spent, he decided to stay with Anne in the hospital. He would sleep in a chair by the side of her bed. Erin, Cait, Donna and I left them shortly before nightfall.

There would be no rest for the weary this night, however.

Less than three hours later, a neonatologist came to Anne's room to talk about Wyatt. He had the results of their son's echocardiogram. The test revealed a *moderate to large patent ductus arteriosus* (PDA). The doctor explained that if the heart's ductus arteriosus remained patent or open, it would lead to abnormal blood flow between the aorta and the pulmonary artery. Wyatt's already critical lung problems would be worsened by abnormal blood circulation between his heart and struggling lungs. The neonatologist recommended that they act immediately to address the condition. He would prescribe a medication called Indomethacin. There were risks using the medication — in some rare instances it had resulted in a perforation of the bowels — but the alternative was surgery and given Wyatt's condition that was not a viable option. The PDA might spontaneously close in a few days on its own, but that was an unrealistic time frame for Wyatt. He needed every opportunity to improve his lung function as soon as possible.

If Rob had been home that Saturday night he might have pulled out his wife's medical school textbook, *Pathologic Basis of Disease*, to find what he could about PDA. He would have read about the respiratory distress syndrome with which his children, Wyatt especially, were all struggling. No doubt, he would have found the final sentence in the section about this lung condition unsettling. The paragraph, while noting that infants who survive RDS are at an increased risk for PDA, as well as a variety of other complications, closed with this statement: "Thus, although current high technology saves many infants with RDS, it also brings to the surface the exquisite fragility of the immature neonate." The premise that the gains from life-saving technology exposed preemies to more grave risks in the future might have seemed tragically ironic to Rob, the engineer, but what was he as a father expected to make of his children's "*exquisite* fragility"? It sounded so elegant, and not at all like the menacing, life-threatening mess in which Timmy, Edda, Lily and, especially, Wyatt were trapped. But Rob was in the hospital with his wife that night and her textbooks — which weren't written for parents, in any event — were at home. Anne and Rob opted for the Indomethacin.

After the neonatologist left their room for the evening and, thankfully, for the night, Anne fell asleep while Rob, waiting until he was sure his wife was sleeping soundly, opened his laptop to learn what he could about PDA. He would sleep only fitfully that night.

I wanted to know nothing about it. If Anne and I felt safer with our heads in the sand, Rob and Donna were the opposite. They were eager to learn everything, as if understanding the problem might also let them begin to see its solution. I remember Erin painting the picture for them.

"Lungs look something like an upside down tree," she said, "with a trunk, two large branches and then smaller and smaller branches with twigs." Instead of having leaves, though, she described the tips of the twigs as being "like little clusters of grapes." Donna knew enough from her EMT training to know these were really the air sacs where the work of the lungs took place: oxygen in; carbon dioxide out. "I don't know if babies this young even have aveolar sacs yet," Erin continued.

"What about the steroids?" Rob wanted to know.

"That helps the lungs mature some, but breathing is still so difficult for them. Every baby's first breath is hard. It's like a balloon, I guess — you really have to blow to get it started, but every time you blow after that it's easier. Unfortunately, for some preemies the lungs just collapse after each breath. They lose all the air out of the balloon."

"That's what the surfactant is for, right?" Rob countered. "The doctors told me they gave it to each of the babies when they were intubated."

"It helps. If it wasn't for surfactant —" but Erin cut herself off before stating what she knew was obvious.

"Why's it so much harder for Wyatt?" Donna wanted to know.

"He's the smallest. His lungs are probably even less mature than Timmy and the girls'."

"But he's so feisty," Rob countered.

"That's part of the problem. He's exhausting himself," Erin said.

Donna slumped at that. "So his fighting to live is killing him?"

"And now this heart issue — his PDA — what about that?" Rob wanted to know.

"It complicates things. We have to hope the medication works," Erin said. "Really, what Wyatt needs — what they all need — is time. That's really the only cure for immature lungs."

"How long can they stay on the ventilators?" Donna asked.

"I don't know, Mom. You should ask the pulmonologist. The vents can cause tears and scarring of the lung tissue. Fluctuations in their oxygen levels can lead to blood pressure issues. Severe RDS can lead to eye problems, chronic lung disease —"

"Brain bleeds?" Rob interrupted.

"The tissue in these babies' brains is so soft," Erin said, but before she could explain more Rob dropped his head and turned to walk away. He had heard enough.

For the NICU team at Wilford Hall, balancing the oxygenation requirements of Anne's babies against the side effects of mechanical ventilation would be a high wire balancing act. Timmy, Edda and Lily would creep slowly forward, making precarious progress inch by inch in the days to come, but there were no guarantees. Wyatt was proof enough of that, having fallen from the wire altogether on DOL 3. Though the HFOV rescue treatment was a safety net that caught him in time, how long it would continue to hold, no one knew.

When we returned to the hospital on the morning of DOL 4 we learned that Anne was going to be discharged by late afternoon. Whether that cheered her or not, I wasn't sure, but she seemed in better spirits than the day before. She was even a little sassy.

When she suggested she might take Erin and Cait with her to the NICU, Rob cautioned that one parent escorting two aunts into the nursery was a breach of the visitation rules. Anne barked back at him, "To hell with the rules! I'm bringing my sisters with me to see my babies!" She even told us that she was encouraged that Wyatt was fighting so hard to hang on and that she thought Timmy and Edda were maybe doing just a little bit better.

Donna and I grabbed a quick lunch in the hospital cafeteria while the others went to the NICU. When we returned to the Labor & Delivery ward Anne was lying on top of the thin blanket stretched across her bed. The sheet was pulled up in a ball that she held against her belly. Cait and Erin had been helping their sister pack but whispered to Mom that Anne had quickly become exasperated. Try as she might, Anne couldn't keep the façade going. As morning turned into afternoon, it was obvious she was crumbling from the strain. Donna sat down gently on the opposite side of the bed and placed a hand on Anne's shoulder.

"Annie? Are you okay, sweetheart?"

She didn't respond.

"Not doing so good, honey?"

Anne shook her head.

"Does the incision hurt?"

She shrugged.

"Do you want me to help you get up? We can try to give you another bath. Dad can wait outside until we're done."

She shrugged again and shook her head.

I walked around the corner of the bed so I could see Anne's face. With one hand she was holding the corner of the sheet, pressing it against her mouth and nose. I could see her eyes. They were puffy and wet.

"Come on, honey," Donna said and pulled at her daughter's shoulder with a firm tug. "Your father is going to go." She gestured for me to leave. "Come on, soldier! Up and at 'em."

Anne pulled hard away from her, covering her face with the sheet. I didn't make any move to leave.

Donna turned from Anne to look at Erin. "I don't think she's doing very well," she said, reaching back toward Anne once more, this time placing her hand on top of Anne's hip.

Erin nodded and said in a low voice, "It's a lot, I know."

"I don't think she should leave the hospital tonight. She's not ready."

"Well, that's not our choice."

"You can talk to the doctor for your sister. Go talk to the residents."

"I already did. They need the room because the ward is full. They were doing her a favor letting her recover here because it's just down the hall from the NICU."

"Then they can move her."

"It's not that easy."

"I just don't think Annie's ready to go home yet. She should be near her babies."

"It's been 72 hours since her surgery," Erin explained. "They send mothers home who've had caesarean sections after 48 hours in most cases." She paused before adding, "And they send them home without their babies if they have to."

Anne pushed her face into her pillow.

The room was quiet. "I'll keep working on Anne's suitcase," Caitlin finally said.

I sat down on the corner of Anne's bed and began running my fingers through the long curls of her hair. When she didn't look up at me I bent down toward her and whispered, "Let's you and I go together to see the babies."

Still she didn't move.

"I want you to introduce me to your little guys. You've been in the NICU with everybody but me."

"I don't want to see them," she said and began to sob.

"It's okay, honey," I replied. "It's okay."

But it wasn't and I didn't have any idea how to make it better. I got up and left the room without saying anything. In the hall I noticed a wheelchair next to the nurse's station. I remembered Nurse Johnson's words, that my daughter's children were favored by God. If they were, it was hard to see how. And what about their mother? What was His plan for her? I didn't know. For now, I decided, a plan of my own would have to do.

"I think this little girl needs to go for a walk," I announced as I pushed the chair into the room. I grabbed Anne under her arms and, without asking, pulled her slowly up out of her bed and placed her carefully into the wheelchair.

"She doesn't want to go to the NICU," Donna said emphatically.

"I said I was taking her for a walk. I didn't say where." Then I pushed the wheelchair out of the room, out of Labor & Delivery and away from the NICU. We took the elevator to the first floor, and when the doors slid open I headed down the main hall toward the front entrance and the daylight beyond.

On the way we passed a wall of pictures. There was a photograph of the President. Beneath him was the Secretary of Defense and framed photos of the Chairmen of the Joint Chiefs of Staff, the Joint Chief of Staff of the Air Force, the picture of the Commanding Officer of the 59th Medical Wing, every general who had ever been the CO of the Wing, and then, in the bottom two rows, a photograph of the current Chief Master Sergeant of the Air Force, followed by all the former Chief Master Sergeants since the Air Force was founded. I noted that the chiefs all had more "bling" on their uniforms and more stripes on their arms than the generals. I remembered Anne and Erin telling me that it was the non-commissioned officers who *really* ran things in the military.

Anne motioned suddenly for me to stop. "There," she said with a proud smile. "That's him!" She pointed at a photo of one of the former Chief Master Sergeants of the Air Force. "He's my patient."

"You're kidding."

"Nope, and he's the nicest guy."

I thought about what a privilege it must have been for my daughter, just a new doctor and already seeing patients like that, and then asked, "So, does *he* have to call you sir?"

She laughed. "He does call me Ma'am."

"Well, all right then, Ma'am. Shall we march on?"

"Forward march, Papa," she replied, pointing to the wide set of glass doors that led outside. They opened automatically and I pushed Anne out, stopping in the shade of the hospital overhang. Access ramps for wheelchairs branched to both sides of the steps leading down to the street. To our left, another young woman sat in a wheelchair. She was holding a newborn, swaddled in a colorful blanket. Her husband was at the bottom of the steps, his head stuck inside the back door of their car, nervously adjusting the infant seat. To our right, a young man was helping a pregnant woman out of a car.

"Afternoon, Sir," he said as he walked past Anne and me. He stopped to look at the wheelchair, but before he could ask, the very pregnant woman at his side said, "I'm fine. I can walk to the elevator myself."

So *damn* routine, I thought. Pregnant woman walks in one day and comes out in a wheelchair with a baby in her arms the next. That's the way it was supposed to be, wasn't it?

"Best wishes," I called after the couple disappearing into the corridor beyond, then pushed Anne out from under the protection of the hospital's overhang and into the sunlight. It was bright and hot. The crepe myrtles that lined the road leading to Wilford Hall were filled with lavender and fuchsia blossoms. Beautiful though they were, the thin-limbed trees weren't very tall and didn't provide much in the way of shade. Anne was quick to protest. "If you get me sunburned, I'll kill you! I'm supposed to be a dermatologist, remember?" I pulled the black baseball cap with the gold and white star on its front and U.S. Army stitched in white thread beneath it from my brow and placed it on my daughter's head.

"There!" I said. "Sunscreen."

"But what about you, Papa?"

"I worked outside for twenty-some years with nothing more than a tee shirt wrapped around my head. It's too late for me now." I pushed Anne away from the hospital, past large parking lots that were not even half full on the weekend and turned onto a lane that led toward a few outbuildings that dotted the sprawling Air Force base. When we reached a spot that was shaded by short, thick trees I stopped, pulled Anne's chair onto the grass and sat on the curb by her feet. Further down the road I could see a wide fenced-in lot filled with swings, slides, see-saws and jungle gyms. The playground was attached to the base's day care center, but there was no one there on a Sunday.

I put my hand on my daughter's knee, and we sat there staring blankly into the distance. Even in the shade the sun seemed so close I could reach up and touch it. I wiped the sweat from my forehead. It was too hot, I realized. I shouldn't have brought Anne outside. I didn't know exactly what I'd wanted to say to my daughter when I brought here out here. Now, whatever thoughts I'd had were melting away. "I love you, Annie," I finally said. My eyes were welling with tears, but I did not let her see them.

Anne rose slowly up out of her chair and eased herself down beside me on the curb. "I love you, too, Papa," she whispered.

We sat quietly for what seemed a long time, both looking straight into the hazy Texas afternoon. An occasional car drove by. I wondered if anyone noticed us — a gray haired guy and a young woman in a hospital gown with only ankle socks on her feet, both looking lost on a curb in the middle of an Air Force base.

"Why is it so hot here?" Anne asked, breaking the silence as she pulled my Army cap from her head and set it on her lap.

I shrugged. "And it's only April."

"I miss the changing seasons, the changing colors of the leaves in the fall. The leaves only turn brown here."

"For what it's worth, the spring is beautiful," I countered. "Did you see the bluebonnets along the highway when you came to the hospital?"

"I don't know. I think it was dark when we got here. I missed them, I guess." She was looking around as she answered, but there were no flowers in sight. "I miss the winter," she continued. "I miss being cold, I miss the snow. You know what? What I really miss is Christmas. There's no Christmas here. How can you have Christmas when it's 70 degrees?"

I chuckled until I noticed that she was sniffling. She raised one hand and wiped away a tear. "I miss home, Papa," she said, and leaning against me she began to cry. "I want to go home. I just want to be home."

I held her while she sobbed, while she fought the emotions that needed to come pouring out. She hated to cry in front of me. "It's okay, sweetheart." The tears were rolling down both her cheeks, dripping from the tip of her nose. "I'm so proud of you," I told her, hoping that would make things seem right. I so wanted to make things better, wanted to tell her that they would be soon, but I knew they'd be empty words. I'd never felt so helpless. I could no more help Anne than she could her own babies. Like them, she was only surviving minute by minute, from one painful hour to the next. Tomorrow, or the day after tomorrow, was a place that no longer existed for her. Telling her things would get better would be telling her nothing at all.

What I finally did say was more a promise than anything else. I told her that her mom and I would be there for her through this whole thing, no matter what. And then I apologized to her. "I'm not a very good father," I said.

"Don't say that, Papa," she replied.

"It's just that — I don't know. Dads are supposed to make things right. And now when you really need me to, I don't even know how to begin."

"If you're a bad parent, what's that make me?" she asked.

"You'll be a great mom someday," I said. Then I added, "You're already an amazing mother."

She laughed, as though the notion was so absurd it was funny.

But I told her I believed that with all my heart. "I don't know why this is happening, why this has happened to you. But if I was Timmy or Edda, or Lily or Wyatt, if I was in their shoes I wouldn't want anybody else in the world to be my mother besides you."

She rested her head against my arm.

"It's okay if you're afraid to love them right now. I get that. It's okay if you don't even *want* to love them, too. But you will. I promise you, you will."

She shrugged.

I looked back toward Wilford Hall, at the hospital's aged brick veneer shimmering in the afternoon sun. "You know one of my favorite Psalms is Psalm 100?"

"I know how much you like the Psalms," she replied quietly. "I like reading them, too."

"I've read it so many times you'd think I'd know it by heart," I said, "but what I never forget is where it says it is the Lord who made us. And that we didn't make ourselves. That makes us His — you and me; all of us. We are His people; the sheep of His pasture is what the Psalm says. He loves us no matter what."

"I know," she said, lifting her head. "I want to believe that."

"I don't know how this is going to turn out, Annie, but Timmy, Edda, Lily and Wyatt..." I stopped as a swell of emotion caught in my throat, "even little Wyatt, they're all His. Before they were yours, they were His. He loves them. They're in His pasture, too, His little lambs."

We were quiet again for a minute or two. Then I laughed. Anne looked up at me curiously.

"Now that the sermon's over you probably think I'm going to start singing, right — the old Sunday school song? 'Jesus loves me this I know, for the Bible tells me so.'"

She smiled at me for poking fun at myself.

"That's how the Psalm ends," I said. "His love for us carries on forever. And He is faithful not to forget us. Not me, not you, not your children. 'Little ones to Him belong. They are weak but He is strong.'"

We sat for a few more minutes, but with the heat stifling us, I told Anne we should get back to the room; her mother would be wondering what I'd done with her daughter.

I could not get the Sunday school song out of my mind as I pushed Anne back toward the hospital. Little ones to Him belong. We are weak. He would have to be strong for all of us.

By late that afternoon, Anne was packed and ready to leave Wilford Hall. She and Rob said good night to the babies and drove away, leaving the fifth floor windows of the neonatal nursery shrinking behind them until, heading west on Highway 90, the entire hospital complex disappeared from view. When they arrived home there were no pink or blue balloons, no stork in the front lawn announcing a new baby's homecoming, no well-wishing relatives waiting anxiously with cameras poised to capture the first photos of Mom, Dad and baby arriving.

Inside, after we'd brought Anne's things in from the car, we busied ourselves with all that needed doing. Rob dumped a hamper full of clothes into the washer and then fell fast asleep on the living room floor. Erin printed boarding passes for herself and Cait, and then the two of them set about packing for their flights out of San Antonio the next day. Donna uploaded photos of the babies on her laptop and typed out an email announcing that Anne had come home. She closed the update by noting that, hopefully, the babies would be coming home to be with Anne and Rob in another 12 to 16 weeks. That would have them leaving the NICU around what had been their due date: July 24. Whether that was wishful thinking or not — it was so far in the future and the future was so uncertain for Timmy, Edda, Lily and Wyatt — we all realized that there was no sense in circling that or any other date on our calendars.

I had Anne sit on the loveseat in the living room and when she did, her two cats, Bravo and Zulu, came bounding out of the master bedroom to throw themselves into their mommy's lap. Anne was so happy to see them as they rubbed against her and purred, pushing each other out of the way as they vied for her attention. I made Anne a Manhattan — she loved the maraschino cherry I always put in it for her, so this evening I put in two — and for the first time since late October she took a sip of a cocktail. By the time I returned from the kitchen with a cocktail of my own, Anne was lying down, wrapped in the afghan her mother had knit for her years before. Both cats were tucked in with her, their heads on either side of her chin. She was fast asleep.

I would never really know what Anne went through in those first days after her babies were born. Certainly I could never feel the anguish she did. She had suffered a terrible loss. The pain she felt was as though someone very close to her had died, and while she was overwhelmed with grief, she was confused as to why. No one *had* died. Still she felt a gnawing ache, a stabbing pain that dug deeply into her, and she could not find the thing that had pierced her, let alone begin pulling it out. It wasn't for lack of trying. She desperately wanted to feel joy. But any notion that something should be celebrated — the birth of her children — was offset by the sense of grief that followed having her pregnancy cut short.

Anne had been deprived of an *experience*; she had lost her entire final trimester with her babies. For a mother, especially for a new mom, that is the time for the physical and psychological preparations preceding the birth. Few mothers-to-be are as excited about the birth of their child in the first few months as they are in the last months when the imminent arrival of their babies (and the associated preparations) makes it all feel real. Anne and Rob had yet to decorate their nursery. They had no stroller, not even car seats to bring the babies home. Anne hadn't even had time for a baby shower. All the happy anticipation that usually surrounds an expectant mother in the last month or so of her pregnancy was lost.

In its place there was only uncertainty, confusion and an overwhelming sense of loss. Anne was deprived in so many ways of "real" motherhood. Instead, she carried the guilt of feeling she had failed her babies, the guilt of ever having considered hormonal therapy, the guilt of forcing her husband to have children when he was not sure he was ready. Anne had only wanted what so many women have wanted: a child of her own. She wanted to squeeze the cheeks of her chubby, happy baby and to kiss her warm lips. She wanted to experience the delights of the first time her child latched upon her breast, the first time she changed her little diaper, the first time she gave her a bath. Instead, she was given the unwieldy weight of four micro-preemies who were barely clinging to life and facing a harrowing future. Try as she might to convince herself she should feel joyful, to persuade herself — in spite of all that had transpired — that there were still things she should be thankful for, she could not. She was being crushed by the looming prospect of even greater loss and grief. It was so hard for her to hold onto hope.

Had Anne remained pregnant, her babies would have been entering their 25th week that Sunday. Anne would have been only weeks shy of her third trimester. She would've been done with morning sickness and packing on pounds while her uterus continued to expand with her growing babies. Had she been carrying a single fetus it would be tipping the scales at around 1 pound, 9 ounces. It would be nearly a foot long, measured head to toe, but in the womb the tiny baby would appear more like a miniature bear hibernating, its head pushed down against its chest, arms folded just beneath the chin and legs crossed and drawn up tight. With four babies hibernating, Anne's tummy would have been getting crowded. Her "cubs" would be looking more and more like babies every day, with fully developed fingers and toes, eyes, ears and a nose. Though their eyes would still be closed in the womb, they would be able to sense changes in light and darkness as small amounts of light filtered into the uterus. And they would have been able to hear, too — the whooshing and swooshing of mom's heartbeat, digestion and other body functions giving them their first taste of a life beyond their own. Developmentally, things would be further behind inside them, however. Their internal organs would be far from mature and their bones would have only recently begun growing firmer. At 25 weeks, Anne's womb would have been their perfect home. There really was no better place on earth for them, and nothing Anne had wanted more than to keep them there.

CHAPTER 8

San Antonio
Winter 2010

"One of the reasons this issue hasn't been out of the closet is that usually one brings to the pregnancy experience an expectation of pleasure and joy."
Catherine Monk, Ph.D.

By THE END OF HER first trimester, Anne's pregnancy had become a guilt-ridden struggle to eat more, drink more, rest more (but don't work less) and for heaven's sake, don't worry — be happy! I had little doubt that what Dr. Monk's research suggested about how prenatal stress and maternal mood affected fetal development was true: the kinds of messages Anne's babies received from her in the womb could go a long way in shaping the kind of people they turned out to be. I was hoping Anne would finally get to a quiet place in her pregnancy where she could impart to her babies something of her own sweet spirit. I hoped she would think of her womb as more than a factory where a fetus developed fingers and toes; instead, I wanted Anne to think of it as a garden where she was sowing seeds that would blossom throughout her children's lives. But everything seemed to be working against Anne as she struggled to do that, and it was driving Rob, Donna and me toward utter frustration.

Donna flew from Philadelphia to San Antonio on Thursday, January 21. Anne was scheduled for a cervical cerclage the next day; she would be prepped for surgery and ready for the procedure to begin as early as seven in the morning. Donna would be with her from early dawn until they took her into the operating room. Rob would join his mother-in-law later and together they'd wait for Anne to come out of recovery. No one anticipated there would be any problems. It was a routine procedure. Rob expected to take his wife home that evening.

Nothing happened at seven that morning. The anesthesiologist didn't come to see Anne. No one had come by eight o'clock. By nine, Anne and her mom were still in good humor, Donna only half-seriously suggesting that the waiting game Anne was experiencing as a patient should be part of the curriculum for all doctors-in-training. By mid-morning, still without any explanation for the delay, Donna went to the nurses' station for some answers. There were none forthcoming. The staff was waiting for notice from the attending physician, but they'd heard nothing. Anne would have to keep waiting. She had become an "invisible patient" — that wide-eyed person so ubiquitous in hospitals, peering anxiously out from her room into the hall every time she heard steps approach.

Though Anne remained calm throughout the morning, Donna and Rob were concerned. In fact, they were becoming alarmed. Anne had not eaten or drunk anything since the night before. Now, with no chance of the procedure being performed before early afternoon, by the time Anne was out of recovery and able to eat and drink again 24 hours without food or drink would have elapsed. Donna said it was absurd considering her condition. Rob feared it was dangerous for the babies. But despite their protestations there was still no word from the OB-GYN team.

What exactly was said when the department head of the OB unit — a "full-bird" Air Force Colonel — arrived in Anne's hospital room that afternoon, I will never know. Donna called me that evening, her voice filled with exasperation; she was at the point of tears, and she was infuriated. They'd *declined* to do Anne's cervical cerclage, she told me. The reason was nearly incomprehensible. The Colonel, upon entering Anne's room, had gone on something of a tirade. He informed Anne that he had decided that his department would no longer provide care to Anne or any other soldier for that matter who was openly critical of the quality or professionalism that his doctors offered. He made it clear that he was offended that another physician, and a junior officer at that, had framed his department in such a bad light. With seething vitriol he rejected the premise that he was responsible any longer for her care. Rather, he said, it was incumbent on Captain Spillane that she and her husband make plain their intentions to him regarding whether they wanted to pursue prenatal care from his department or not. His surgeon would not be doing Anne's scheduled cerclage today, nor would he at any other time in the future, unless and until she was fully committed to placing herself and her babies in their care. His point made, the Colonel left Anne alone in the hospital room.

Anne was devastated by the dressing down she'd received at the hands of another doctor and senior officer. When I talked to her the following day she was confused by what had happened and embarrassed that, whatever it was she had done, she had managed to put herself professionally into disrepute. Worse, she was mad at herself for having gotten pregnant. She was feeling guilty that she had begun something that was going awfully wrong, something that was spiraling out of control.

I quickly realized there wasn't much to be gained dredging facts out of the mud. In the end, it wouldn't matter anyway; the damage was done. From what I could tell the whole situation was the result of a volatile mix of ego, intra-service rivalry and misunderstood intentions. That none of it needed to happen was the most frustrating thing of all.

Perhaps by probing for data from the OB-GYN department about their success in handling high-risk/multiple-birth pregnancies, Rob had ruffled some feathers. For her part, Anne had looked into the possibility of transferring her care to the Phoenix clinic and learned that obtaining insured care outside the military would require a special waiver.

Anne's department head tried to see if such a waiver would float. That had the unfortunate consequence of pitting two branches of the Armed Forces against one another. Anne's Dermatology Department, though it contained both Army and Air Force staff, was essentially an Army unit. The OB-GYN team also had physicians from both branches but it was, administratively, an Air Force unit. In the days before Anne's scheduled cervical cerclage the informal request apparently made its way up the Army chain of command. When it reached as high as it could go it had to cross over to the Air Force's decision-makers. But when it jumped across the aisle it had the effect of setting off fireworks. Since "shit flows downhill," as any veteran of the Armed Forces can tell you, the fallout from the informal request went cascading down the Air Force chain of command until the "shit" ended up being hand delivered by an Air Force colonel to an Army captain who just happened to be my daughter.

I don't know if the Colonel who dumped on Anne felt warranted in his indignation toward her, but that was beside the point. Maybe he was already upset by what he perceived to be a challenge to his department's integrity; maybe the "shit" that fell in his lap from the chain of command above him represented a breach in protocol. I don't know. But Anne was not just some junior officer to be chewed out to assuage the Colonel's ego; she was his patient — a pregnant woman carrying four tiny lives!

I was as infuriated as Donna and Rob by the episode and even more frustrated to be so far away. My gut reaction was to avenge the wrong that I felt my daughter had suffered. I actually came close to buying a ticket for the next flight to San Antonio, but as the weekend slowly passed I knew there was little to be gained by doing that. I would probably end up making things worse.

When my brother Mike called on Sunday to ask for an update on Anne's surgery, he seemed nonplussed. "We have someone else to fight our battles for us," he counseled. And when we prayed together, as we often did on the phone, he quoted these words of Jesus: *These things I have spoken to you, that in Me you may have peace. In the world you have tribulation, but take courage; I have overcome the world.* He concluded his prayer with words that I would hold fast to over the coming weeks and months: "Lord, let the troubled waters around Anne be stilled."

On Monday, Donna called from Texas to tell me that after a difficult and emotional weekend, Anne and Rob decided not to transfer their care to the specialty clinic in Phoenix. They realized it had become an untenable situation and just wasn't worth the trouble. They spent that morning in meetings with various members of the Army and Air Force "brass" to iron out any more misunderstandings, and Anne was rescheduled for her cervical cerclage the following Friday. Donna would stay on with Anne until she was through the procedure.

As for the Air Force Colonel, he never bothered to see Anne as a patient again. Though his team would provide her excellent prenatal care and agreed to incorporate some of the protocols used by the Phoenix facility, he remained conspicuously absent. Even after the crisis in the last days of Anne's pregnancy and the ensuing trauma of her delivery, he would never return to check on her. He had washed his hands of the whole affair.

The following weekend, I sat down and wrote Anne a long email. Glad to have the "cerclage crisis" behind us, I offered some encouragement. The crux of my message was found in a few short paragraphs:

> I know how hard this pregnancy has been for you, what with the shock of first learning that you're having quadruplets, the nausea, the imbroglio with the military over your care, the recent surgery, the fight to gain weight, the anemia... it just must seem like it goes on and on for you.
>
> One of Mom's favorite scriptures is Psalm 139, which begins, "O Lord, Thou hast searched me and known me." What a great and comforting thought that our God knows us even when we sometimes fail to understand what's going on in our very own lives. God has been busy searching and knowing us from the day we were first conceived and what I know Mom especially loves in this Psalm is the description of the life that grows in a mother's womb: *"Thou didst form my inward parts; Thou didst weave me in my mother's womb. I will give thanks to Thee, for I am fearfully and wonderfully made."*
>
> Hopefully, in a few more weeks Mom or I will be back out with you. Until then, know that you, too, have been fearfully and wonderfully made and that process is what has made you the special person you are today. Sometimes, it just takes patience getting there!

Anne's pregnancy had reached 15 weeks when I sent her that email. On Skype the day before, she'd lifted her sweatshirt to show me her belly. There was a lot more than the "small melon" that was there when we went hiking just a few weeks before. No doubt about it, the forming and weaving that takes in place in a mother's womb was certainly happening in Anne's. Only for her, with both fear and wonder, it was happening times four.

By the 15th week of a normal pregnancy, a developing fetus would look so much like a baby that calling it anything but that seems absurd. Its head is sitting on a sturdy neck, raised up above the shoulders. Its eyes have begun to grow eyebrows and tiny lashes. Hair is growing on the scalp, too. Most babies by this point are practicing swallowing, sometimes even hiccupping. Some have begun to suck their thumbs. From the ultrasounds, we knew that Anne's babies were keeping pace. They were growing quickly, getting close to four inches long and weighing a couple of ounces each. Their little hearts were working furiously. As for Anne, her heart had been working hard, too. A woman will have to pump 20% more blood than before she was pregnant; we all knew how imperative it was for Anne to stay well hydrated. That fact alone made the Air Force Colonel's decision to leave Anne waiting without food or fluid while he debated delaying her scheduled surgery a ghastly mistake in judgment.

The morning after Donna flew back home I put together my third update to keep family and friends apprised of Anne's situation. There had been another ultrasound earlier the same day so I included some exciting news from that: there was reasonable speculation concerning the babies' sexes! Unfortunately, there was also increasing concern about Anne's health.

> Another ultrasound today — this week's images has it at two boys and two girls but nothing definitive yet — and then a cardio exam is scheduled for tomorrow since Anne seems to have an elevated HR, shortness of breath and constant

state of exhaustion that is causing some concern. Maybe this is just the toll carrying quads has on her rather small frame but the docs want to make sure it's not something to worry about.

We are nearing week #16 and that puts Anne right around halftime in this journey; 14-16 more weeks and by God's grace Donna & I will go from zero grandchildren to having four!

Though the ultrasound hinted at two boys and two girls, it would be another three weeks before the doctors were confident of that. What was more important was the 16 week milestone I'd mentioned. It meant that Anne was halfway to her goal. The first four months had not been easy, but I was hopeful that the worst was behind her. The end was almost in sight — a couple more months working at the Derm Clinic and then four to six weeks of bed rest at home before Anne would be admitted for full time observation. Then she would remain in the hospital until they delivered her. My own mental calendar looked something like this: 8 more weeks and the babies would be approaching viability; 12 weeks and their lungs would be mature enough to give them a much better shot at life; and 32 weeks? That would be almost ideal for quadruplets. Unless you were Rob and you wanted the babies to make it to 34 weeks. To me, that was like wishing upon a star, but who could blame him?

February was a month of blizzards in Pennsylvania. Donna loved it. Being home-bound in a winter storm with nothing to do but sit by the fire and knit was heaven for her. And with four babies to knit for, it could have snowed for 40 days and nights for all she cared. For me, the endless hours pushing the snow blower up and down the driveway helped speed the passage of time. By the end of the month, Anne was 19 weeks pregnant.

Between Skype, phone calls and email, Donna and I talked with Anne frequently. She told us she was envious of our weather since the closest thing to snow she'd seen in Texas was a morning frost, and she regularly updated us on her condition. She told us she was settling into something of a routine, finally, and that she was eating more and had gained 25 pounds.

The babies were growing, too. By the middle of February, when we were in the midst of our second blizzard, Anne's babies were each about as big as a baked potato — almost five inches long and nearly five ounces in weight. By the end of the month they were more than half a foot long and about half a pound each. Tiny though they were, Anne said she was sure she was beginning to feel the babies moving.

In early March, with the worst of winter behind us, Donna packed her bag and flew once more to Texas to see her daughter and the grandbabies who were starting to make Anne look like she'd tucked a basketball under her blouse. With Anne tiring easily at work, the Dermatology Department Head went out of her way to lessen Anne's patient load. She allowed her extra time between appointments to grab an energy bar and a big glass of juice and even let Anne squeeze a nap in some afternoons. But by the end of the first week of March, when it came to work, enough was enough: Anne was going home. As Donna explained in the update she sent upon her return from that brief visit, everything was still going according to plan.

> Anne is doing well. She's on home bed rest now and is just finishing up week 20. A home health service dropped off a monitor that she wears for an hour in the morning and an hour in the evening. It sends its info wirelessly to the OB docs, who then check back in with Anne. So far, her uterus

is just "irritable." For gosh sakes, I'd be irritable, too! She's the size of a 40 week single pregnancy now, so things will begin to get really interesting soon!

No sooner was Donna back home than Caitlin went to visit her sister. For Cait, it was especially enjoyable to be with Anne again. She hadn't seen her big sister for nearly a year, and when she called us from Texas she reported that Anne was getting to be a really *big,* big sister. She told us she thought it unfathomable Anne would carry the babies for another two months. "She'll just explode!" she said, noting that every part of Anne was still Anne, small boned and thin except her belly, which was already way huge.

Not long after, it was my turn for a visit to San Antonio. When I arrived Anne had been on bed rest at home for two weeks. Her appetite was better than ever and, as she was hardly burning any calories resting, she was gaining weight rapidly. Cait was right about her "big" sister. By the time of my visit she had gained nearly 60 pounds. But being home was no picnic…

She is fighting depression. The days at home seem endless to her. She is bored to death. "All I do is eat, drink and sleep," she tells me. "And pee. A lot!" She dreads knowing she will begin *real* bed rest in the hospital before long. There she won't be allowed out of bed at all.

"Not even to pee," she laments.

So much has changed in the two months since I'd last seen her. Then we'd spent an afternoon hiking in the Texas Hill Country. We laugh as I show her the photos I took that day. "I don't even know who that is anymore," she says, smiling. She is sitting on a rock, her hair flowing freely from under a black cowboy hat, her thin face bright and smiling. She's glowing. Now, however, Anne is someone else. Her face is puffy, her hair limp. When she smiles, instead of exhilaration, her eyes look tired.

"Can I get you anything?" I ask.

She shakes her head, her eyes still on the camera in her hands, her fingers clicking through its images one after another. She is wearing a gray hooded sweatshirt with large red letters spelling CORNELL on the front. Its waistband is pulled up toward her chest, exposing the bulbous mass of her belly. A small monitor is resting on top of her tummy; elastic straps stretched around her torso hold the device in place. One of her cats, Bravo, is resting contentedly on her lap, eyes only half-open.

"You should keep drinking," I tell her, seeing an empty water glass and a half-filled mug of tea on the end table. A prescription pill bottle sits there, too. "Can't I get something for you?"

"Can you get me out of here?" she asks, putting the camera down. "Is there such a thing as a 'Get out of pregnancy free card'?"

We both laugh.

"What was it — only eight weeks ago that we were hiking above that canyon?" I remind her. "In another ten you'll be thirty-two weeks pregnant and free to deliver."

She chuckles, but says she thinks she'll die first.

"Well, how about eight weeks?"

She sighs.

"Okay," I tell her, looking around to be sure Rob is not in earshot. "This is between you and me; it's our secret. You hang in there six more weeks. You make it to 28 weeks and your babies should have a decent shot. You can do that, right?"

"I'll do my best."

"That's a good soldier."

"But what do I do in the meantime?"

I ponder that and then, showing her the book I'd brought for her, I ask Anne if I can read her one of its short stories.

"I'd like that, Papa," she says smiling. "You'll be the first person to read to my babies. It'll be their very first story."

"It's by Annie Proulx, one of my favorite authors," I say before announcing its title, *Deep-Blood-Greasy-Bowl*. Admittedly, it is an awful name for a baby's first story, but Proulx's words are almost lyrical. I begin to read aloud to Anne about a band of anxious hunters who'd been waiting for days for some word or omen from the tribe's holy man.

> *Gradually the familiar sounds of night and sleep gave way. A few men came awake at once and raised up on their elbows, listening to the change. The chill air presaged autumn. In the blue draw coyotes argued. A sated owl on the island hooted and the river choked through sun-baked stones. But these were common sounds, and had not wakened the men. Silence disturbed their sleep, the cessation of a voice. The shaman had stopped chanting.*

I read on, the story exploring the subtle wonder of nature, the cycle of life-death-life again, and the fragile thread of the spiritual that binds one generation to the next. It is a tale of cunning hunters and the almost mystical appearance of an eagerly sought herd of bison; of a courageous warrior-band whose reverence for the tradition of the hunt tempers their impatience; of the instinctual rush to survive that drives their prey head-long over a cliff's edge and into the grateful clutches of the hungry tribe below. It is about the deep stone bowl handed down from one generation to the next and how it is filled once more with the grease and blood of the sacrificed bison. The final scene is of a young boy. He had never witnessed such a spectacle. His gaze is transfixed by the warm liquid, and as he stares into the overflowing bowl, he begins to feel for the first time a kinship with the past and a hope for the future that will become "twined into his lifelong sense of being."

I do not look at Anne as I close the book. Instead, I stare at her belly. For a moment I cannot escape the absurd notion that her babies and I have somehow connected through the story.

"Thanks, Papa," Anne says. "That was beautiful." She places my hand atop her tummy and smiles. "I think they're all asleep. That's a good bedtime story."

I laugh at the thought of having put them all to sleep. But what I could not know then is that perhaps there was also portent in the tale I'd read. Maybe like the hunters spending long, lonely nights waiting for a sign, the babies would soon hear in their own solitude the cessation of a voice. Like the waking warriors, they, too, would hear that the shaman had stopped chanting. Their time was about to come.

On Tuesday, March 30, five days before Easter, Anne went into labor. She wasn't sure that the contractions were strong enough — in fact, she could hardly feel them — but the growing number recorded by her belly-monitor started to worry her. She called the group that remotely interpreted the monitoring data. A nurse told Anne not to be too concerned. The number of contractions *was* high, but experience told her if Anne would relax and increase her intake of fluids over the next two hours, they might diminish. The strategy had actually worked for Anne in the past; on several occasions when her contractions had gone into the "red zone" she'd been able to bring them back down with water and rest. The nurse assured her they would monitor the contractions again in a few hours to see what the data looked like then.

This time, though, the contractions persisted. The nurse said she would call the OB at Wilford Hall to apprise him of the situation. "Hold tight," she told Anne, "and let's see what the doctor wants us to do." But the OB was in an emergency delivery and could not be reached. She would keep trying to contact him, but in the interim the nurse thought it best that Anne get to the hospital.

By the early hours of Wednesday morning, Anne was stable and resting in a room at Wilford Hall. Her contractions had subsided. She was seen by her doctor later that morning, and the news was both good and bad. The number of contractions was in a safer range and Anne's cervix was in good shape. Anne's blood pressure, however, was too high and not coming down. They would watch that closely. Anne sent Rob home with a list of the things she needed. She wasn't going anywhere until the babies were born.

A patient once again, Anne knew the daily routine from her own experience doing hospital rotations. By the time the doctors made their morning rounds the patient had already had vitals taken and any prescribed meds administered. The team usually consisted of a senior on-call resident, one or two less experienced residents and sometimes a medical student. But on Thursday's rounds, Anne was greeted by the chief resident and the attending OB. That was unusual and, as she rightly suspected, not a good sign.

Anne's labs from the previous day showed she had proteinuria. Her high blood pressure was one thing, but the presence of protein in her urine had pushed her diagnosis past its tipping point. She had preeclampsia. Though not critical yet, the attending made it clear the end game was on. Anne *might* carry her babies for weeks more, but with preeclampsia there were no guarantees.

Donna and I had been down this road when she was carrying Anne and Erin. Nearly 30 years later, the pathology of preeclampsia was still poorly understood. In spite of continuing research, it remained a pernicious problem in pregnancy. It was like a game of dominoes; once the first piece falls all the others follow. For Anne, that first piece had already toppled. How long before the next pieces fell was anybody's guess. The looming challenge for her doctors was how to maintain a tenuous balance between the health of their patient and the health of her babies. High blood pressure put Anne in danger of kidney failure, not to mention seizure or stroke. If the doctor treated the hypertension too aggressively, Anne's blood pressure could drop to the point where her placenta would not be sufficiently perfused — cutting off the supply of blood to her babies. It was like a see-saw with Anne on one side and her babies on the other.

No sooner had the doctor given Anne the news about her condition than she was on the phone with her mother. Donna later told me Anne was surprised by her diagnosis, but didn't seem to think the situation warranted more than close observation by the OB team yet. She sounded more like a doctor than a patient, Donna said, and Anne seemed almost detached about her condition. We're just going one day at a time now, Anne told her, and there was no reason to panic. On the positive side, Anne said that they had done an extensive ultrasound the day before and the babies seemed to be doing well.

Before I left the office later that morning I sent out a quick update. The subject line read: "Anne update — Urgent!" Though I didn't want to cause alarm I thought that the sooner people got praying the better. As it turned out, Anne would need serious prayer support sooner than I imagined possible. Donna called me a few hours later to say she needed me to come home as soon as I could. She would only tell me that Anne had called minutes earlier and was crying uncontrollably. Donna wanted to get on a flight to San Antonio that evening. She told me she needed to be with Anne ASAP.

What I learned when I got home was that additional blood work showed Anne developing HELLP Syndrome, a condition much more dangerous than preeclampsia. Further lab work would be necessary to verify the diagnosis, but if the preliminary results were correct, Anne was facing possible damage to her liver and worse. Like preeclampsia, the only effective treatment for the disease was delivery.

What sent Anne into near-hysteria, however, wasn't the preliminary diagnosis of HELLP, but the later discussion with the OB team and the neonatologists. HELLP is a life-threatening condition and if confirmed in her case, the combination of it with preeclampsia would present acute obstetric complications. It was their duty in light of the circumstances, the doctors explained, to present Anne with all the options available.

It *was* possible for Anne to continue to carry her babies; their condition remained good. It was possible, but highly unlikely, she would carry them for a few more weeks. More likely, her condition would become critical, and they would have to deliver the babies to save her life. Realistically, an emergency caesarean section would have to take place within days, perhaps sooner. If that was the case, it was possible, but highly unlikely, that all her babies would survive for very long; and if any did, the long term prognosis would include an array of serious developmental issues and severe disability. Anne's own health was being jeopardized by continuing the pregnancy. Her babies' very quality of life would be jeopardized by ending it.

The babies' gestational age on Thursday, April 1, was 23 weeks, 5 days. The team informed her that 24 weeks was considered the threshold for viability in the State of Texas. If the babies were delivered before Saturday, the doctors would not be legally required to resuscitate them. The option was Anne's to choose. She needed to consider whether to terminate her pregnancy in order to protect her own life.

Anne called Rob first. They had to talk, she said. Then she called her mom and that's when she fell completely apart. I knew she needed her mother. We booked the last available seat on the last flight out of Philadelphia bound for Texas. Donna threw whatever she could grab into a carry-on and we headed for the airport. Once I returned home I put together another update. The subject line read: "Anne's update — Urgent 2."

> Hey — Donna is flying to San Antonio and will be w/Anne in the hospital by midnight tonight. Things are something of a high-wire walk right now with complications arising quickly that may make delivery soon necessary. We just don't know yet. Viability for the babies at this point is not good according to the neonatal team. We stand in God's strength and believe in His goodness. We will update as time goes on and as we learn more.

On Friday morning, Anne told her doctors she was unwilling to give up the babies. Her resolve was strengthened when her blood work looked better later in the day. After the difficult afternoon before, Anne had decided that if she got knocked down she would do all she could to get back up on her feet. If she was going to lose this fight it would have to be by knockout. And by late in the day, it looked like she was improving. The OB told Anne he was pleased with her condition — her vital signs were stable and though her blood pressure was still high, he thought it was manageable. He promised he would fight along with her to get every day, every hour they could for her babies. While he knew it was rare for a woman to carry on with her pregnancy more than a couple weeks after a diagnosis like hers, if Anne was lucky she might. That would get her babies beyond what Donna called the "really scary delivery zone of 24–26 weeks." The waiting game was back on.

Nothing eventful happened over Easter weekend. In an email sent from the hospital on Sunday, Donna closed by saying, "The docs continue to be guarded and make very clear how quickly things can turn and force an immediate delivery. We continue to believe God for getting these babies to the 28 week mark and to protect Anne's body as she takes care of these little guys, and I have no qualms about letting the docs know we have a great God!" Reading it made me smile. Donna wasn't about to throw in the towel, either.

With Donna in Texas, Erin decided to spend Easter weekend with Cait and me. The two of us had been on pins and needles, not knowing exactly what was happening with Anne, so it was great to have Erin. She offered reassurance, but when I couldn't get her to say whether Anne was out of the woods or not, I pressed for more.

"The real problem is her blood pressure," Erin began.

"High blood pressure — that's it?" It didn't seem an insurmountable problem to me.

"Proteinuria can be indicative of renal damage. Malfunctioning capillaries in the kidneys suggest a broader hemodynamic problem. Low blood volume eventually leads to arterial muscle constriction resulting in increasing blood pressure."

Cait interrupted to point out that, in case Erin had forgotten, she hadn't gone to medical school. I nodded appreciatively.

"It's like this," Erin said. "Since they are finding protein in Anne's urine it's likely that her blood vessels are leaking protein in other parts of her body, too. As proteins leach into the surrounding tissue they draw water after them. This reduces blood volume. The arteries constrict in response and blood pressure goes up. High blood pressure damages the kidneys and that just makes things worse."

"So what do you do?" I asked.

"They're pumping fluids into Anne on a regular basis."

"Will that work?" Cait wanted to know.

"The extra fluids will replenish the blood supply and help control the blood pressure."

"Is that it?" I asked.

"The problem is that once the blood makes its way from the arteries to the weaker walls and valves found in the veins the added fluid just leaks out again. It can be a difficult cycle to manage."

"So the doctors are really just buying time?"

"I guess you could say that. Dealing with hypertension is so much more complicated in the late stages of pregnancy than in other situations."

"Is that where we are now — the end of Anne's pregnancy?" Cait was caught off guard by what Erin was saying. "She's got a few more weeks, at least — right?"

"I don't know," Erin answered. "I don't think anybody knows right now."

Uncertainty aside, whatever Anne's doctors were doing seemed to be working. Over the next two days, her heart rate, respiratory rate, blood pressure and oxygen saturation level were all stable. Her contractions remained within an acceptable range. Daily ultrasounds showed the babies continuing to do well. Anne was able to stop thinking about her own health problems long enough to focus on her babies. One of them was a bit smaller than the others, so he was being monitored closely for any signs of distress. "He jumps around so much," Anne told me when I talked to her on the phone on Monday, "he's definitely the one with the most 'attitude.'" She had taken to affectionately calling him the runt.

Things seemed to be going so well that Donna decided to keep the reservations for her flight home on Wednesday. Anne had assured her mom she was going to be all right. Go home to Dad, she told her. And she insisted the two of us should go on the trip to Chicago we had booked for the coming weekend. "It's Papa's birthday," she reminded her mom. "Go and enjoy it."

But even before Donna and Rob had left the hospital late Tuesday night Anne started to feel worse — much worse. She couldn't get comfortable. Her breathing was labored; she felt like someone was sitting on her chest. She convinced herself it was probably nothing and didn't tell anyone. Whatever it was, I think she figured it could wait until rounds in the morning.

But the pressure on her chest worsened throughout the night. Anne was barely able to breathe. She would later recount to me how she could not even reach the toilet only ten feet from her bed. Collapsing to her knees after each step, she broke down crying and gave up. Lying on the cold floor she could see the clock by her bed. It was 4:30 in the morning. Morning rounds were still hours away. She was scared enough she crawled to reach her phone to call her sister. When Erin answered she was shocked by Anne's voice. "What the heck is going on?" she demanded. "You sound like you just ran a marathon!" Anne tried to apologize for calling so early, but she couldn't even finish the sentence. Erin insisted Anne ring for the nurse. "Get the resident to order up a chest x-ray," Erin told her. "You need to find out what's going on. You need to do it now!"

The trip to Radiology seemed to last forever, Anne told me. She was taken in a wheelchair from the fifth floor down into the bowels of Wilford Hall and wheeled through its long corridors. It was gray, cold and eerily quiet. Things felt surreal. After the orderly who'd pushed her into the waiting room left, time seemed to stand still for her. There was no one else around; no other patients and no staff. She remembered thinking it was too early in the morning. Someone might not come to get her for an hour or more. Anne told herself not to be afraid. She was going to be a mom, she reminded herself. She would have to stay strong. And that was when she realized she'd made a mistake.

She should have seen this coming. She'd had a dry cough for weeks, hadn't she? There was the sensation of subtle but unmistakable pressure on her chest. She had become increasingly short of breath. In her last couple weeks at the Derm Clinic, she'd stopped using the stairs and instead had to take the elevator to make it from the first floor to the second. She had tried to make light of it all then. In her last week at the clinic she'd given a lecture to staff and residents. "You'll all have to forgive me in advance," she'd told them then. "I'm going to have to take a few short breaks from talking because my four babies are taking up so much space in my belly they're starting to squish my lungs!" But the joke had been on her. She'd never told anyone a thing more about the growing weight on her chest. Now as she sat in the wheelchair, she struggled to breathe. The short, labored breaths did little good. She thought she might be suffocating. She wondered if she was dying.

X-rays revealed that, overnight, Anne's lungs had begun rapidly filling with fluid. That was why she was having difficulty breathing. She was slowly drowning. Back in her room, Anne called her sister with the news. Erin did her best not to sound alarmed. There was probably some way for the OB team to manage the pulmonary edema, she said, and told Anne that a simple diuretic might be all it would take.

"You'll be all right," she insisted, wanting with all her heart to believe that Anne would.

But when the attending physician and chief resident arrived later that morning the news they brought with them was worse. They had completed a careful review of Anne's most recent lab work. The results showed that Anne now had extensive anemia. Her red blood cell count was dangerously low. The risks to Anne and her babies were plain. The attending physician told Anne bluntly that, for the sake of her own life, she should consent to delivering the babies now. He knew how important every day in the womb was to Anne's babies, but she was his patient. He could not guarantee a safe outcome for her if she remained pregnant for much longer. And he would not be able to save her babies if she went into cardiac arrest or had a seizure.

Anne did not hesitate. She knew that each hour she could fight to keep her babies was one more hour that might make all the difference. She told the attending that delivery was not an option, not yet. She asked him if there wasn't something more he could do. There was, he said, but he thought the prospects of it working were bleak. Anne said she understood she was taking a risk. He told her that she was asking him to act against his own best judgment, but admitted to admiring her resolve. Together they agreed on a treatment protocol designed to buy more time.

Administering a standard diuretic alone to treat the pulmonary edema was not really feasible in Anne's case. Because her blood vessels had been losing fluid as a result of the proteins that were leaching out of them, a diuretic would only exacerbate the problem. The best the doctor thought he could do was use blood transfusions to fight the anemia and temporarily pump up Anne's blood volume. The new blood, flush with proteins, would serve to draw fluid back into the vessels and create a window of opportunity to give Anne a diuretic that would then remove fluid from her lung tissue. The OB didn't think this was a procedure they could repeat more than a few times, if that. Anne told him she was onboard with the plan. The attending was hardly sanguine about it. This was only a temporary solution; nothing he could do would really change the underlying problem or the dynamics of his patient's circumstance. He could not deter the effects or progression of preeclampsia and HELLP syndrome. Only delivering the babies would do that. He ordered the blood transfusions. The dominoes were falling rapidly now, he knew. He prescribed a course of glucocorticoids to stimulate the production of surfactants in fetal lungs. And he had Anne moved to a room in Labor & Delivery.

My conversation with Donna did not go well when she called to say she wasn't coming home.

"What about tomorrow? Can't you get a flight home tomorrow morning? We'd still be able to catch our Friday flight to Chicago."

"I'm afraid to leave Anne."

"We'll only be gone for the weekend. If something happens I'll be able to get you on a flight to San Antonio in a few hours."

"You're not listening to me. Anne is sick."

"She's pregnant. Everybody knew there would be complications."

"Pulmonary edema means she's sick."

"You told me she had fluid in her lungs. They can use a diuretic or something, right?"

"It's not that simple."

"What am I supposed to do? I've spent a lot of time putting plans for this weekend together."

"You go if it's that important to you."

"I don't want to go without you. We've got reservations for my birthday Friday night at a real nice restaurant in town. I guaranteed the reservations at the hotel. I don't know what it'll cost to cancel the flights."

"I'm not leaving *my* daughter. I don't care about the money."

"She's *our* daughter."

"You don't seem to get that right now."

"What I don't get is what is going on out there. You were supposed to fly home today. A day ago you told me Anne was doing OK. You told me she wanted you to come home, that she would be all right. I thought we were talking about Anne maybe getting to 28 weeks. I don't get it."

"I don't feel like I can leave her now."

"Well, what I am I supposed to do?"

"I think you should come here and be with your daughter."

"I don't want to do that. Not yet."

"Then go to Chicago. Do what you want."

I didn't want to go to San Antonio. I was afraid of what would happen if I did. Anne was only a couple days beyond the 24 week mark. She needed to carry her babies longer. She needed to keep them in her womb as long as possible. I knew she would fight for every day, every last hour for them. I was afraid if I came to San Antonio now it would show her that her situation was hopeless. I was afraid that when she saw me she would break down. She would know I was coming to tell her it was okay to let go.

I felt all the hope oozing out of me. I knew Donna's intuition was likely right. Anne was in serious trouble. As a mom, my wife knew she needed to be there with our daughter, but it wasn't so straightforward for me. I didn't care about the Chicago trip any more than Donna; I just didn't want to give in to the notion that we had run out of time. Not yet. I could feel my own resolve crumbling and if I gave in, then what?

The next few hours were long and lonely for me. I sat in the office cancelling the hotel reservations, the dinner reservations and the flight to Chicago. When I could sit no longer I got in my truck and drove out to the construction site where our crew was working. I told my foreman, Fergus, and our guys that things were getting a little bit sketchy for my daughter. I said I might have to fly to Texas at the drop of a hat. When Fergus asked about the babies I felt my face flush and tears well up in my eyes. "I don't know," I told him. I didn't know what was going to happen. And from what I could gather, the prospects for Anne carrying them much longer did not seem good.

When I returned home it was nearly four in the afternoon. I hadn't heard anything more from Donna. I didn't know if it was because there was nothing more to tell me or if she was infuriated with me. I didn't think I'd be able to reach her on her phone in the hospital. Instead, I sat and waited. When the phone finally rang, it was Erin.

"What's going on, honey?"

"Mom told me you wouldn't listen to her, so I should call you."

"I don't understand what's going on. I thought we were talking about Anne hanging in there for a few more weeks. You told me that yourself."

"I know, Dad."

"So, what am I supposed to do? Mom wants me out there to be with Anne. You know what will happen if I come. That's what I was trying to tell your mother. If I come out there Anne will think we're giving up. She can still hang in there, can't she — another week or at least a few more days?"

"When I talked to her this morning, I thought so."

"Well?"

"Her lab work is getting worse. Her platelet count is dropping. That might be from the additional blood volume from the transfusions. The doctors aren't sure yet."

"Transfusions? Mom didn't say anything about transfusions."

"Maybe they weren't giving them to Anne yet. She said you weren't listening to anything she was saying anyway."

She was right; I wasn't listening. I didn't want to hear about anemia and blood transfusions. I didn't want to think about preeclampsia and HELLP syndrome or any of that stuff. What I wanted was somebody to tell me that everything was going to be okay.

"You need to go, Dad. You and Cait need to get out there as soon as you can. I'm going to try and get out there tomorrow night if I can get emergency leave."

That was it, then. There was nothing to argue anymore.

"Is Anne going to be OK?"

"They need to deliver the babies to give her a chance."

"A chance?"

"It's a very tenuous situation. But they're good doctors. They are on top of this thing. They're going do everything they can for Anne. It's just that they can only push the envelope so far. I think the doctors have gone beyond what they'd do for any other patient in her condition. Everybody wants to give her babies the best chance they can."

"What about them?"

"They're so young, Dad."

"Will they make it?"

"Maybe."

I was quiet for a long moment.

"Dad?"

"They have a chance, don't they?"

"All we can do is hope."

"But 24 weeks is the threshold for viability. That's what everybody has been saying." I was grasping at straws.

"They'll have a lot of problems if they live."

"Like what?"

"There's a lot of disability associated with very premature babies."

"Disabilities?"

"Lung problems for sure. Physical and cognitive developmental issues. The disabilities can range from needing eye glasses to severe cerebral palsy. It's hard to say for sure."

"There's nothing they can do to buy more time?"

"You need to go, Dad." She hesitated, and then added, "Anne needs you. I'll call Mom and tell her we talked."

When I hung up the phone I turned to my computer and pulled up the Southwest website. There was a flight to Houston that would connect to San Antonio by early afternoon. The only tickets left were business class. I booked two. And then I sent out an email with a subject line that simply read: "Anne."

Pray if you have a moment when you get this, please... Anne has run into some more complications and the serious nature for her & the babies is escalating. Sorry I don't have more details to share but at least Donna is still in San Antonio w/

her and will continue to be... We are fighting for hours now; by God's grace maybe days. Thanks. More to follow as I get it.

When Caitlin came home from work I gave her the news. As I was telling her what time we would need to leave in the morning to catch our flight she broke down. I pulled her close to me and hugged her, but I cried, too.

Donna and Rob spent the night in the hospital with Anne. Rob finally fell asleep in an armchair a few feet from his wife. Donna barely slept at all. She had pushed a physician's stool against Anne's bedrail, placed her hand on her daughter's chest so she could feel her breathing and closed her eyes.

In the morning, an echocardiogram showed significant strain on Anne's heart, its pumping function beginning to fail. She was on the precipice of heart failure. She was in imminent danger. There were only hours left now.

In the air somewhere east of the Mississippi, Cait and I had no way of knowing what was happening in San Antonio. But deep within, I think we both sensed the inevitable. The last domino had fallen for Anne and her babies.

CHAPTER 9
DOL 5 to 7
April, 2010

THERE WAS NO NEWS FROM the NICU Sunday night. It was a brief reprieve, but it was one Anne needed. She was emotionally spent, in pain and the trauma of the last ten days had exhausted her. Another trip to the hospital was the last thing she needed. Donna encouraged her to spend a few hours with Erin and Cait before they flew home. Rob agreed that the best place for her was in her own bed. I told Anne that after driving her sisters to the airport, I would stay home with her the whole day. If something happened to one of their babies, I would be there with her when the news came, and if necessary, we would drive together to the hospital. But nothing traumatic happened that day, and when Rob and Donna returned from Wilford Hall in the evening they were upbeat.

Wyatt was hanging in there. With each passing hour the HFOV therapy was looking more and more like a life-saver. Wyatt was also maintaining weight. "He's catching up to his brother and sisters!" Rob announced before admitting that was only because the other babies were losing weight. By Monday morning Timmy,

Edda and Lily had each lost nearly 50 grams. They were down to 1lb 4½oz, 1lb 2½oz, and 1lb 6oz, respectively. Some loss was anticipated in the first few days, but a significant decrease would be worrisome.

Intraventricular hemorrhages remained a concern. Though the 72 hour window when brain bleeds usually appear had passed, the babies were not out of the woods yet. "That's just how things go with extremely premature babies," Rob said, trying to stay positive. "The most recent head ultrasounds aren't great, but they're not terrible, either."

Lily's hemorrhage was stable. Unfortunately for Timmy, his bleeding, which like Lily's had been confined to one part of his brain, was now found to be leaking into the ventricles on both sides. When I asked what that meant, Donna told me that he now had a Grade II IVH, but that did not necessarily mean there would be developmental problems down the road. She hoped the brain bleed would resolve on its own. As for Edda and Wyatt, they didn't do quite so well this time, either. Edda's test revealed a small Grade I hemorrhage much like her sister's. Wyatt's ultrasound showed new bleeding in two ventricles, similar to his brother's.

Anne, who'd slumped at the first mention of Timmy's bleed, protested that Edda and Wyatt had been fine only the day before. Rob responded by saying she should listen to her mom. "Let's not jump the gun on this, not yet. Besides, things could be a lot worse."

"Any more 'good news'?" Anne asked.

Donna sat down beside her on the couch, lifting Anne's feet onto her lap. "You're forgetting something, aren't you, Rob?"

Rob looked perplexed. Even a "good" day in the NICU was so full of frenzy that it wasn't always easy to remember everything — or separate what was progress from what wasn't. But after a moment his eyes brightened and a broad smile appeared on his face. "You know what? There really is good news," he said.

"They looked at Wyatt's heart again today and his PDA is closing. The medication is working."

Anne brightened. "That's a big plus. Will they test the other babies, too?"

"They did echocardiograms on Edda and Lily this afternoon," Rob answered. "They're waiting for the results. Timmy gets one tomorrow morning. We'll know his results by evening rounds."

DOL 6: Tuesday, April 13

The human heart begins beating about three weeks after conception. If a newborn lives an average lifespan, its heart will have beat three and a half billion times. Though their hearts were only the size of cashews, according to the echocardiograms taken in the Wilford Hall NICU, Timmy, Edda, Lily and Wyatt each had strong hearts. The very premature infant might have severe lung issues; its brain would likely be so underdeveloped that the soft tissues could be easily torn and subject to bleeding; its liver and kidneys are not completely formed; but its heart? If anything was working in the favor of a baby born so prematurely, it was its heart.

With one exception: The *patent ductus arteriosus.*

Inside the womb, a baby gets its oxygen needs met by its mother. With no need to enter the lungs, the baby's blood follows a more direct path to its growing organs and tissues. That path is through the ductus arteriosus. The duct is basically a shunt — an alternate route — that allows the blood to bypass the pulmonary arteries and connect directly to the aorta. Once born, however, the baby's blood will have to travel the longer route from the heart into its lungs and back again before continuing to the rest of the body. For virtually all full-term babies, as the flow of blood moves away from the ductus arteriosus permanently, the small blood vessel that had served as a shunt prior to birth begins to spontaneously constrict and eventually close.

Why the PDA doesn't close in some preemies is not clearly understood. But the problem that results is plain: not all the baby's blood gets oxygenated. In severe cases, heart failure can follow and the results for the very premature infant can be deadly.

Wyatt's PDA closing was great news, and though Lily's echo-cardiogram also had a PDA finding, it was very small. But we were learning that in the NICU good news would often be tempered by bad. Edda's PDA was too big to ignore. And Timmy's PDA was larger yet. His PDA, and Edda's, would have to be closed. As they had for Wyatt, the doctors recommended Indomethacin.

They reiterated the possible side effects of the medication. But the alternative was surgery and that obviously had risks of its own. Surgery would also require transferring care to an outside facility — Wilford Hall did not have a pediatric cardiologist with the expertise to perform the surgery required on such a premature baby. The decision seemed straightforward to Anne and Rob; they opted for the medication. It made sense to me. With Anne trying to rest and recuperate at home and Rob spending as much time with their babies at Wilford Hall as he could, it would be hard to cope with babies in different hospitals.

On Tuesday morning, Donna and I stayed at the house. We printed boarding passes and packed. Well, *I* packed. Donna wasn't sure that we'd be going anywhere. It was her intuition again. She set her clothes out neatly on the floor beside her suitcase and said she would pack in the morning, but not until then. That was fine with me. I had pushed her to come home only a week before when, in hindsight, she was right to have resisted my urging. And I was wrong when I resisted coming to San Antonio only a day or so later myself when I should have. I decided it best to avoid similar mistakes in the future.

We met Rob later at the NICU. Anne had left him to get more training — and encouragement — on how to use the breast pump. She was having little success getting her milk to let down and it was frustrating, Rob said, but left it at that. He was more concerned about the results of Timmy's latest head ultrasound. His ventricles were still growing and there was increased blood in the left lateral ventricle. To compound Rob's anxiety, one of the residents apparently mentioned a Grade III IVH, but the fellow on call quickly interrupted, saying that was overstating the case. Still, it had clearly unsettled Rob. "A Grade III brain bleed would be disastrous for Tim," he said as we followed him into the NICU.

Inside the unit, I felt that same sense of something almost sacred or hallowed that I had the very first time I'd entered. Donna and I stood motionless by the girls' isolettes for a minute, but when I turned to look for Rob he was gone. I caught a glimpse of him a moment later standing in the adjacent staff room. He was rubbing his palms together. I couldn't hear a word or see who he was talking to. He began to nod slowly, put his hands on his waist and then he looked up at the ceiling. I kept watching him until he turned back toward the NICU. As he did, his eyes fixed on mine momentarily, but it seemed as though he were looking right past me. The last thing I could see before someone pushed the door closed was Rob sit down at the table and drop his head into his hands.

"Honey! Tim!" Donna was motioning to me. I took a few steps toward her, stopping several feet from the isolette labeled C.

"Doesn't she look great?"

"Sure," I agreed, nodding though I wasn't able to see much of the tiny infant's face. A pink knit wool hat was pulled down to her dime-sized ears, and there was still a thick plastic tube inserted into her mouth. "Which of the girls is this?"

Donna gave me a perplexed look.

"Lily or Edda?" I asked.

My wife stared at me, dismayed. Then she turned back to the isolette, bent down and said, "Lily Joy, I want you to meet your grandfather. He's apparently forgotten that he's ever met you."

I took the last few steps toward the isolette and said, "All right, so now you're *sure* this is Lily. It's just that I thought, or Erin said anyway, that there was some confusion —" but before I could finish Donna grabbed my hand and pulled me down next to her.

"You're sure?" I asked.

"This child could only be Lily."

"Hi, Lily," I whispered and reached up to touch the side of her crib. As I did, she squeezed her fused eyelids closed even tighter and turned bright red. I pulled away, but it was too late. In a flash her skin changed from red and rosy to pale pink and then to blue, and the alarms on her monitor began to make their infernal racket.

"Oh, yes, that's your granddaughter Lily," Donna said. "It couldn't be anyone but her."

Lily's nurse rose and after studying the monitors and their flashing numbers, carefully reached down into the isolette, rotated Lily onto her side and rubbed her back. Shortly, the alarm went quiet.

"Is she always like that? I mean, does she get that fussy with everybody or is it just me?"

"Anne says the nurses told her she's quite the diva. Amazing they have personalities already, isn't it?"

In the next instant, I saw Rob come out of the staff room, but he slipped out of the NICU without saying a word to us. I turned to follow him, and then thought better of it. Maybe he needed some time alone.

Left to our own devices, my wife and I were able to spend some time getting to know each of the babies' nurses a little bit better. We also got a primer on all the machines and monitors in the NICU. Seeing the confidence of the nurses, and their unfailing commitment to the tiny infants in their care, we got a sense that *somehow* things might turn out all right. Every minute that went by, every breath brought them one step further down the long road ahead. At the same time, my newfound optimism was tempered by the sober realization that in less than 24 hours Donna and I would leave San Antonio, leaving our daughter and her husband alone in the middle of a tempest. And as for their new babies, Timmy, Edda, Lily and Wyatt, we would be leaving without knowing for sure which, if any of them, we would ever see again.

As that morning turned to afternoon I began to feel for the first time I desperately wanted the babies to survive. I wanted them *all* to survive. Ludicrous as it seems to me now to suggest that there ever was a time when I wouldn't have wanted that, the truth is that really wanting something is a wide world removed from simply wishing it could be true. I'd desperately wanted Anne to survive her emergency caesarean surgery; it was only wishful thinking to imagine that all her babies would, too. After that, I'd wanted all the babies to live long enough to hear their mom's voice, to feel her touch, to sense her presence though they could not yet open their eyes to see her face. To want them all to live longer than that was an impossible dream. Given Wyatt's extreme respiratory distress and the unresolved heart issues in Timmy and Edda, seriously contemplating that they all might survive seemed like setting myself up for hurt. But in the NICU that afternoon with my wife, I began to cling to each of their lives in a way I had not before, in a way I could not easily articulate. It was Donna who did it for me.

"I feel like we're interlopers here, you know?" she said.

"I feel out of place, too," I agreed, not grasping her meaning. "All the machines, the doctors, the nurses — I feel I'm always in the way here."

We were standing next to the boys' isolettes. The girls were getting a dose of the glowing blue bili lights again. Wyatt's crib was entirely covered by the small quilt draped over it. Only Timmy was in plain view. The blue knit wool cap he was wearing covered half his ears and his eyes entirely; the rest of the hat formed a funny cone shape as it extended up beyond the top of his head. He was lying flat on his back, his arms and legs stretching away from his torso. There was an IV line piercing his lower left arm; it was carefully taped to keep it in place, but the wrapping was so bulky and his arm so small that it made his wrist look as if it had been casted.

"Not that," Donna continued. "It's not the NICU. I mean the babies. It's like we're seeing something I feel like we shouldn't be seeing, something not meant for anybody to see."

It took another moment for me to catch what she was saying. I remembered what I'd thought when Erin introduced me to my first grandchild: that what I was seeing was the unfinished work of God. I looked at Donna and then down into the crib again. Timmy's face was turned toward us. The plastic straps that braced the tube running down his throat were secured to his rosy cheeks with wide swaths of gauzy, white bandage. His mouth was round and red, like a cherry tomato skewered on the tube that penetrated his thin lips.

"You know what I mean, don't you?" Donna asked. "When the Psalm talks about our inward parts being formed by God — where it says that we're weaved by Him in our mother's womb?"

I recalled the verses. I had told Anne when she was pregnant that it had always been her mom's favorite. "We're fearfully and wonderfully made," I said. It was the line I remembered best.

Donna reached for my hand. "I can't believe that we're actually seeing this. It's like we're being allowed a glimpse into the true miracle that grows in a mother's womb."

Beneath us, Timmy's chest moved rhythmically up and down with every breath. I noticed that his ribs were blotched in places with mottled spots of maroon and purple beneath his translucent skin. He was still a frightening sight to see, something so fragile and vulnerable, barely clinging to life. My wife slipped her hand around my upper arm and pulled me closer.

"I just love these little guys so much," she said.

I nodded, smiling at the thought of actually loving the babies. They had come into our world so unexpectedly. I was so unprepared for this. We stood staring at Timmy for I don't know how long. It was as though we were transfixed.

"I want him to live, honey," I finally said.

Donna let her head rest against my shoulder.

"I want them all to live." I don't recall saying anything after that. I only remember the feelings that followed: the flood of barely controllable emotion, the tug-of-war that pitted hope against the prospect of inevitable loss. My words were only a desperate prayer; a prayer that was realistically our only hope.

When Rob returned that afternoon to the NICU, he brought Anne with him. He was still looking discomfited and out of sorts. Sensing his mood, and knowing that Anne and I hadn't spent any time together with her children, Donna cajoled her son-in-law into having a late lunch with her. She would not, she told him, take no for an answer.

Anne and I were finally in the NICU together. She stood with her arms folded, resting them on top of her belly — a tummy that just a few days ago had been so large she could scarcely support it. Already it was so much smaller that the bump practically disappeared beneath her loose fitting blouse. She was peering down into an isolette beside her and saying nothing.

"You did good, sweetheart. You did real well," I said to break the silence.

"But look at them."

"You got them this far, you know. A few days ago none of us knew if we'd meet even one of them. We didn't even know for sure that we'd still have you."

Anne moved closer to me, and sighed. "I know," she said, "but I should have carried them longer, Papa."

I put my arm around my daughter. "You did all you could, honey. You know how proud you've made me, how proud we all are of you? Annie, you have four babies alive right now," I said, "and they are clinging to life because of you. They know you are here waiting for them. Maybe that's all they'll need to get through this — just knowing that you are here for them."

She started to cry quietly.

"Talk to them, honey. Talk to them every chance you get. I know it sounds silly, but they know your voice. They need to hear from you now more than ever."

Anne wiped her eyes and looked right at me. "They know your voice, too, Papa. You read to them. You read them their very first story."

I dropped my gaze; the memory of that time seemed so far away — a hopeful time — somehow no longer part of what we were experiencing. We were standing in the nursery between the sterile plastic isolettes that contained the daughters of my daughter. The blue lights were shut off, but both girls still wore the cotton bili-shields over their eyes.

"Lily? Lily, it's Papa. You remember me, right?" I looked at the granddaughter who was either peacefully sleeping or, perhaps, seeing how still she lay in her crib, stone, cold dead. "Lily? Lily Joy?"

The tiny baby girl twitched, turning her head first to one side then the other. Oh boy, I thought, here she goes! But she settled again.

"Lily? It's Mommy." Anne's words, their intonation so soft, so full of love and tenderness, crushed me. Lily turned again so that she was facing Anne and me, but between the bili-shields and the tubes and plastic support braces surrounding her mouth, there was not much face to see.

"Lily?" Anne said, almost cooing.

The child turned her head away at first and then in the next instant, lifted her left arm straight up as if to grasp for something that she sensed, but could not see. Instinctively, Anne reached toward her daughter.

I reached for the camera in my pocket. "Hold her hand, Annie," I implored.

Anne reached through the opening on the side of the isolette, a clear plastic hatchway that swung on a hinge. "Lily?" Anne called, as she let her first finger stretch far into the isolette. The infant's own arm and hand remained outstretched, her fingers so small, so tiny that they seemed to belong to a doll. Anne's finger met hers and she clasped Lily's palm, clutching it between her own forefinger and thumb, the moment frozen in time by the picture I took.

"She needs you, honey. They need you so much."

"I'm so afraid for them, Papa," she whispered to me.

I wanted to tell her that it was okay, that they all would live, but that had been, until an hour or so before, something I didn't even really consider possible. And what if they didn't? The last thing I wanted to do was to give false hope to my daughter. She had already suffered so much disappointment, felt such guilt.

Lily's hand slipped from Annie's grasp and fell lightly to her side. She was asleep again.

"I love you, Dad," Anne said as she turned back to me. "I'm so glad you and Mom are here."

I smiled and put my arm around her shoulders. But we wouldn't be there for much longer. If not tomorrow then the next day or next week, we would eventually have to leave. We could not stay indefinitely with Anne and her babies. Anne knew as much, too.

"You need to promise me you'll stay strong for them, honey."

Anne looked at the floor.

What I saw in her in that moment reminded me of the same kind of fear, the same fragile hope, the same flickering light of faith that I had seen in myself 30 years before when Anne and Erin were tiny babies brought home to live with her mom and me. *Just one more breath*, I remember thinking at the time; just let Anne and Erin keep breathing through the night, I'd asked God those many years before. I pulled Anne away from Lily's isolette, drew her close and prayed the words I had with her so, so many times before, beginning when she was only a baby herself. "Lord God give you good rest and peace, and keep you in His care tonight," I whispered.

She pushed her face into my chest.

I knew her fears were so much more real than mine had been. And faith? My daughter's faith would be tried in ways that mine never was, in ways that until now, I had never imagined. "Come on," I said, trying to comfort her. "Let's pray for your babies."

We went to Timmy's isolette first. I held one of Anne's hands in mine and rested the other against the side of the sterile plastic, high-tech hospital crib that was his bed and for now, his home. Timmy lay motionless inside it except for the rise and fall of his chest. It did not matter to me that it was a machine that kept the boy breathing. All that mattered to me was that he did.

I looked across the top of his isolette and out the NICU's windows. Out there was a separate world, something close at hand yet beyond our grasp. Out there was a world which held the promise of a future that was still far too distant to see. I knew what I wanted that future to hold for my grandson.

"Lord God let you live, Timmy," I said.

Anne squeezed my hands.

"Lord God let you live to bless your mom and dad."

I thought about the other babies.

"Lord God let you live to bring joy and encouragement to your brother, Wyatt, and your sisters, Edda and Lily."

I hesitated, searching for something more.

"And the Lord God let you live so that one day you can call out with your own voice to Him who made you, 'Abba, my Father and my God.'"

My words hung in the air, as if the reality of what lay before us was weighing them down, holding them in that place. I could not honestly say that I had the faith that my prayer would go anywhere. The world outside the hospital windows was an impossible journey away. Though the NICU nursery had seemed from the first moment I'd entered it an almost holy place, it was also a foreboding place — sterile, cold and isolated. It would take more than a miracle of medicine to get Timmy out of it.

As I gazed at the tiny boy and the web of wires and hoses that entangled him, the invisible weight, which clung like heavy chains to my words, made the hope that my prayer might rise up from that room seem nearly absurd. Still, it was all I could do. And there were three more lives that hung on little more than a thread, waiting.

I moved with Anne to Wyatt's isolette, and as Anne gently lifted the quilt that covered it I put my hands on top of the plastic shell to pray the same prayer for him. We prayed those same words over Edda and Lily, too.

And then we left them.

I knew that afternoon I would not see Timmy, Edda, Lily or Wyatt for some time. Before we left, I stopped and looked directly down the long hall that led to the elevator bank. But I diverted my eyes from the pictures and plaques hung on the corridor walls, the photographs that celebrated life and the ones that memorialized it. I was too afraid to imagine what kind of memento might one day hang there among the others to mark the days my grandchildren had spent in the Wilford Hall NICU.

Lord God, let them live.

That was my only thought.

That was my prayer.

Sometime in the late afternoon of DOL 6 Timmy was given his first dose of Indomethacin to help close his PDA. Edda's dosing had begun earlier. The goal was straightforward: to interrupt blood flow through the PDA via constriction of the vessel. What the exact means are by which Indomethacin works is not clearly understood, but it has been repeatedly proven effective in closing PDAs in newborns. It's the first-line therapy for PDA closure in most NICUs today and has been for many years. It usually works.

Timmy's experience, unfortunately, was anything but successful. After a first dose of Indomethacin, his ductus arteriosus remained open. His condition became increasingly unstable as his little heart struggled. Excess blood was accumulating in his lungs. His heart rate was increasing, his blood pressure rising. But it wasn't only his heart that was in distress. A battery of x-rays in the early morning hours of DOL 7 revealed air leaking in his gastrointestinal tract. The right side of his abdomen was beginning to discolor. The immediate diagnosis was bad. Timmy's bowel was perforated. Indomethacin was the likely culprit. The NICU docs knew that bleeding in the GI tract was a possible side-effect, but none of them had ever seen the medication lead to an actual tear in the bowel. The fellow in charge of Timmy's care was devastated; a reaction like this to the Indomethacin caught him completely by surprise and he felt personally responsible. But the truth was that no one could be sure if the bowel perforation was due to the medication or not. If it wasn't, then this might be the first sign of a serious intestinal illness known as necrotizing enterocolitis or NEC. Whatever the cause, Timmy's condition had quickly deteriorated. In the parlance of the NICU, he was suddenly "trending down."

DOL 7: Wednesday, April 14

Donna's intuition had been right again, though neither of us knew as much when we finalized our departure plans. While she thought it a mistake to leave Anne and her babies with their health in such flux, she also recognized that status quo for the babies would be anything but stable for the foreseeable future. Whether we stayed wouldn't change that, and we couldn't stay indefinitely. We had our own responsibilities back home; our business needed attention from both of us. So deciding not to heed her own sense that something was wrong — possibly seriously wrong — with one of the babies, Donna relented and agreed to return to Pennsylvania with me.

We were up at dawn on Wednesday. One of Anne's fellow derm residents was coming to drive us to the airport, and we were scurrying to be sure we would be ready. Donna was closing her suitcase when Anne came into the guest room. Always the good mom, Donna pushed the suitcase aside and began clawing at the sheets and blankets on the bed. "I'm going to put these into the wash and run it in a minute, honey. I just don't know if I'll have time before we leave to put them into the dryer."

"You don't have to worry about it, Mom. I can do the sheets."

"You've got enough to worry about," Donna said as she pulled the comforter off the bed. She turned to me. "What time are we leaving?"

Instead of answering, I took a step toward the door where Anne stood leaning against the jamb. She looked tired, her eyes swollen and cheeks hollow. "Are you okay, sweetheart?"

Anne looked at the floor.

"Didn't sleep well last night?" I asked.

"The NICU called a couple times last night and early this morning."

Donna dropped the comforter she'd been carefully folding. "And?"

Anne didn't look at either her mom or me.

"Who is it?" Donna asked. "Is something the matter with Wyatt?"

She shook her head.

"Why was the NICU calling, honey? They wouldn't be calling in the middle of the night for no reason."

"Rob talks to them every night, Mom," she said matter-of-factly.

"In the middle of the night — in the early morning hours?"

Still she didn't answer.

But Donna persisted, practically pleading, "Annie, you've got to tell us what's wrong!"

Anne looked confused, like she wanted to say something, but was at a loss for words. Then she said our ride to the airport would be here soon.

"Annie!" I said, softly but firmly.

When she lifted her eyes to mine there were tears in them. "It's Timmy."

My heart sank.

"What's the matter with Timmy?" Donna asked, quickly adding that we could cancel our flight. "What else can we do, sweetheart?"

"You can go home." She said it without any emotion; a simple statement of fact. "You and Dad need to go home," she continued. "You've been here for two weeks, Mom."

"Is it Timmy's heart?" I asked, knowing they were concerned about his PDA.

I watched her composure return as she considered the question. "His tummy — they think he might be bleeding internally," she finally said.

"Don't tell me he's got NEC," Donna said. She sounded suddenly defeated.

"NEC?" I didn't recognize the term let alone have any idea what it might mean for my grandson.

Anne shook her head, her eyes still distant. "They think he might have a little tear in his bowel. Maybe it was a reaction to the medication for the PDA that they started him on."

"Oh, honey!"

"Where's Rob?" I asked. As I did, Donna picked up her suitcase and with a lurch, cast it on top of the bed. She practically tore at the zipper, trying to open the bag.

"He went to the hospital," Anne replied, pulling the suitcase away from her mom's hands.

"Annie!" Donna protested.

"The doctors wanted to meet with one of us. He'll call me if there's a problem." She sat down on the corner of the bed, pulled a pillow onto her lap and shook it until the pillow dropped free from its case. "I'll call you when you get home tonight," she continued, and then reached out with her free arm to grab the remaining pillow, grimacing slightly as she did.

"Annie — honey!" Donna pleaded.

"You and Dad need to go home," she said again.

Donna turned to me before looking back to Anne.

I opened my mouth but realized I didn't know what to say.

"What about Timmy? And Wyatt — what about him?" Donna sat down on the rumpled bed beside Anne. "And what about you, honey? What about you?"

"I'll be all right. I'm not as sore as before." She slid the pillow off her stomach and got up from the bed, then began pulling the sheets up into a pile.

The tough soldier routine, I thought as I watched her stand up and try to carry on as though there wasn't anything to be concerned about. She could be so determined.

"Besides," Anne suddenly said, "it's important to Rob that you and Dad get home for at least a little while. He's worried about your business..." She hesitated before adding with a wry smile and little conviction, "Life goes on, right?" and then reached for Donna's suitcase, somehow still on top of the bed.

But I stepped between her and the bag. With one arm I grabbed the suitcase and pulled it from the top of the now-wadded sheets; with the other I pulled my daughter close to my side. She looked up at me for a moment, trying to smile, trying at least not to cry. And then she turned her face away, reaching once more for the bed sheet.

"You and Mom go home, okay, Papa?"

There was something different in her voice, something other than determination. It was an odd mix of both resolve and resignation. She was facing a fate that she could do nothing to change. She also knew she and Rob would have to face it alone, and as much as her mom and I would have wanted to spare her from it, we could not. She was simply steeling herself for that reality.

Breakfast — an Egg McMuffin and hash browns — tasted like newspaper. I have nothing against fast food, but on that Wednesday morning in the San Antonio airport not even eggs benedict and a mimosa would have gone down easily.

Donna and I ate without saying much. The rest of the day is a blur. By nightfall, San Antonio and my daughter and Rob and their four babies were eighteen hundred miles away. There was business to take care of at home. We had to make payroll, vendor invoices were coming due, and checks had to be cut. My crew was struggling to get a leg up on a job we had intentionally underbid just to get enough work to keep our business open during the economic downturn. Life had to go on. We knew that.

What we didn't know was that before our plane had even left San Antonio, Timmy had been operated on. Anne received a call from Rob only minutes after we'd left for the airport and she rushed to the NICU without calling us. Later, she would tell me that when she arrived at the hospital and saw her son he looked as though he'd already died. Timmy's belly was a dusky, ashen-gray color; mottled blotches of brown and red were scattered like splashes of muddy clay beneath his translucent skin. He lay motionless in his crib; the only movement was the rhythmic rise and sink of his chest as the mechanical ventilator breathed for him.

In a small room outside the NICU, the surgeon, a tall woman with piercing eyes and a very direct manner about her, told Anne and Rob what she intended to do for Timmy, what her expectations were and what might go wrong. They signed the consent forms, and the surgeon left for the secluded corner of the neonatal unit where she would perform the surgery. There were no guarantees, she had told them; there never were. In that moment, both Anne and Rob wondered whether Timmy would be the first of their children to whom they would have to say good bye.

It was too risky for the surgeon to search for the small tear in Timmy's bowel. That would have meant pulling part of his intestine out and combing through it inch by inch. There would be too much blood loss; the resulting trauma would be lethal. Instead, she used a needle to insert two small tubes, one on either side of his abdomen, to drain the contents of the bowel where it spilled out into Timmy's gut. The hope was that the tear would be small enough to heal itself; the drains would keep the area around the tear free from infection.

The idea was to buy a little more time for Timmy. His heart was struggling, and they had to stabilize his condition before he could be transported for the surgical ligation he now needed to close his PDA. If he developed sepsis — a severe infection that would travel through his bloodstream to infect other parts of his body — they would be unable to transport him, much less do the surgery. The pathology was straightforward. If the drains did not prevent bacterial infection at the site of Timmy's bowel perforation, neonatal septicemia would ensue, his already overburdened heart would be even further taxed by the infection, and it would fail… resuscitation attempts would follow, but the trauma would prove too much for a body already so fragile. He would die.

The surgery was quick. But the surgeon was no more optimistic than she had been before the operation. The next 24 hours would be critical. The x-ray an hour after surgery showed the drainage devices properly positioned in Timmy's abdomen. The evidence of air that had alerted the NICU staff to the bowel perforation originally on the right side of his tummy appeared gone, but now there were air pockets appearing on his left side. The NICU docs would continue to order additional radiographs throughout the course of the day to monitor the situation. They could do little else.

Anne called Donna after the surgery, but by that time our connecting flight had already left Houston. We were skirting the Gulf Coast when Anne left a brief message: "Timmy's hanging in there. I'll call you tonight." But her assessment of her son's condition was far from the truth. It wasn't that Anne was lying to protect us. At the time, she didn't have any real idea herself of what Timmy was about to go through.

Within hours of the surgery, Timmy was no longer trending down. He was dying. His heart rate was elevated and his blood pressure was dropping. The hypertension he'd had over the previous 24 hours was reverting to a *hypo*tensive situation. Dealing with that required the use of vasopressors to elevate his blood pressure. But doing so would require careful management by the doctors to balance the needs of all the major organs in a maddening struggle for survival.

By 11 a.m. on DOL 7, Timmy was facing major challenges on virtually all fronts. By noon his organs were failing. They were not getting enough oxygen. Timmy's gall bladder was distended and there was still free air and blood in the abdominal cavity. His kidneys were similarly distended and dilated, unable to effectively remove the urine accumulating in them. Later x-rays showed still more excessive bleeding in his abdomen and around the surgically-placed drains. Timmy was in a world of hurt. His lungs were tiring. His heart was overworked trying to push more blood to his organs. Without enough oxygen the kidneys and other organs were being pushed to the point of failure.

This tug-of-war between Timmy's organs was taking its toll. The fight over a continually decreasing supply of oxygen meant that the blood vessels leading to the kidneys, bowels, muscles and skin were becoming constricted. His body was doing this automatically. It was working to ensure that the blood flow to his heart and brain remained stable, or even increased; the need for adequate oxygen delivery to those most vital organs would trump everything else. But this redistribution of blood flow could only work for so long. In time, his heart function would deteriorate if the oxygen deprivation continued; his blood pressure would continue to fall, and the blood flow to all his organs, heart and brain included, would become insufficient to sustain him.

As his grueling day wore on, the only good news was that a mid-afternoon follow-up echocardiogram showed that the Indomethacin had helped to reduce Timmy's PDA from large to moderate. But that was almost unimportant now. Timmy was walking on a high wire separating morbidity from mortality. If things did not improve he would die. The medical regimen being employed to keep him alive could cause damage to his heart and lungs that would lead to pulmonary vascular disease and, ultimately, only delay his death. And if somehow Timmy avoided that, there was still a significant likelihood that the lack of oxygen in his blood might also result in irreversible brain damage.

But somehow, against all reasonable odds, Timmy kept his balance on the high wire. He lived through the night.

When Donna and I arrived back home the only news from Anne was the brief message she had left earlier in the day. We still didn't know that Timmy had undergone surgery; we had no idea how critical he was. I can't fault my daughter or son-in-law for that. I'm not even sure Anne and Rob, who were both in the NICU with him the whole time, understood the gravity of their son's situation. Things had been happening so quickly with him. And they still had three other babies competing for their attention.

I tossed our suitcases on the bedroom floor when we arrived home — Donna was unwilling to unpack just yet — and we both threw ourselves into the work of sorting out the world we had left behind. There was a pile of newspapers on the kitchen counter, a stack of mail beside it. There were a dozen messages on the business line and more on our home phone. There were faxes, a string of unopened emails. From my desk in our little home office I looked out the window: the grass needed to be cut and weeds were already wrestling with the fresh blooms of the Johnny-jump-ups for space in the gardens. Things were not so different, I told myself, than if we had been returning from an extended vacation. It was always the chaos that made me wonder why we went away at all. But this *was* different. We were not returning to our comfortable life; we were not easing back into its familiar rhythm and flow. This was all a distraction now. This did not feel like home at all. Our hearts were elsewhere.

After an hour or so, I turned to check on Donna's progress. She did all the bookkeeping for our business — the payroll, managing the accounts payable and receivable, she even did a sizeable chunk of the company accounting. That meant she had considerably more to catch up with than me. She was staring intently at the screen of her computer, brows furrowed and eyes squinting.

"How are you making out, honey?"

She didn't answer. I wondered if she'd heard me.

"I'm going to need to bring paychecks to the job tomorrow morning."

Still no reply. She was moving her mouse and clicking, her gaze fixed on the monitor.

"Donna?"

She snapped her head up.

"Payroll?"

"Later tonight or first thing tomorrow morning. What time are you leaving to meet the guys?"

"Are you all right, honey?"

Donna sighed and admitted she hadn't been thinking about work at all, not for the last half hour. Instead, she'd been searching the Internet, reading anything and everything she could find about micro-preemies. She was reading blogs and articles, and looking at pictures of babies in the same condition as Timmy, Edda, Lily and Wyatt. It was overwhelming, she said. She couldn't believe that until a week ago she'd had no idea what it was like for these tiny babies or how hard it was for their parents. She remembered, she told me, how hard it had seemed when they'd taken Anne and Erin from her and placed them in the intensive care unit. Anne had been so unbelievably small, but she'd been nothing like these babies. Erin was out of intensive care in 48 hours; Anne just a few days after her sister. Donna knew babies were being born and surviving smaller all the time. Everybody knew that. Still, until she had seen a micro-preemie for herself, she said she couldn't have imagined a baby so little, so fragile, possibly surviving.

"I'm sorry," she said, rubbing her eyes before dropping her hands into her lap. "I'm having a really hard time focusing."

We were both quiet for a minute.

"Nothing more from Annie, yet?" I asked, already knowing the answer.

Donna shook her head. She was starting to cry. I got up from my chair and walked the few steps to her desk to stand behind her. I put my hands on her shoulders. Her browser was open to a website with pictures of babies in incubators, and they were all covered with wires and tubes. There were pictures of tiny infants in their parents' arms, the babies so small that they were all but hidden by the cupped hands holding them against exposed skin. There were pictures of smiling parents holding happy toddlers in their arms, too. There were articles and links to articles about the experience of premature birth. At the top of the page was a boy's name, scrawled with blue crayon, written the way a young child might write it, and next to it, one small blue balloon rising from his name toward the sky.

My wife turned from the computer and rested her cheek against my midsection. "I don't know how we're going to get through this," she said.

I stroked her hair. I didn't know, either. I had no idea at all.

The common metaphor for the journey through prematurity likens it to a roller coaster ride. We heard it from the doctors and nurses in the very first hours after Anne's babies were born. In the NICU, there would be good days and bad, some weeks better than others. If things were good more often than not, the roller coaster would slow and finally stop. The ride could stretch on interminably, though, a seemingly endless series of undulations that drained the deepest reservoirs of a family's hope and resilience. The ups and downs in any premature baby's condition can be relentless, the emotional toll on a family at times nearly unbearable. Later, on a Facebook page dedicated to parents of preemies I would find a post from a mother whose premature son was struggling to survive. It captured that desperation in one poignant line: "I would like this roller coaster ride to be over — now!"

Micro-preemies like Timmy, Edda, Lily and Wyatt are vulnerable to medical problems and complications that are so pervasive that overcoming one often means it's time to prepare to do battle with another. Being born at the limits of viability, these babies have to face a harrowing gauntlet of problems affecting every major bodily system. Respiratory problems are almost unavoidable for the very premature; cardiovascular and neurological complications are nearly as common. Surmounting one obstacle is little assurance that there is not something bigger, more ominous still ahead.

But the image of the roller coaster ride never fully captured for me what Anne and Rob were experiencing. There was something more subtle, almost sinister, about their journey. To borrow from military parlance they were becoming lost in the "fog of war." Their whole situation had unraveled so suddenly: a pregnancy that nearly killed Anne; her babies born so early it was a miracle they survived the delivery. A mother physically exhausted and wracked with guilt. A father who only a few short months before had not been sure he wanted any children now passionately fighting for his wife's health and her babies' lives. And not one — though that would have been enough of a burden for any parents — not even two, but four children isolated in a critical care unit where the joy of seeing one of their babies doing well was always countered with news that another was not. The only thing certain for them was that nothing was certain. In that sense it was a war. They were becoming lost in what Tim O'Brien describes in his stories about Vietnam, *The Things They Carried*, as "a great ghostly fog, thick and permanent. There is no clarity. Everything swirls.... You can't tell where you are, or why you're there, and the only certainty is overwhelming ambiguity."

In the time Donna and I spent apart from Anne and her children, if our daughter and son-in-law were living in a war zone, then we were the home front. We committed to being their support system, trying to help them in any way we could. And we would seek the same from others on their behalf, too. I thought if there would be any rescue coming for Anne and Rob at all it might be discovering that other parents had weathered the same kind of storms.

Seven and a half months after Timmy, Edda, Lily and Wyatt were born, a little girl living more than a thousand miles away celebrated her fourth birthday. As was the family tradition, she and her mom and dad also marked another birthday. Reece was a twin. She'd had a brother. They were born together via emergency caesarean section on Thanksgiving Day, 2006. Their mother had been very sick; preeclampsia had put her on strict bed rest since Halloween. Even with that her condition grew increasingly perilous. In the end, things became touch-and-go. When her blood pressure rose to a point where the doctors told her she could no longer carry her two babies, she delivered her twins. Jenn and her husband, Nick, named the tiny boy Graham. He and his sister were only 25 weeks and 3 days gestational age.

Jenn was so ill she remained on best rest for another six weeks after the babies were born; she was only allowed to visit Reece and Graham for brief periods. Nick scurried back and forth between his wife, recuperating at home, and the NICU where his new son and daughter were fighting to survive. It was an overwhelming experience, physically exhausting and emotionally draining. The tiny girl was doing better than her brother, but young Graham was a tenacious little guy and he fought on. His mother was finally able to hold him for the first time shortly after the New Year. He was still on his ventilator, but Jenn was able to cuddle him, gently holding his head against her chest. It was the best day of Graham's life.

Nick would only get to hold his son once. That was the day he and Jenn said good bye to their little boy. On January 7 every year, Reece and her mom and dad observe another tradition. They gather with friends and family to release blue and white balloons into the sky. And they remember Graham, who lived for only 45 days.

It was on our first evening home that Donna discovered Graham's Foundation. She read everything she could on the website with the blue balloon, the story of the twins, Reece and Graham, and how their dad, Nick Hall, had started a foundation with his wife, Jenn, in memory of their son. Donna sent an email to the foundation and was surprised to hear back from Nick in an hour by phone. His heart went out to Anne and Rob. He knew how hard the road ahead would be for them. He knew the kind of loss that he hoped they would never have to bear. But four babies in the NICU at once? He admitted he couldn't imagine that. He promised Donna he would be thinking of our family, and before hanging up told her to remind Anne and Rob that no matter what, to keep hopeful, stay resilient and believe in miracles.

The news and updates from the "front lines" came in bits and pieces, in irregular intervals, and were often laden with inconsistency and ambiguity. There was just too much happening in the Wilford Hall NICU at any given time to expect that the news we received would be anything more. Still, we longed to hear from Anne and, though we were careful not to pry or to push too much, we were desperate for news about the condition of our grandchildren. That was the hardest thing for us — not knowing. Ignorance might be bliss, but for us, the hours and sometimes the days that went by without knowing were nothing short of torture.

Anne did finally call later that night. She was tired and had not been feeling well. She told her mom about Timmy's surgery, that it had gone well, but he was still having blood pressure problems, and it was causing the NICU staff consternation. Their goal, she said, was to get him stabilized so he could be transferred to Christus Santa Rosa, the downtown San Antonio hospital that had a pediatric cardiac surgeon on staff. Then she dropped the subject of Timmy altogether and proceeded to work through the list of how her other babies were doing.

Edda's situation was becoming complicated. She'd had some bouts with respiratory distress throughout the morning, and the NICU doctors thought that was being caused by her PDA. She was tolerating the Indomethacin well, but the follow-up test showed the duct smaller but still open. The cardiologists had also found a murmur in her heart. Thereafter, a debate ensued between Neonatology and Cardiology about the proper course of action. The heart guys felt that the findings, even with the new-found murmur, did not amount to "hemodynamic significance." They were content to continue with follow-ups and would revisit the whole scenario in four to six weeks unless Edda's situation worsened. The NICU docs were more inclined to think in increments of four to six hours and, not wanting to risk an acute issue down the road, were pushing for a surgical intervention to close the duct sooner rather than later. They did not want a heart problem — no matter how small — complicating or extending the time frame it would take to get Edda off mechanical ventilation and the problems it often caused in such premature lungs. Cardiology insisted that unless the need was acute, there would be no transfer to Christus Santa Rosa. For the time being, Edda would remain with her siblings.

Anne told us she and Rob had no idea what the right course of action was. They'd let them sort it out. She was more concerned that Edda was continuing to lose weight and nobody seemed to know why. "There's not a whole lot left to lose," she said. "Maybe one morning we'll come to the NICU and find that little Edda has just disappeared."

For Wyatt, no news was good news. He was still on his oscillating ventilator and tolerating it. There was no timetable for getting him off it. But at least he was stable.

Anne saved the good news for last, and just saying it out loud seemed to lift her spirits. Lily was officially off her ventilator! "She has the cutest little face!" Anne said.

That was enough to make Donna cry, and it let the two of them forget about how sick Timmy was for a few minutes. Anne recounted to her mom how, cute though she was, Lily could be downright pernicious. After they'd extubated her, not without a fight, the little girl spent the ensuing hours either trying to rip off the tiny tubes of the nasal cannula that blew the extra oxygen she still needed into her nostrils or pulling out the plastic tube that passed nutrients through her mouth and into her tummy. She only wanted to suck her thumb, Anne said. By the time the nurses got done taping and then adding more tape to hold everything in place, Anne lamented with a chuckle, you could hardly see the poor girl's face again!

This good news reminded Donna to tell Anne the babies should expect a care package in another week or so. "Well, not for them; it's more for you and Rob, but each of the babies will receive one." Donna told her a bit about what would be in the packages — a disposable camera to leave by the babies' bedsides, hand lotion, tiny blankets meant to absorb mom's scent that could be placed right in the isolette, preemie-sized hats, snacks, a journal and more.

Anne wanted to know where it was all coming from.

Donna told Anne about Graham's Foundation. "There'll be bracelets you and Rob can wear, too," she said. The bracelets would read *Hope*Resilience*Miracles*. She also told Anne that when she'd showed me the website, the care packages and the bracelets, I'd insisted on making two donations to order bracelets for both of us, as well. "Your father says he'll wear his until this whole NICU ordeal is finally through." What none of could know then was that I would wear mine for another 188 days.

CHAPTER 10
DOL 8 to 23
April, 2010

Lɪᴋᴇ ᴠɪʀᴛᴜᴀʟʟʏ ᴇᴠᴇʀʏ ᴏᴛʜᴇʀ part of their bodies, Timmy, Edda, Lily and Wyatt's brains were much smaller than a full term baby's. In fact, their brains were only about one quarter the size they would have been if they'd been carried to term by Anne. Consequently, their immature brains were also extremely vulnerable to the rupturing of blood vessels that led to hemorrhaging. The bleeding was an almost unavoidable byproduct of their acute respiratory problems. In simple terms, their underdeveloped brains could not readily adapt to oxygen fluctuations in their blood supply. Like virtually everything else that undermined the health of a very premature baby, the root causes of their intraventricular hemorrhages came down to their lungs.

As a baby matures it gradually gains the innate ability to regulate its own cerebral blood flow. This process allows the brain to quickly adapt to abrupt changes in blood pressure. But for Timmy, his bowel tear and his unresolved PDA combined to exacerbate his already existing pulmonary problems. That produced the significant swings in the oxygenation levels in his blood that his tiny brain was not yet suited to handle. Timmy's Grade I IVH (where a minimal amount of hemorrhaging is restricted to one portion of the brain) moved quickly to Grade II (where the bleeding begins to manifest in the brain's lateral ventricles). By DOL 8 it was pushing toward Grade III (when the ventricles begin to enlarge significantly due to the blood accumulating in them). This was what had Rob on edge when I'd last seen him in the NICU. A Grade III intraventricular hemorrhage was not the shot across the bow that the first two stages generally are; it was a direct hit amidships. All kinds of developmental issues are associated it. The diagnosis is a chilling nightmare for any parent.

There were, by Thursday, no good choices left for Anne and Rob's firstborn. Continued low blood pressure meant inevitable organ failure. An increase in blood pressure put his brain at risk for further hemorrhaging. If he lived at all, keeping him alive would be something of a Pyrrhic victory: pulling Timmy back from the brink of death was likely costing him any hope of having anything approaching a "normal" life.

There was more devastating news. The results of the day's head ultrasound showed a new, large intracerebellar hemorrhage. Timmy was bleeding openly into his brain. His ventricles were growing larger as blood accumulated in them. The white matter of his brain was being destroyed by the blood. His cerebellum was at great risk. His brain stem was endangered, as well. It was as if a dam had burst. So much was being lost and so quickly.

But he was alive.

By late afternoon, the doctors had pulled off a small miracle by stabilizing Timmy's blood pressure. It was the only window they might have to move him. They placed the tiny boy they had worked so desperately to save in an ambulance for emergency transfer and sent him to Christus Santa Rosa Hospital for surgery to close his PDA. When the baby boy left them that evening, the department head, the neonatologists, the fellows, the interns and residents, the nurses and techs all knew they had done everything they could for Timmy. But none of them knew whether they would ever see him alive again.

There were no tearful good-byes. There were no cheerful balloons or hugs. His transfer was strictly business-like. When the ambulance doors closed with Timmy inside, the vehicle rushed out of the hospital's emergency bay with lights and sirens blaring and headed into the night. It was considered a high-risk transport. Anne and Rob were not allowed to travel with their son. No doubt they wondered, too, if they would see Timmy alive again. The truth is they didn't know, either. No one did.

They would not be allowed to visit him until his condition was stabilized in the NICU at Christus Santa Rosa. They did not know how long that would take. At the very least, they hoped to be able to visit with him before his surgery in the morning. Until then, they still had three babies to care for. Edda, Lily and Wyatt had each survived their first week of life. Anne and Rob tried to take some solace in that.

"That's such good news about Edda, honey. I'm so happy for her."

Donna was on the phone and for the first few minutes, the tone of the conversation seemed light and animated. She, Caitlin and I were downstairs in the family room. The gas fireplace was glowing, its blue and orange flame taking the chill out of the early spring evening. Caitlin sat on the floor in front of the little stove, our two Irish setters lying on the floor on either side of her. She was nursing a beer and eating Goldfish crackers. We'd been watching television together when Anne called. Alex Trebec's face was frozen in place on the screen — I'd pushed pause when the telephone rang.

"He did not! He said that about Lily? ...Oh, I want to be there when you do!"

As the conversation between Anne and her mom continued, the excitement in Donna's voice began to wane.

"Okay," Donna said softly. "Okay."

There followed a long stretch were my wife said nothing before I heard her whisper, "I know, honey, I know. We're going to just believe God for good."

Their conversation continued like this for a few more minutes. Donna was standing in the corner, to the side of the TV, and though from time to time I could hear the muffled voice of my daughter, I couldn't understand anything she was saying. Caitlin and I sat motionless, our eyes moving from the frozen television screen to Donna and back. Occasionally, our eyes met one another's. Time was crawling for us both.

"I love you, honey. We're all thinking of you. Cait and Dad send their love."

I couldn't hear Anne's response.

Donna suddenly turned her back to Cait and me and dropped her head. I could see her nodding, then heard her whisper something to Anne. Finally she lowered the phone, but as she did she remained standing with her back to us.

"How's Anne doing?" I asked meekly.

Donna turned around and took a step toward the center of the room. I sat forward in my chair. Cait tilted her head so she could see her mother's face. The dogs were sound asleep in front of the fire. Alex Trebec was still motionless on the TV.

"She's hanging in there. She's so tired."

"And?"

"And there's good news and not so good news. I think this is just the way it's going to be for a really long time."

"Good news?" Cait asked, trying to be upbeat.

"Lily's still doing real well breathing on her own."

"She's breathing on her own?"

"Well, she's on a high-flow nasal cannula. But she's going to need that for weeks, maybe months."

I nodded.

"And she's still driving the nurses crazy by trying to pull all the tape off her face."

"She's a little pistol, isn't she?"

"Like her Aunt Erin," Caitlin suggested.

"The really good news — ready? — Edda's off the ventilator, too!"

Cait let out a little whoop and smiled.

"Oh, and I almost forgot," Donna added with a smile. "One of the Neonatology fellows told Anne he thought she would be able to hold Lily before long. And then he said to her, 'You know, it's still a long road ahead, but this bird's gonna fly!'"

"Gotta love those little girls," I said.

Knowing more was to come, Cait and I savored this good news before prodding Donna for the rest. The boys' update was not so great. Wyatt remained on the oscillating vent; his lungs were not getting any better. He was still having a difficult time expelling carbon dioxide from his lungs. His battle with RDS was not going well.

"RDS?" There were so many acronyms. I couldn't keep track.

"Respiratory distress syndrome," Donna explained. "Wyatt is going to require intensive respiratory care for some time. Anne says the NICU is working hard to manage it for him."

"Right," I said, the rush of the good news already dissipating.

"And Timmy?" Caitlin forced a smile, still mustering all the enthusiasm she could.

"Well, Timmy got to ride in an ambulance this evening," Donna began.

Cait and I looked at each other.

"Annie said that Rob crowed about how lucky Timmy was — only a week old and already getting to ride in an ambulance with lights flashing and sirens going. All the traffic moving out of Timmy's way. How many little boys ever get to do something cool like that?"

Cait smiled, for real this time, at Rob's attempt at gallows' humor.

"They took him to the hospital downtown?" I asked.

Donna nodded. "Looks like they'll try to do the PDA ligation in the morning."

"PDA?" It was Cait asking about acronyms this time.

"It's a heart thing," I said, remembering a conversation I'd overheard about a PDA in the NICU a few days before. "A duct — a valve kind of thing that isn't closing on its own. They have to operate to get it shut. That's what a 'ligation' is, I think."

"I thought that's what they gave him that medicine for. And they just did an operation on him yesterday, didn't they?"

"He had a tear in his bowel, honey. They think maybe it was the heart medication that caused that. But he still has a problem with his heart."

"He's going to be all right, isn't he?" Caitlin asked, now frowning. "I mean we're talking about heart surgery, right?"

Donna stepped around the coffee table and sat down on the couch opposite from Cait. She looked at the phone still in her hand.

"Mom?"

The words came slowly. "He's such a tough little guy, but it's just that..."

We waited for the hammer to drop.

"The last day or so has been really hard for him. His situation has gotten really critical."

"They're all in critical condition! Even the girls are," I interrupted. But I knew Timmy's condition was much more serious than that of his sisters.

"It's not just his heart," she said. "It's more than that now."

The issues Timmy had faced over the last few days were putting a great deal of stress on his brain, Donna told us. That

I understood, but how his heart problem or bleeding in his gut caused that was beyond me. The medical jargon left me drifting. Ventricles? I knew the heart had ventricles, but the brain? How did the brain bleed fit in? Was it okay to have a Grade II IVH but not a Grade III or IV? Timmy's gut had perforated and bled but nobody gave that a grade. It was too much. I felt like I was swimming in quicksand. When Donna began outlining the long term implications — developmental problems; that Timmy might have severe emotional issues; that his motor skills might be nonexistent — I cut her off. I didn't want to hear any more.

"I'm just trying to explain what Timmy's up against now," she said.

"I know, honey, I know. It's just that we're not going to get through this by looking much further down the road than one day at a time. Maybe not even more than one hour at a time."

Caitlin was still staring at her Mom, but she wasn't feigning a smile anymore. "Timmy's dying, isn't he?"

"I don't know. Nobody has said that yet."

"And if he lives?"

"We're just going to believe God for the best," I answered, but Caitlin ignored me.

"What are you saying, Mom? What about his brain?" Her expression was now grave.

"If Timmy survives... It's just that everything that has happened to him in the last couple days... I guess nobody really knows at this point how things will turn out for him."

"Is Timmy going to be retarded?"

I flinched. The word caught me off guard. Is that what we were really talking about for Timmy now?

"Mom?"

"I don't know, honey."

Cait pressed on. "He'll have to be in a wheelchair?"

"We don't know. Nobody knows that for sure, yet. It's just going to be very difficult for him…" Donna said. Then she turned to me. "I don't have to tell you how hard this is for Anne and Rob."

I nodded, slumping in my chair.

Donna looked down at Cait sitting motionless on the floor. "Tomorrow's a new day right? We'll see how Timmy does after his surgery in the morning."

But her words brought no comfort. I watched Caitlin's expression grow taut and her lips begin to tremor. A week ago she'd flown to Texas not knowing if she'd see her sister alive again — the babies just an afterthought. But Anne survived and her children were all born alive. Seeing them for the first time had obviously changed Cait. They had made her an aunt; she had become part of them and they were now a part of her heart. She had only left Timmy three days ago. He'd been doing fine. He was going to be okay. This was so disorienting for all of us. Caitlin locked eyes with me, pressing her lips together. Then she burst into tears.

DOL 9: Friday, April 16

Anne and Rob rose early on Friday morning, got onto the highway before rush hour began, and made it quickly to Christus Santa Rosa. Once inside the unfamiliar hospital and its labyrinth of halls and floors, they had some trouble navigating their way to the Level III neonatal intensive care unit before finding it. It was larger and busier than they expected, but after a few minutes of confusion with the admissions staff — there was no record of a Timothy Spillane because he'd been admitted under his father's name — Anne and Rob were led to their son's isolette.

Timmy seemed to have even more lines and tubes, more wires and leads, more tape and wraps on him then when they'd seen him last. His color was worse. The little of his flesh they could see — the bits and pieces of him that weren't obscured by the medical paraphernalia that all but engulfed his tiny body — was dusky and blotched. He hardly looked alive. He lay motionless, animated only by the ventilator pushing air into him.

They waited for what seemed an interminable time for the surgeon. Rob studied the array of monitors and machines keeping his son alive. Anne sat beside Timmy, her knees drawn up against her chest in a chair, but she could hardly bear to look at him. She could not forgive herself for what she was putting her baby through.

When the surgeon finally arrived he explained what the PDA ligation entailed. They would have to put Timmy under general anesthesia, and he would perform the surgery right where the baby lay; they could not risk destabilizing him by moving him to an operating suite. Barring complications, he expected the procedure would take less than half an hour.

As with any surgery there was always the possibility of complications. Infection and bleeding. Fluid could build up around the lungs. Because Timmy was so small, the area where the procedure was performed was also very near a nerve that led to his larynx; any inadvertent contact with that nerve could result in injury or paralysis to his left vocal cord. But the risk of complications was relatively low; for a pediatric cardiothoracic surgeon in a large city hospital, the procedure was routine. After answering the few questions they had, the surgeon asked Anne and Rob to sign the consent form that would allow him to begin the procedure. They did. Without the ligation, they knew Timmy would certainly die. What else could they do?

I was out at a job site when Anne called her mom to tell her Timmy pulled through. Donna told me shortly afterwards, and then she sent out an email to our growing list of concerned friends and family members. In it she explained the move to the downtown hospital and Timmy's surgery there. She said she thought it had gone well and then added this:

> We are all working on resiliency. It's our word and thought of the day. We've all been so consumed with the setbacks that we've failed to really see the miracles happening right in front of our eyes. Lily & Edda both off of the ventilators and breathing on their own is awesome. And little Wyatt... his tenacity continues to surprise us all as well. Today is really the first day that I'm working on being happy and excited about being a Grandmom; shame on me!

But my wife's enthusiasm was short-lived. Less than three hours after her first email, she sent out another with the subject, "Sad news."

> Well, so here come some downs... Anne and Rob were just called by the hospital and Timmy is not doing well. The NICU at Lackland AFB has also contacted them and it looks like Wyatt has contracted a very serious infection.

> Please pray for Anne and Rob as they deal with two of their babies growing very sick. I think they're going back to the downtown San Antonio hospital to spend some time with Tim and then will get back to Wilford Hall to Wyatt and the girls.

Resilience — rebounding from adversity — would become the word of the day for all of us. It was clear by now we would need it every day for many weeks to come. When I got home there was not a lot more Donna could tell me about either of the boys. Anne had been too upset to share much other than that although the surgery had gone well, Timmy's condition was trending down again. He'd been so debilitated by his battles over the last 48 hours that the NICU team was having a very hard time keeping him stable. He'd fought so hard to hang on, but the neonatologists at Santa Rosa did not know if he could hold on much longer.

Back at the Air Force hospital, Wyatt was facing new challenges. Even though he was already on the high frequency oscillating ventilator, he needed more and more intensive respiratory management. His increased vent settings and low blood pressure alarmed everyone on the NICU team. His platelet count was too low. But they were also concerned about something else. Wyatt's mounting problems might well be caused by an infection that up until now had gone undetected.

The doctors called for an early morning consult with the Pediatric Infectious Disease specialists. The worry was that Wyatt was becoming septic. Sepsis would lower his blood pressure even further. Shock could follow; his major organs and internal systems would then begin to falter. In time, they would shut down entirely. The specialist noted that Wyatt was at high risk for fungal infection, given his extreme prematurity, very low birth weight and his indwelling lines. They ordered cultures to be taken and processed ASAP.

With their phones off in Christus Santa Rosa's NICU, Anne and Rob could not be reached. When they finally checked voicemail, Anne saw that Donna had been calling for updates, and Rob discovered he had missed multiple calls from Wilford Hall. While Anne spoke with her mom, explaining that Timmy had made it through surgery and it was possible that his newly closed PDA would help his bleak prognosis improve, Rob was on the phone with a neonatologist at Wilford Hall. The doctor told Rob that he and Anne needed to see him as soon as possible to discuss

Wyatt's condition. What he didn't say was that Wyatt was about to be pushed to the brink again.

If a roller coaster ride is a metaphor for the ups and downs parents of preemies experience in the NICU, I can only guess what it's like for the babies themselves. When searching for an analogy, I thought of the lyrics from an old Jim Croce song: *Bad, Bad Leroy Brown*. Premature babies start their lives in the NICU "like a jigsaw puzzle with a couple of pieces gone." Except the earliest preemies have more than just a couple of pieces missing. They're lacking scores of them. But it's more than that.

In this analogy, the mother's womb is the sturdy tabletop upon which all the pieces are fit together. Early in the pregnancy, the key pieces — the brain, the heart and the lungs — all begin to take shape. The progress that follows is dependent on the sections preceding it being completed, much in the same way it's easiest to complete a puzzle when the border pieces are fit together first. Though a 24-weeker will have a lot of pieces in place, no part of the puzzle is completely joined with the others. And since none of the body's major systems is finished, none of the others can function fully, either. For the micro-preemie, taken from its mother's womb at the very edge of viability, the whole puzzle has been knocked to the floor. That's why so few babies born before 24 weeks can survive.

Timmy, Edda, Lily and Wyatt were born only five days removed from that critical threshold. None of their bodies' major systems were complete; they hadn't even made it to what could be called the "fine tuning" period before they were born. In week 27, a still developing baby will start filling in the last puzzle pieces that will prepare it for the transition to the world outside the womb. By week 38, the lungs will be ready to breathe without difficulty; the circulatory system will be ready to move oxygen and nutrients with its own blood; the bones will be stronger, the skin thicker and the body fatter.

Anne's babies would have to do their fine tuning alone, separated from the foundation she would have provided. Moving from womb to world was a staggering endeavor for babies born so early. The NICU would do — was doing — everything possible to recreate the conditions that would help them sort out the pieces and complete the picture, but in the end, it would be up to each of the babies to finish putting the missing puzzle pieces in place on their own.

Caitlin received the email about Timmy and Wyatt's problems at work. She was in meetings all afternoon and couldn't call home. Instead, she emailed Donna and me from her phone when she could steal a minute. Her message was waiting for me when I sat down at my office computer, and good thing it was. Donna and I were despondent after discussing the deteriorating conditions of the boys. But Cait wasn't giving up; she was going to take the bull by the horns.

> Remember the Miracles. This is what we need to do in the down times... We still have Anne and we still do have 2 healthy girls and 4 BABIES.

I smiled. The girl had spunk; I had to give her that. If she'd been a prize fighter, she would have been the type of boxer who might get tagged from time to time, but once she realized you'd bloodied her nose, she wouldn't stop swinging until she'd broken yours. That's just the way she is. After she'd been so upset about Timmy the night before, it buoyed my spirits to see her pulling herself back up off the mat so soon. But I was still having a hard time keeping focused. Donna and I spent another half hour staring blankly at the work in front of us before I decided to take my bike out for a spin. I could try to enjoy the last hour of sunshine and at the very least, clear my head.

I rolled my bike down the driveway, clipped the cleats of my riding shoes into the pedals, and headed for Devereux Road. The "Devereux Ride" was a short route I'd ridden a hundred times. When they were younger, I'd taken each of my daughters on it because I thought, since the ride was short — little more than a ten mile loop — they'd enjoy it, but they disdained it because it was so hilly. Even Anne, with her lithe, long build that let her float up hills like a leaf carried by the wind, complained about how hard it was. I loved it for precisely that reason. The tough terrain provided a good workout that could be done in a short span of time, and it was a ride I could slip away on when I needed to relax. I could lose myself enjoying the countryside as I turned the pedals slowly over while climbing the hills; feeling the rush of wind against my skin while racing through the sweeping downhill turns; daydreaming while soft-pedaling the flatlands in between.

It was also a ride I took when I wanted to work through hard times. I rode the loop to forget about work when jobs got particularly frustrating; I rode it to get over my anger after arguments with my wife. And I'd ridden the loop in the painfully dark days after losing my nephew, Dave. On those rides I'd laughed remembering silly things about my brother's son, and I'd wept thinking about how his life had been cut tragically short. And as I climbed the ride's hills I groped for what meaning or good could possibly come from such loss.

It was beautiful outside — the last rays of a setting sun briefly bringing a fresh palette of color to the fading light of a mid-April day. But I hardly noticed. I was thinking instead about Dave as I turned from Creek Road and headed down toward the bridge which, once crossed, gave way to the hills of Devereux Road. And then I started applying the brakes; not to the bike, but to my thoughts. The memory of my brother burying his son was bringing to mind the awful realization that I might be burying one or both of my own daughter's sons soon. I was not ready for that. I told myself that I shouldn't be thinking about that at all.

There were daffodils, bright yellow and pastel green, growing wild in the grasses sprouting along the banks of the approaching stream. This was the upper east branch of the Brandywine River, and where the old iron truss bridge crossed the water, the river was not much more than 40 or 50 feet wide. The sinking sun left gleaming flickers of light dancing on the water; tall sycamores leaned inward from either bank, casting their wide, long shadows downstream. Coasting my bicycle to the other side of the bridge, I pushed hard against the pedals and, rising out of the saddle as I began to climb, I tried to push the gnawing pain out of my soul and down into my legs.

The road wound uphill, snaking between the small, scattered buildings of the Devereux Day School before leveling out as it split a boulder-strewn pasture. The road rose again then, more steeply than before. Still breathing hard from the last hill, I stood on the pedals and pushed the bike forward. In a minute I had crested the top and, gasping for breath, let the bike coast downhill before beginning to climb once more. The adjacent fields were dotted with steer, grazing lazily in the waning hours of the day. Just ahead, an old stone farmhouse and whitewashed barn hugged the roadside. And in the distance, rising above the tree line that marked the top of the road's final incline, a church steeple pointed skyward, the painted white and shingle-sided spire still capturing the full light of the setting sun.

But the ride was little help. My heart still pounding, I soft-pedaled the final length of Devereux Road, passed the 150-year-old church and the aging post and beam carriage shed where worshippers once left their horses and buggies tied. To the rear of the church and nearly hidden behind the more modern parish house, the weathered gray and white stones of the cemetery marked the graves of lives come and gone. The names and dates etched into the oldest stones were now mostly eroded, though some family surnames remained legible: Byers and Trego, Krauser and Griffith. These were now the familiar names of local roads and hamlets in the area. And among the oldest clusters of family graves, one or two — in a few spots even more — smallish, squat stones were set in front of two taller markers. There, placed to rest at the feet of their moms and dads who hadn't joined them until years later, laid the remains of children who'd perished before their time.

There could be no escaping it. Death followed life, so the saying goes, as surely as night follows day. For the unfortunate few, it came far too early. And as for Timmy and Wyatt? I felt like we were looking down the wrong end of a gun with both barrels loaded. No escape. In a sudden, unexpected moment or over a stretch of agonizing days or weeks, life is snuffed out. As I rolled my bike past the church and back towards home, I thought again about my nephew, Dave. I thought about the young girl Reece, and her parents, Nick and Jenn Hall, about the brother and son they had lost, the boy for whom Graham's Foundation was named. I thought about the long corridor that led to the NICU in Wilford Hall and its wall of plaques and pictures documenting both celebrations of lives still being lived and the poignant reminders of lives no one could save.

The mail had come while I was gone. In it were the bracelets we had ordered from Graham's Foundation. Donna handed me mine when I got home, and as I slipped it around my wrist I read its inscription of *Hope*Resilience*Miracles*. Like a talisman's magic, I wanted to believe there might be something gained by wearing the band, but truth be told, I found myself wondering what help those words could possibly bring.

Our good friends, Rick and Barb, our neighbors across the street for the better part of 20 years, came to visit Donna and me two days later. Things hadn't improved for Timmy or Wyatt in the intervening 48 hours but, in Caitlin's words, at least we still had 4 BABIES!

Donna started to cry as soon as she saw Barb. She and Rick had nearly a dozen grandchildren of their own, and Barb said she couldn't stand the thought of having to watch any of them suffer so much. And I cried, too, unable to help myself when Barb pulled out a gift they'd brought. It was small picture album with a cover made from birch veneer. On the front, lettering carefully burned into the wood read:

Our Grandchildren ~
Timothy David, Edda Grace, Lily Joy, Wyatt Lee

Seeing their names carved into the wood created a new feeling of permanence. The four of them had come into our lives so suddenly; we also knew that they could be just as quickly gone. But as I held the album in my hands I began to realize that, no matter what the future held, they would all be a part of our lives, always.

We spent a few hours together, the four of us sitting on the porch, laughing together and sharing our concerns about the future. Just before they left, when the ladies had gone inside for a moment, Rick leaned toward me and raised the glass of beer in his hand in a toast.

"To grandkids," he simply said.

I smiled and nodded, taking a long swallow of my own.

"You gonna be all right, bud?"

I nodded again. "Yeah."

He caught my eye and said, "Don't bullshit me. I've known you too long."

I laughed. "Yeah, you have. I'll be okay. Donna's a strong woman, you know that. We'll be okay."

Rick kept his gaze fixed on me and then raised one eyebrow. He still wasn't buying it, and he was right not to.

"It's Annie I'm worried about," I said. "It's such a helpless feeling, you know. She's my daughter, her babies are out there a couple thousand miles away in a critical care unit, two of them are probably going to die and there's nothing I can do about it."

"You know if there's anything Barb or I can do…"

"I know. You've already done a lot."

He raised an eyebrow again as if to brush aside the suggestion they'd done anything at all.

"No, I mean it. Just bringing that little book…" I felt my eyes filling. "Sometimes it's the little things that make all the difference in the world."

"That was Barb," he said with a grin. "I just brought the beer."

We sipped in silence for a while, until Rick drained the last of his glass and took a deep breath. "How are you gonna get through this? I mean, really, how are you going to do it?"

I looked at the ground and shook my head.

"Hey, I'm sorry, I didn't mean to —"

"No, it's all right. I've been asking myself the same question for a week now. Nothing makes sense."

"You've got a great family. You've got each other. God knows, it won't be easy. But if anybody can get through this, it's you guys."

I told him that his encouragement meant the world, and then I felt driven to add that though nothing seemed very hopeful at the moment, I was discovering that other people had faced the same things, the same uncertainty. I told him the story of the Hall family and how they'd had a son and a daughter in the NICU hanging onto life by a thread. I told him how they'd come out of a very dark period in their own lives and were now reaching out to help others. And when I'd finished telling him what I knew about Graham's Foundation, I said, "I guess I'm going all in on 'hope, resilience and miracles.'"

He gave me that funny look again, the one that said, "Don't bullshit me."

"I'm serious," I told him and then paused. Rick kept his eyes on mine as I tried to gather my thoughts. "Why those words, why not three other words, I don't know. But I've been thinking about them a lot for the last couple days. I'm starting to think that maybe they're a framework for getting through this mess. I mean you have to have something to hold onto, right?"

Rick didn't say anything, but motioned me to go on.

"Start every day with hope, right? When hope goes bust, resilience has to take its place. You have to keep getting back up after you're knocked down. I guess that's where we are with Timmy and Wyatt. Get back up and try to hope again. You keep getting up until you can't any more. That's the only way I suppose I can help Anne. Stay hopeful for her; always try to get back on my feet so I can help her get back on hers. And when you can't do it any longer, well —"

"You believe in miracles, bud?" Rick interrupted.

I hesitated, but he was expecting an answer.

"That's the place that you never want to come to, isn't it? Miracles sound great until you actually need one," I said. "And it's looking like we need some in a big way."

DOL 12: Monday, April 19

We knew by the end of the weekend that Timmy was only living on borrowed time. There was not much hope he would ever return to his brother and sisters back at Lackland AFB. Things looked grim for Wyatt, too. His infection had become extremely grave. Even the girls, having done so well for the first two weeks of life, were beginning to experience more serious problems as they entered their third week. And while Donna and I were not there to see it happening, it was becoming evident that our daughter was hour by hour, day after day, slowly being crushed by the weight of her babies' suffering.

Her children's problems swept over Anne like the waves of a pounding, storm-tossed sea. There was nowhere to hide, no opportunity to catch her breath, virtually nothing stable enough to cling to. She only had Rob to hold onto through the dark days and nights, but he was suffering, too. As much as we all tried to stay in touch, daily phone calls and emails couldn't drag my daughter and her husband up out of the flood of diagnoses, prognoses and medical procedures that was now their everyday reality. They were on their own, alone and horribly frightened.

I knew if Timmy suddenly died over the course of the coming days, he would do so without ever being held by his mother; Anne would never even have the chance to see him open his eyes. Maybe he knew that, too. Inexplicably, her little boy pressed on, clinging precariously to life. Every hour that Timmy lived created the hope that he could survive a few more. But before any of his doctors ventured to say he might pull through, Timmy took a turn for the worse. By midweek, Anne started to see more and more "dark, sludgy stuff" passing through the tubes that drained his abdomen. When she told her mom about it Anne was demoralized. She explained that he was once again approaching systemic failure. And while she never came out and said it to either of us, we knew Anne was sure she would lose her Timmy. He'd held on against all odds, but she didn't know how much more he could take.

I didn't know how much more *she* could take considering that Timmy was not her only concern. The infection Wyatt had contracted days earlier had destabilized him. It was a simple common cold, but for Wyatt, it was enough to push him toward the edge. The biggest threat came from episodes of dramatically decreased blood pressure that put his heart and brain at risk, but artificially controlling Wyatt's blood pressure meant taking other risks. Not treating the hypotension would mean his body's systems would ultimately fail; he would die. Like Timmy, the doctors would have to manage Wyatt's blood pressure with the use of vasopressors, and like his brother, that meant subjecting his brain to the potential trauma that the changes in blood pressure could entail. There was no other choice.

The vasopressors did their job. But when Wyatt was finally deemed stable enough to undergo a follow-up exam of his brain, the results of the head ultrasound revealed a progression of his hemorrhage. His IVH, which had only been minimal before, was now advanced bilaterally to Grade III on the left side of his brain and Grade IV on the right. Like his brother, the question for Wyatt was not whether — should he survive — he would have cognitive and developmental issues as a result of the bleeding in his brain, but how severe the disabilities would be.

The news was almost too much for Anne and Rob to bear. First Timmy and now Wyatt. Perhaps they could rationalize Timmy's PDA complications, which were almost de rigueur for micro-preemies. If his situation was extreme, at least they could make some sense out of it. But a cold virus? Wyatt had been brought nearly to the point of death and suffered considerable brain damage by a common cold — and why? Because someone didn't properly wash their hands, because a piece of equipment hadn't been completely sanitized, because another mom or dad had come into the NICU with the sniffles? It just made no sense.

I don't know how Anne and Rob kept up or how they coped, going back and forth every day between Wilford Hall and Christus Santa Rosa. Anne was pumping milk constantly, filling the small plastic bottles the NICU provided one after another, storing them in her freezer like a squirrel gathering nuts for the winter. Her babies would need it someday but more importantly, pumping all day and through the long nights was the only thing that gave her some sense she was doing something for her babies. Rob didn't sleep much at night, either. He took calls from the NICU teams and called them himself late into the night and again before dawn. He spent hour upon hour researching everything he could about preemies and followed blogs by parents who had experienced the same awful circumstances. I think he thought the more he learned, the better prepared he'd be to deal with the angst and uncertainty. But Anne was moving in the opposite direction. She wanted to know less and less. Some days, I sensed, she wanted to know nothing at all. Anne was pushing back, as though not knowing could safeguard her children from the worst. But the flood of information was relentless. There was no avoiding it.

There was so much for the doctors to convey. How was the baby's respiratory system adapting? Was the cardiac and pulmonary circulation pattern improving? Were the body's fluid and chemical levels being balanced by the kidneys? Was the liver beginning to function properly? Did the ultrasounds reveal further brain abnormality? Did the most recent x-rays uncover any problems within the GI tract? It was an almost endless recitation of medical jargon delivered twice a day after rounds; in acute situations sometimes even more frequently. All this times four, once each for Timmy, Edda, Lily and Wyatt.

How Anne and Rob kept track was anybody's guess. Had it been me, the glut of information would have been paralyzing. Keeping track wasn't the only problem, though. By the third week of the babies' lives, it was beginning to have a corrosive effect on Anne. Swallowing it all day after day was like being slowly poisoned. Atelectasis, bacteremia and chronic lung disease… the lexicon of conditions and symptoms was becoming an alphabet soup of heartache and pain for her. She did not want to be a doctor for her children; she wanted to be their mother. What she wanted to hear was that her babies were going to be okay. What she wanted was hope.

But hope was in short supply. Because the babies were still so young and vulnerable, their conditions could go from bad to much worse in only a few hours. The problems that Edda and Lily began to encounter by the end of their second week were proof enough of that.

By DOL 12 both girls were showing signs of difficulty with tube feedings that now included small amounts of Anne's breast milk. X-rays of Lily's GI tract were beginning to show prominent loops of gas-filled bowel. That could be an early indicator of necrotizing enterocolitis. Edda was not producing enough urine. But Edda's potential problems were not restricted to her kidneys. Ultrasounds also found possible nephropathy of the newborn (another kidney problem), a possible liver lesion, a fluid-filled stomach and several gas-filled bowel loops, as well as distensions of the bladder and gall bladder. As with their boys, there was little Anne and Rob could do for Edda and Lily but watch and wait. Potential problems materialized and got worse — often quickly — or just disappeared altogether.

The yo-yoing in the babies' conditions was seemingly endless. At one point during the week Edda had to undergo a lumbar puncture to rule out possible meningitis. Though the cerebrospinal fluid drawn during the lumbar puncture was bloody and clotted, the subsequent culture analysis revealed no infection. She was also experiencing apnea episodes and increasing pulmonary problems. The NICU docs had every reason to be suspicious. Edda's lung volumes were decreasing; the chest x-rays showed a small collapse of the left lung, while the appearance of the right lung was also becoming suspect.

Lily began to develop her own lung problems, too. Her chest x-rays were showing signs of pneumothorax, where the accumulation of gases in the chest cavity presses against the lungs and hinders their ability to expand. The respiratory specialist was also concerned about air leaking *between* the lungs. It had the same compressive effect, making Lily's breathing more difficult. Regardless of the cause, the end result was the same: Lily was requiring increased respiratory support. She was re-intubated.

In less than 48 hours, Edda joined her sister on the mechanical ventilator, too. In her case, though chest x-rays showed no sign of pneumothorax she was continually de-satting; Edda just couldn't keep a sufficient level of oxygen in her blood. The doctors said her lungs were simply "tiring out."

It had to be overwhelming for Anne, but she always tried to tell her mom and me about the hopeful moments. The morning before she was re-intubated, Lily opened her eyes. Within a day, she was spending more and more time awake and looking around. Edda cried during her lumbar puncture, and though it was difficult for Anne and Rob to watch, it was also the first robust cry they'd heard from any of the babies. A day later, Edda opened her eyes, too. Anne was so excited to see her daughters with open eyes that she taped tiny, pink bows to the tops of their little bald heads. "They're so beautiful," she cried when talking to Donna on the phone that night.

And for a brief minute, in the middle of the frenzy and fury of Timmy and Wyatt's struggle to survive, of the despair of watching Edda and Lily regress, Anne finally got the chance to hold one of her babies. It was the day before Lily was re-intubated. One nurse pulled a rocking chair close to an incubator and motioned for Anne to sit. A second nurse lifted the tiny baby up from her bed before the two of them carefully placed the wire and tube-laden child into Anne's arms and helped her pull the infant up against her breast, just under the nape of her neck. Fittingly, it was Lily, the one a NICU fellow had called the "bird that's gonna fly!" It was also unfortunately Lily — the one the NICU nurses had already christened "the Diva." Anne held her for less than a minute. "The brat!" she laughed on the phone with her mom. "She turned beet red, shrieked and then held her breath until she started to turn blue." Even so, I knew that holding Lily was an unexpected joy for Anne, and something of a triumph, short-lived though it was.

Our phone rang in the middle of the night. It was the office line that we sometimes left turned on in our bedroom. Donna's cell phone was on her nightstand, and the land line was also set to ring in our room. We wanted to be sure Anne could get hold of us at any time. I pushed against Donna's shoulder; the phone was on the dresser on her side of our bed. "Grab it, honey! It might be Anne."

"That's the business line, isn't it?" She was still half asleep.

"Maybe she pushed the wrong button on her phone. She's probably got all our numbers plugged in it. Just answer it!"

Donna threw back the covers, stepped out of bed and grabbed the phone.

"Annie?"

I didn't hear anything and couldn't make out the expression on my wife's face in the dark.

"Annie? What is it, honey?"

Still nothing.

"Is it Timmy, honey?

There was only silence.

"What is it, Annie? Did Timmy pass?"

It felt like a long time before she spoke again.

"It's okay, Anne. Just tell me what we can do. I'm right here, honey." Donna paused. "Annie, honey? Anne, I'm going to put Dad on the phone. Talk to him, honey."

She sat down on the edge of the bed and handed me the phone. "She won't say anything to me. I can hear her breathing and sniffling, but it's like she can't bring herself to say a thing."

I didn't know what to think. Timmy must have died during the night. And now Anne could not bring herself to utter so much as a word.

"It's Papa, Anne. Honey, we're here for you. We're going to get through this together, okay?"

There was only the odd sound of breathing and static in the background.

"Annie?"

Still nothing.

"Anne? Talk to me, honey." I waited for a few moments, maybe a minute. Still she said nothing. I put the phone on my lap and looked at Donna in the darkness. "Maybe it's not her. I can hear somebody in the background, but I can't get her to say a word."

Donna put her hand out and I gave her the phone. "Hello? Hello!" She got up and walked to the dresser, turned on the bedroom light and started pushing buttons on the receiver. Thirty seconds later, she turned off the light and came back to bed. "Wrong number, I guess. I don't recognize it. It's not Anne's or Rob's." She sighed. "I guess that's good news."

I fell back down against my pillow, wide awake.

"Honey," she whispered. "Are we going to get through this?"

"I don't know."

She rolled over and said, "I'm going back out there. I can't take this. I can't take not knowing. I can't keep doing nothing."

We bought tickets to San Antonio the next morning. And we continued praying.

I don't know if they were answers to my prayers, but the emails I received the following day were a blessing.

The first came from Anne. There was no message in the email, only a photo. Rob had taken it Saturday afternoon in Wilford Hall. Anne is sitting in an armchair, the photo framing her from mid-torso to the top of her head. She is wearing only a spaghetti-strapped, cotton camisole; her arms and shoulders are bare. Her long, brown hair hangs loosely on her shoulders. Cradled in her hands, a tiny baby is pressed against my daughter's breasts. It is Anne's first time holding Edda. The baby is so small in her mother's hands that hardly any part of her child is visible. What I see first is the medical paraphernalia: the four white vinyl I.D. bracelets that the hospital has given Anne to wear, one for each of her children. They hang around her wrist in a disorderly jumble. There are tubes and wires that reach like tentacles around and through her elbows, forearms and hands, weaving their way to the baby whose life support they provide. There is the white of a disposable diaper, the diaper's yellow, blue and purple decorations standing brightly out against the soft cream color of Anne's camisole. That diaper nestled in the palm of her left hand seems to hold little more than air. A small bit of Edda's leg can be seen just below it; the meat-red color of her fragile flesh visible through the scotch tape that wraps around the tiny limb, holding a medical line in place. Though Edda's feet do not even reach to her mother's wrist, Anne's hand and long fingers stretch all the way to the middle of her infant daughter's back. And tucked just below her mother's chin, Edda's small, round, fuzzy-bald head rests gently against Anne's chest. Her right hand is cupped so tentatively around her daughter's head that it seems to me as if she is clutching a hot mug of tea close to her bosom — wanting the warmth but wary of pressing too hard and getting burned by its heat. Edda's eyes are closed. The clear tubing of a nasal cannula extends around her cheek to her mouth where her one hand is clenched into a fist so small that it nearly disappears from the photograph altogether. When I look more closely I can see her tiny thumb pushed up against her lips as though, perhaps, she is giving thought to sucking it. Edda would stay like that, cuddled and quiet, resting contently against her mother's bare skin for more than 30 minutes.

For Anne, holding Edda was the first time she truly felt like a mother, and it brought with it all the conflicting emotions new mothers know too well: tenderness tempered with anxiety, longing weighted with the fear of the unexpected. As I looked at the picture of my daughter, the intertwining of hope and hopelessness within her seemed almost palpable — the joy of the one at odds with the despair of the other. Anne would later say that holding Edda for the first time, though wonderful, filled her with dread. Sadly, her sense of foreboding had been prescient. It was in the early hours of the following morning that Edda would lapse into respiratory trouble. Anne would not hold her again until she was removed from the mechanical ventilator and no one could tell her when that would be.

The second email I received that day brought with it some timely encouragement in the form of a story. The dean of the school where I'd earned my Master's Degree was a good friend. Though our paths had crossed infrequently in the years since, Marla kept tabs on me and my family. She was a medical doctor herself and when she'd heard of Anne and her babies' plight, she was quick to reach out.

> I am sure you hear a lot of stories now. We have one too. My sister-in-law had her daughter, Molly, some 20+ years ago — in the 6th month at an Albany NY hospital. Molly was barely a 1 pound speck of life amidst technology and hope — and that was over 20 years ago! When she finally went to 3 pounds, she was allowed to go home.

> Two years ago she married. Several months ago, *my* daughter's baby furniture went traveling to NY — where Molly's new baby now sleeps.

It isn't always this way, we all know. But it is possible.

Again, I am thinking about all of you.

Marla

The truth was we hadn't yet heard any such stories from people we actually knew. It meant the world to hear that good things really were possible for Timmy, Edda, Lily and Wyatt. While it was true there were no guarantees — Marla knew to point as much out — the message was a reminder that there is always hope. I forwarded Marla's story on to Anne. She was struggling. The hope she'd held in her heart while holding Edda on Saturday afternoon was slipping from her grasp by Sunday morning as she learned her baby had been intubated again. All four of her children were on mechanical ventilators once more, the machines doing for them what they were too sick or too weak to do for themselves. More than two and a half weeks had passed since the babies were born and none were getting better. It seemed they were all getting worse.

I've heard it said that a person can live for forty days without food, four days without water, and four minutes without air, but can't survive for even four seconds without hope. I suppose that's overstating the case, but what was clear to me that Sunday was that we were all in need of something to hang our hopes on. Thinking about Molly helped us find a measure of hope. It wasn't a lot, but it was something to build on. Whatever hopes we had left — with storm clouds growing on the horizon once more — we would have to cling to them with everything we had.

DOL 19: Monday, April 26

It was not a grandiose plan, but it was elegant in a simple way. Donna decided the best thing we could do for Anne and Rob when we returned to San Antonio was to tend their flowerbeds. As the unusually wet winter had given way to a warm spring in south central Texas, flowers were blooming everywhere. Everywhere, that is, except in front of our daughter's small brick rancher. There, the gardens had been untended since late fall when Anne and Rob learned they were expecting quadruplets. By spring the plot of ground was overgrown and choked with weeds. It gave their home the appearance of being almost abandoned, and now with four babies clinging to life in two different hospitals, it nearly was. Donna's plan to bring the flowerbeds back to life gave us the pretense of doing something to make existence for our daughter and her husband a little more pleasant.

We left for San Antonio early on Monday, rented a car at the airport and drove directly to Anne's house, only stopping at the local grocery so Donna could pick up some things to make dinner. We had decided not to try and meet Anne or Rob at either of the hospitals where their babies were. Donna wanted to do something more practical and making dinner fit the bill. She doubted either Anne or Rob had eaten a decent meal in days. What we didn't want to do was return to Texas and start bombarding them with questions about how the babies were doing. The last few days had been so hard for them. More than anything else, we wanted to give them a chance to unwind, even if it would only be for a few hours in the evenings.

When Anne and Rob returned home that night they were exhausted. They had been in the downtown hospital with Timmy for several hours and then spent the rest of the afternoon at Wilford Hall. Anne had just enough energy left to give us a quick rundown. Both Edda and Lily were still on vents; neither one could breathe adequately without the machines. Anne tried to smile, reminding us that her girls' lungs were just tired and needed some time to rest. We wouldn't find out until later that the pulmonologist was increasingly concerned about Lily and that Edda's respiratory distress was necessitating frequent blood transfusions. Maybe Anne forgot to mention it; probably she was just too numb to recall.

Timmy was somehow hanging on, but little had changed. It was Wyatt who was the day's big headline-grabber. His head ultrasound showed indications of the early stages of hydrocephalus. The severe hemorrhaging that was a result of the cold virus he'd caught a week before had left his brain ventricles inflamed and filling with debris. The lateral ventricles were being clogged with residual blood and unable to drain the cerebral spinal fluid accumulating in them. A third ventricle was also increasing in size. Rob, I could tell, was having a very difficult time coming to terms with the diagnosis. He barely greeted us when he and Anne arrived home from the hospital. He went almost immediately to the master bedroom where he called his parents and then stayed in there, alone, well into the evening. The weight of what his little boys were going through was catching up to him. I knew that more than anything, he had always hated the thought of children suffering because it seemed so unfair. Now those suffering children were his, and fairness was only a philosophical footnote.

Donna made enough food so that there was plenty remaining after dinner, and she packed the leftovers in the freezer. She told Anne she would cook dinner each of the remaining nights we were in town and make extra portions to be put away every time. She also mentioned that we planned to head to a local garden store in the morning to get the supplies we would need to begin working on the front flowerbeds. Anne and Rob could spend as long as they wanted in the two NICUs. We would hold down the fort for them and wait to see the babies until they felt the time was right. Life for Anne and Rob was difficult enough; they didn't need to worry about us.

But our plans to work outside after breakfast never materialized. Anne woke us just after dawn on Tuesday to tell us that they were going to the hospital immediately. Timmy had suffered another bowel perforation, and his situation was acute. He required emergency abdominal surgery. She and Rob were leaving to see him. They would call us when the operation was over. There was no need for us to come, she said. I told her she was crazy. Donna and I followed them out the door in a matter of minutes. The gardening could wait.

At Christus Santa Rosa, the surgeon explained the necessary procedure. While the earlier drainage surgery involved only two small incisions on either side of his abdomen, she now would be cutting Timmy all the way across his tummy below the belly button. This was the same pediatric general surgeon who'd done the initial surgery, and although she felt it had been successful, she explained that such a limited procedure could not confirm the severity or extent of the intestinal damage. But it *had* bought Timmy time and allowed him the window for his PDA surgery. Now, though, it was apparent that the drains were no longer enough. There was too much waste accumulating in his bowels; the risk of bacterial infection was serious. The laparotomy would allow for a thorough visual exploration of Timmy's intestines. It was highly risky, but there was no other option now. She would then resection, or remove, any damaged areas of the intestine. Lastly, she would do an enterostomy, opening a passageway through the muscle layer below the skin, pulling the cut end of the intestine through it and turning it inside out so she could sew it to the opening in Timmy's belly. This would be where she attached an ostomy bag, a plastic pouch used to collect fecal material and other waste that passed through Timmy's intestinal tract. She was frank about the surgery and the trauma it would cause such an unstable infant. But because babies as premature as Timmy also have very immature immune systems, doing nothing meant that peritonitis — a life-threatening infection — would almost certainly kill him. The surgeon was kind-mannered in her explanations, but she was also blunt: Timmy might not survive the procedure.

She gave Anne and Rob yet another consent form to sign. And then she gently told them to take their time deciding what was best for their baby boy.

Neither considered any other course. They signed the form almost immediately. Then Rob met me and Donna in the waiting room. He needed to call his parents and respond to the calls he had been getting from Wilford Hall. He asked me if I would go be with Anne in the NICU before they started prepping Timmy. He didn't want her to be alone.

After washing and putting on a hospital gown, I was allowed to join Anne beside Timmy's incubator. He lay motionless on his back, arms and legs extending limply to the side, chest rising with each breath the ventilator pushed into him. His face was puffy and his eyes were closed. It was almost painful to look at him. He had already gone through so much. When Anne told me what the surgeon was proposing I sighed. And when she confessed that she couldn't come up with any explanation for why her little boy was even still alive other than wanting to be with his Papa again, I could barely keep from crying.

We sat together, watching Timmy sleep. They would close part of the NICU and operate right there. Moving him to the OR was still too risky. All but essential personnel were evacuating the area to provide as sterile an environment as they could. We waited, anxious, wondering when someone would finally come and ask us to leave, too.

It was not a nurse, but the neonatologist in charge of Timmy's care who came. Anne introduced me to him, and he congratulated me on my grandson, assuring me they were doing everything possible for the boy. He said he was looking forward to meeting Timmy's brother and sisters one day. And then he turned to Anne and said what he had really come to Timmy's side to say: "You don't have to do this. Do you understand that?"

Anne stared at him, confused, and then turned to me. I looked back at her, trying to reassure her with my eyes alone. When she didn't speak, I did. "Both my daughter and her husband already talked at length with the surgeon."

The doctor nodded. His expression was warm, his demeanor gentle and calming, but his eyes were telling. "Your son will die without the surgery," he said to Anne. "But I just want you to know that he doesn't have to go through it if you don't want him to."

Had it come to that? Timmy lay there unmoving in his incubator. We both looked down at the tiny boy. He was alive, even if it was the ventilator breathing for him. He had hung on through so much already. He was the resilient one. Should we give up hope on him now? I looked at my daughter, putting my arm around her shoulders, but said nothing. It was her decision and Rob's. It had to be that way.

"We want to do this," she said. Then she lifted her eyes to stare into mine. "Don't we?"

"We need you to tell us when you think it's been enough."

The words hung in the air. No one moved. No one said anything. The hospital social worker pulled a tissue from a box and nudged it toward the center of the table where Anne could easily reach it. The silence was like a heavy weight pushing against us from all sides. I kept my eyes on the team of doctors sitting across from us. I was afraid to make eye contact with any of them. The doctor who had spoken finally folded his hands on the tabletop and leaned ever so slightly forward. He looked at Anne and then Rob and then again at Anne.

"We can't make this decision for you," he said softly.

Another awkward silence followed.

Anne turned toward me, and I met her eyes full on. They were wide and quivering, like the eyes of a confused animal. Finding no answers in my face, she turned toward Rob. He was staring straight ahead, his cheeks flushed and his lips parted as if he was about to ask a question. But before he could speak, Anne looked back at the doctor across the table and asked plaintively, "Sir?"

It was a question and a plea.

The doctor's statement had caught us off guard. Who was he talking about? Timmy had survived his surgery. The pediatric surgeon told Anne and Rob she was pleased; the procedure had gone well and without any serious complication. Though she had done her job for their baby boy, what transpired in the hours and days ahead would be beyond her control.

Even so, we had breathed a collective sigh of relief in the waiting area outside the Christus Santa Rosa NICU after the surgeon left. We would take any good news we could get, and Timmy was continuing to give us hope against all odds. We could, we thought, shift our attention to Wyatt for a time.

Wilford Hall had been calling Rob throughout the morning. Doctors were working on a strategy for dealing with Wyatt's hydrocephalus and wanted to go over the options as soon as possible. The Head of Neonatology was requesting a formal meeting that very afternoon. I sensed that Rob thought Wyatt's condition must have been even worse than he feared. A meeting with the Department Head was never a good sign. But while Rob was right about it not being good news, he was wrong about why.

We were bracing ourselves for more bad news about Wyatt when we arrived at the Air Force hospital. It didn't help when we saw the number of doctors gathered in the conference room down the hall from the NICU: two fellows and a resident, the Department Head and three more neonatologists from his staff, and a social worker assigned to the NICU. Anne and Rob must have known them all; Donna and I had met a few. Their expressions were uniformly grim, like we'd stumbled into a wake. The hospital's social worker wasn't helping things, quietly sobbing as she was. None of us knew what to think or to say. It was Rob who spoke first.

"Things getting more complicated for Wyatt, I guess?"

The Department Head hesitated before replying. The other neonatologists turned their attention to him. The resident kept her eyes on the table.

"I've been in contact with my colleague at Christus Santa Rosa."

Christus Santa Rosa? We were here to talk about Timmy? I suddenly felt sick to my stomach. I feared he was going to tell us that Timmy had died.

"We just came from Christus Santa Rosa," Rob protested. "The surgeon said... has something happened to Timmy?"

The doctor shook his head, but there was nothing reassuring in the gesture. And that's when he said those words. "We need you to tell us when you think it's been enough."

We were frozen by what his message meant.

"We can't make this decision for you."

"Sir?"

When Anne made that plaintive plea, I dropped my hands into my lap and pushed them between my knees to keep them from shaking. I was trembling so hard that I thought it had to be visible to everyone in the room. I could see the fear and confusion in my daughter's face.

And there was the utter incongruity of it all.

We were in a hospital, across the hall from an intensive care unit where the smallest, most fragile of human lives were being cared for. Across the table from us sat soldiers, not just doctors. The Department Head and two of the senior neonatologists were wearing camouflaged combat fatigues. I'd been in military hospitals with Anne and Erin dozens of times before. I had seen them wearing their own white coats over the very same uniforms and smiled with the pride any father would have felt. But this was different. We could have been in an Army hospital in Iraq or Afghanistan discussing a wounded soldier's prognosis, my doctor-daughter asking her superior officer, "Sir?"

In a very real sense, we were in a war zone, enveloped in its disorienting fog. I looked at Anne and could only wonder: Who was this slight, young woman sitting beside me — a soldier, a doctor or a mother? How my daughter survived the rest of the meeting without going to pieces, I can't say. She was experiencing the prospect of her son's death from three fronts at once. She was a junior officer, subordinate to the two Lieutenant Colonels and the Major sitting opposite her. Were they telling her that it was time to retreat, to bury her dead and regroup with the rest of her troops and to focus on them, so at least the survivors might have a chance to live and fight another day? She was also a fellow doctor. Her office in the Dermatology Department was in this very building, three floors below. Were these senior physicians telling her that it was time to face the obvious facts, that the patient was dying and there was no longer anything to be done? Anne knew how much Timmy had endured, how close he had already come to death. She knew that his brain damage was significant and likely irreversible. Facts were facts. As a soldier and a doctor, she should face them. But as a mother? They knew she was that, too, and they were kindly, gently telling her that their hands were tied. They had done the best they could for her son, but there was only so much they could do. What they couldn't do was tell her what to do now. The message was clear: Timmy did not have to go on living like this anymore. But only she and Rob could tell them when their little boy had had enough.

What was the right thing to do? What choice would let Anne and Rob continue on and not blame themselves for the rest of their lives? What was ethical or honorable? Neither Donna nor I could make the decision for them. No one could.

One doctor, however, tried. In what could only be characterized as a senseless, careless interjection lacking any empathy at all, one of the neonatologists added that recent research showed that parents whose children survived the NICU with severe disability had a divorce rate that approached 80%. I was stunned. But if he was trying to pit Anne and Rob against their own son, however good his intentions, he failed. As I watched my daughter and her husband turn to one another, their expressions changed. A moment before they had been scared and unsure; in the next, I think they began to see in one another the resolve to do what they thought was right, no matter what.

The rest of the meeting was a blur. Timmy had been part of our lives for three weeks, but our hopes for him were much older. We found ourselves being lectured about what families like Anne and Rob's faced when hope was gone, when resilience meant finding the courage to deal with everything you'd hoped you'd never have to and when miracles were for someone else.

The social worker explained that there was a local funeral home that worked closely with the NICU. There was also a photographer who specialized in taking the poignantly beautiful pictures of parents holding their babies as they breathed their last breaths. She could help arrange all these things. She would also arrange plaster casting of Timmy's hands and feet, molds that would make durable keepsakes. Families who had gone through the same kind of loss came to appreciate these mementos over the years, she told us. They even made great Christmas tree ornaments.

Every indication, no matter what Anne and Rob decided, was that my daughter's first born — my first grandchild — would live on only in our memories. My head was spinning. The only Timmy we would ever know would be the plaster molds of his hands and feet hung on a Christmas tree? Was that it then? I pushed my chair away from the table. There was only one thing left I could do. Get up, I told myself. Get up off the mat.

The next day, working together in the warm sun, Donna and I tore the front gardens apart. We weeded the beds and cut back the bushes, spread fresh mulch and planted a flower box under the double window in the room that one day would be the babies' nursery. By late afternoon we'd finished. We gave one another a sweaty hug and stepped back to enjoy what we'd done. The sun was sinking behind the rooftops of the neighboring houses, and as I pulled my sunglasses off and reached for my regular glasses, I realized they were gone. Somewhere, while we were buying the things we needed or in the mulch we'd spread or in the trash bags we'd filled, I'd lost them.

When Anne and Rob came home they were delighted with what we'd accomplished. Later, when I complained that in spite of the joy we'd found in doing the work I'd ended the day on a sour note by losing my glasses, Anne took me back outside to help me look again. In the fading light we went through the mulch on our knees and through the trash bags filled with weeds. We even looked under the seats in the rented SUV. But they were nowhere to be found.

"I'm sorry, Papa," Anne said after we gave up hope. "Those were your favorites. And I know they aren't cheap."

"I have an old pair back home — no big deal," I said. And then, thinking about Timmy who was now more than 30 hours removed from his bowel surgery, I added, "If that's the only thing we lose in the next few days, you won't hear me complaining."

She smiled and pulled me to her side, hugging me, and then asked whether I thought she and Rob were making the right decision. I told her I thought they were.

"You gave Timmy life."

"Hasn't been much of a life," she replied.

No, it hadn't been.

"The way I look at it is he'll quit when he's had enough," I told her. "You and Rob are letting him make that decision for himself. I admire you guys for that. It can't be easy. But you know what?"

"What's that, Papa?"

"I'm beginning to think that maybe Timmy's okay with what you've given him. It's a tough road for him, but I think maybe he's doing his best for you."

She smiled.

"And one other thing," I said. "What that doctor said about an 80% chance of divorce..."

"Sometimes doctors don't know when to shut up," Anne said, almost defensively but more, I think, to mollify me. But I wasn't angry anymore.

"I know," I said. "But if Timmy does live — if they all live — what's that mean? Does that mean you and Rob will have a 320% chance that your marriage will fail?"

She laughed. If nothing else, we might have — finally — found something of a rallying cry or a shout of defiance. We weren't going to just sit and let fate run its course roughshod over our lives.

PART III
Miracles

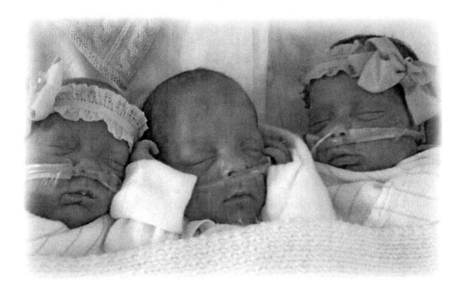

I sit by the restless all the dark night,
some are so young, some suffer so much,
I recall the experiences sweet and sad.
From "The Wound Dresser" by Walt Whitman

CHAPTER 11
DOL 24 to 54
May, 2010

Each was a milestone: their very first hour of life, their first day, their first full week and though it wasn't quite a month, Timmy, Edda, Lily and Wyatt all lived to see April turn to May. It would have been simpler, of course, had the babies remained in Anne's womb. By late April, they would have been beginning their third trimester, that period of fine tuning when the major systems of the developing baby's body begin to integrate. Getting to 28 weeks might have changed so much. But that was moot. Instead, they had been alive outside of the womb for more than three weeks, and it was impossible to say for sure how well things were going. Not one of them had gained more than five ounces since birth, and even Lily who remained in the lead in the chubbiest baby sweepstakes, was by the beginning of May still only 1lb 13oz — about the weight of a tall glass of milk. Both Wyatt's and Edda's weights fluctuated so much — up 50 grams one week only to lose it the next — that by the end of the month neither of them could be said to have gained much weight at all. And Timmy was retaining so much fluid post-surgery — Anne said he looked like the Michelin Man — no one knew what he really weighed.

They each remained in critical condition. The good news: Timmy was alive, and Wyatt's infection was gone and his lungs were improving. The not so good news: Edda and Lily both remained intubated, all the babies were likely candidates for chronic lung disease and necrotizing enterocolitis was a constant threat. To help ward off NEC, feedings were often stopped and then restarted depending on how well their bowels were tolerating the intake. It was little wonder none of them gained significant weight.

But then something amazing happened. The double-barreled gun we'd all been looking down over the course of the last ten days — with one barrel aimed squarely at Timmy and the other swinging toward Wyatt — unexpectedly jammed.

In an effort to improve Wyatt's lung development, the NICU team had started giving him steroids. It's rare for even very premature infants to be given steroids more than a week after birth, but Wyatt's lungs were still not maturing sufficiently on their own. Doing so was not without risk, but with the pulmonologist carefully monitoring him, Wyatt started to improve. In fact, he began doing so well the doctors tried removing him briefly from HFOV therapy and putting him on a high frequency nasal cannula. Though his condition wavered in the days following and he had to go back on the high frequency vent, it was still progress. Both Anne and Rob had practically resigned themselves to the thought that their youngest child might never be able to breathe on his own. The steroids, at least, were giving them some hope. But it was the boys who ultimately decided to take matters into their own hands — literally.

On Monday, the third of May, Wyatt had had enough of the HFOV. While an unsuspecting respiratory tech stood nearby, Wyatt Lee reached up, grabbed the mask enveloping his face and gave it a yank. He pulled so hard that the entire mechanism lifted from around his mouth, bringing up the vent and the feeding tube with it. Bedlam ensued, but once the frenzy of the moment was past the NICU team decided to give Wyatt another shot at breathing with only the help of the high frequency nasal cannula. He remained stable! Anne was in the NICU at the time and while the commotion had been unnerving, it was her first time seeing Wyatt's face unobstructed. She laughed when she told me about it. He looked just like Rob!

If good news travels fast, word of Wyatt's heroics must have quickly reached Christus Santa Rosa. During Friday morning's sponge bath, as two nurses worked carefully together to wash his tiny body, Timothy David wrested his arms from their grip, reached toward his face and thrust his limbs skyward, ripping the vent tube up from his throat and straight out of his mouth. The nurses struggled to regain control of the situation; a neonatologist came running. Capturing the endotracheal tube back from the clutches of the infant boy, they prepared to re-intubate him. But a respiratory specialist also happened to be nearby and, noting that the monitors showed Timmy's oxygen saturation levels little affected, told the team to wait. Instead, he had them place a clear plastic mask over the baby's face and connected him to a continuous positive airway machine to supplement his breathing. Then they watched and waited.

Timmy continued to breathe. After 29 days with a tube in his throat the little boy who had come time and again so very close to taking his last breath was now very nearly breathing on his own. For no good reason the doctors could discern, Timmy was beginning to turn a corner. He was taken off vasopressors as he began to maintain his own blood pressure. As his abdomen healed the NICU team was able to start him on small volume feeds to "prime the gut" for more nutrition-rich feedings later. Not only did Timmy tolerate these little feeds, he seemed to thrive on them.

There was no rational explanation for any of it. The fact that Timmy had demonstrated the coordination to grab the vent tube and pull it out seemed a miracle to me. He hadn't knocked it out by accident; he'd grabbed it with both arms and pulled the wretched thing away! For a baby with such extensive brain damage — well, we took what happened that day as a good sign. Maybe we were just hopelessly naïve, but we were growing surer with each passing day that by giving Timmy the chance to live, his mom and dad were also giving him a chance at life.

Donna and I had been home for nearly a week when Anne called us with the good news about Timmy. I didn't know whether to laugh or cry. I settled on saying a prayer of thanks. That evening as I road my bike across the bridge on Devereux Road I uttered the simple prayer Jesus taught his disciples:

Our Father, who art in heaven, hallowed be Thy name.
Thy kingdom come; *let* Thy will be done on earth
as it is in heaven.
O God let it. Let Timmy live. Let them all live.

DOL 31: Saturday, May 8

It was now a month since Timmy, Edda, Lily and Wyatt had left the warm, dark, watery and secure world of Anne's womb. Not one of them was even two pounds yet. Growing was hard work and their energies were needed elsewhere. It was taking all they had just to survive in a world for which none of them had been remotely ready.

Their first month had not been easy. Neither was the second. Though there were occasional ups, we still faced plenty of downs. Lily became the latest example of how tenuous their grip on life was. She had been the biggest of the four when born and seemed the strongest. Her first two weeks in the NICU had been text-book for a micro-preemie. Her PDA had been small; her brain bleed minimal. By the end of her first week she was off the ventilator. She was feisty and the NICU staff loved to see that. Though she'd later been re-intubated, Anne and Rob still felt Lily really was the "bird that's gonna fly." But her road turned rocky, too, and in the second week of May, Lily's situation became downright scary.

She started experiencing persistent oxygen desats for no apparent reason. When the NICU doctors called for a consult with the Pediatric Infectious Disease team they discovered Lily had bacteria in her blood. The worry was that the bacteria could overwhelm her vascular system; commandeering the blood stream, it could use it as a conduit to spread infections far away from the original port of entry. That could lead to sepsis which would result in a whole-body inflammatory condition. Lily would develop a fever and begin to breathe rapidly. This in turn could bring on hypotension that would threaten to shut down her major organs. As a physician, Anne knew the pathology of sepsis and it was frightening. She also knew if this could happen to Lily — the baby she believed had the best chance to live — then none of her babies were truly safe.

Lily's blood cultures on DOL 27 identified the source of her infection: staphylococcus epidermidis had been found in her peripheral arterial line. Such an infection would be harmless to most healthy children. The bacteria live almost everywhere, both on human skin and on surfaces that people frequently touch. But when staph epi gets into the bloodstream of an extremely low birth weight baby, the lack of a mature, well-functioning immune system makes combating the infection very difficult. Complicating that was the discovery of MSSA (methicillin-sensitive staphylococcus aureus) in Lily's tracheal culture. The mortality from that is more than 25% among babies as small as Lily. The only good news was that the cerebral spinal fluid drawn by the Pediatric Infectious Disease team during a lumbar puncture came back negative. Lily didn't have meningitis.

The NICU staff changed all her indwelling lines and carefully monitored her response to the antibiotics they administered. But it was still touch-and-go for several days. Either Lily would get better or she would get a lot worse.

Two days into her ordeal, Lily's arterial line (which had already been replaced once) tested positive again for staph epi and a third line was now MSSA positive. The persistent infection put additional stress on her lungs. There was concern that they would collapse or fill with fluid. In either case, Lily was teetering on the brink of total respiratory failure. The doctors decided to take the same calculated risk they'd taken already with Wyatt and administered steroids. Anne and Rob gave them free reign. What else could they do?

DOL 32: Sunday, May 9

I was on the phone with Anne.

"They're saying Timmy might be coming home this week. I mean coming back to Wilford Hall, anyway. And Lily's doing a little better. She's not septic, at least. Wyatt is still —"

I interrupted her. "Happy Mother's Day!" It was Anne's first. I told her I was calling to talk to *her*, not about her children. I wanted to know how *she* was doing.

"I don't feel like a mother. I don't even know what it's like being a mom."

"But you will, and you'll be one of the best!" I said. "My mom is a great mother and your mom is, too. My life's flush with good moms. I know one when I see one. You're going to be such a great one, honey."

"Thanks, Papa," she said with mock cheeriness, though I could hear her muffled crying.

"Are you guys doing something special for dinner tonight?" Rob's parents had flown down from Seattle to spend a week with their son, his wife and their four new grandchildren. It was the first time they'd had a chance to see the babies.

"I don't know."

I paused, waiting for her to continue, and then asked if she was okay.

Anne began to openly sob. "I'm just so tired, Papa. I don't care about Mother's Day. I don't want to do this anymore."

I tried to console her but wasn't much help. She was going through so much. Having her in-laws in town and staying at her house for the next week was just one more thing. She felt like she should cook for them, take care of them. She could hardly care for herself. Sometimes she just wanted to be left alone.

"But it's not their fault," she said. "The babies are their grandchildren, too."

She went on to explain how the day had gone awry. As a surprise, Rob had let her sleep in. While she slept, he snuck out with his mom and dad to Wilford Hall to see Edda, Lily and Wyatt. He thought he would call Anne later in the day and make plans to meet for a late lunch together. But Anne went to Christus Santa Rosa to be with Timmy, and they were unable to contact each other during the midday hours since their phones were off in the NICUs. Rob was expecting Anne at Wilford Hall; she assumed he would be meeting her at Timmy's bedside. By the time they finally connected Rob was already having lunch with his parents. He had wanted to do something for his mom on Mother's Day and hadn't known what Anne wanted to do. Until that moment he didn't even know for sure where she was. By the time the Schlenders arrived at Christus Santa Rosa it was already late in the afternoon. Anne introduced Timmy to his grandparents and excused herself. She went home, made a bowl of cereal for dinner and ate it while reading a Dermatology textbook. By the time I reached her that evening she had already gotten into bed for the night. She thanked me for calling, said she was overtired and hung up.

Fortunately, ups often follow downs and the new week began with good news. All of Lily's blood cultures came back negative. Her blood pressure returned to normal levels and remained stable. And by Monday evening, the NICU team decided to extubate her. They put her on a nasal cannula, but she hated it. You'd think she would've been happy to have the tube in her throat gone, but that didn't satisfy Lily. She protested by going *tachycardic* — her heart rate racing to as high as 200 beats per minute. She kept that up, on and off, for another 48 hours. Anne shrugged it off, laughing when she told her mom that Lily was back to being Lily.

There was more. With Wyatt also off his vent, Rob and Anne were finally able to hold one of their sons. The pictures Anne sent us were amazing. Rob's smile as he held the tiny baby boy — his hands so big that his thumb alone covered half of Wyatt's head — was a broader, bigger, more beaming smile than I'd ever seen on him. He was so proud. Anne told me she had to practically pry the little guy from his dad just so she could hold him for a few brief minutes before the nurse insisted on putting Wyatt back in his isolette.

Timmy was next. The nurses at Christus Santa Rosa went out of their way to make sure Anne got a chance to hold Timmy before they transferred him back to Wilford Hall. It was as much a triumph for the NICU team as it was for her. The little boy no one really believed would survive had surprised them all. When a nurse placed him against Anne's bare breast, Timmy immediately burrowed into her, the blue and yellow knit wool cap he wore pressing up under her chin while his face rested on the nape of her neck. He still hadn't opened his eyes. He kept them closed, we guessed, because he wasn't sure if he was ready to look out into a world that hadn't given him much in the way of welcome. The incision from his PDA surgery, which reached from behind Timmy's arm, around his shoulder blade and up toward his neck, was testament enough of that. In the photo she sent, the scar seemed huge. The one on the little boy's belly, Anne later told us, was even bigger. Let him keep his eyes shut for a while longer, I thought. He'd already seen enough pain for a lifetime.

There were more photos. Before Rob's parents left they visited their grandchildren again — and this time, visiting meant more than just looking. In one picture, Grandmom Julie is holding a sleeping Wyatt quietly dozing on her chest, his thumb propped against his lower lip, her hand draped lightly over his back and shoulders while she smiles. Wyatt looked so at peace it seemed inconceivable that up until then most of his life had been one long struggle to survive.

In another photo, Edda is in the arms of Rob's dad, Gene, and while you see none of his face, it's easy to imagine his expression. What you can see are Gene's large hands delicately cradling the baby girl. She is naked save for a miniature diaper that disappears from view in his cupped hands, her legs drawn up against her torso and her arms scrunched against her ribs so that she seems no larger than a sweet potato. Her still translucent skin almost glows with warmth.

Even more amazing: Rob sent us a three generation family portrait that would have been unthinkable only ten days ago. When Anne and the Schlenders arrived later that day at the Christus Santa Rosa NICU, Rob had hoped they could arrange a family photo if Timmy was doing well enough. In the picture, Julie is holding Timmy in a rocking chair. Anne is smiling at her mother-in-law's side, and Gene and Rob are beaming, too. But for the favor and grace of God, neither Gene nor Julie might have ever seen their grandson alive. Had Anne and Rob not given him one more chance at life after his bowel surgery, Timmy would have been taken off his ventilator, wrapped in a receiving blanket and put into his mother's arms to breathe his last. That he was now well enough to lie in his grandmother's arms was a miracle.

Donna cried when she saw the picture.

"Hard to believe, isn't it?" I said.

My wife nodded. The photo filled the monitor's entire screen. Donna moved the mouse carefully, directing the pointer as if by doing so she might touch Timmy, too.

"Babies," I said.

"Babies," she replied, clicking through the other photos Anne sent. "We have grandbabies!"

I know she was happy that Gene and Julie had gotten a chance to hold Wyatt, Timmy and Edda, but I also knew she was desperate to hold her grandchildren herself. Seeing the Schlenders holding the babies made her want it so badly it hurt.

"Bring up the Southwest website," I said. "I hear San Antonio is nice this time of year."

DOL 40: Monday, May 17

Forty days and forty nights is what the biblical record says. After fasting and praying for weeks in the wilderness, Jesus was approached by the tempter offering Him bread. He turned the devil down. And when He did, the Bible says, angels came and began to minister to Him.

Anne and Rob had been in a wilderness of their own for equally long, but no one was offering much in the way of sustenance; not the kind they truly needed. Only the passage of time would bring them that. While there were many who were ministering to them with meals and prayers and offers of help, none could give Anne and Rob what they desperately hungered for: the salvation of their children. We couldn't yet see a reprieve for Timmy, Edda, Lily or Wyatt. Though Anne and Rob had already witnessed each of their children endure trials that seemed designed by the tempter himself, by the middle of May, they knew that what lay ahead for their children was still a wilderness through which they would all wander. This was just the beginning. They were on a journey that would require hope against hope, rivers of resilience and greater miracles than the ones they'd already experienced.

Timmy rejoined his sisters and brother at Wilford Hall. Lily's infection was fully resolved. Everyone was off the vent, though Wyatt and Lily had some difficulty breathing without it. They were all finally growing, too. Each of the babies were now receiving full enteral feeds — nutritionally complete feedings delivered directly to their tummies — supplemented with increasing amounts of breast milk. That was a triumph as much for Anne as it was for her babies. Consequently, both Timmy and Lily had not only crossed the two pound threshold, but were also each over the 1,000 gram milestone. Wyatt was cresting two pounds, too. Edda was holding up the rear in the weight gain derby, lagging behind her siblings. At only 1lb 13oz, she was a full half pound lighter than Timmy. Even if Edda was growing slowly, she was content and happy. She spent most of her waking hours studying the drop ceiling panels above her isolette, unfazed by what was happening around her. Edda did have her opinions, though, and wasn't shy about letting the entire NICU hear them. For a baby who'd suffered respiratory distress, her lungs were astonishingly powerful when it came to making noise. Though usually quiet, when she shrieked it reverberated throughout the room. We called it her "war cry."

The boys' brains, however, remained a significant cause for concern. Timmy had suffered severe brain injury as a result of the trauma surrounding his PDA and bowel surgeries. A recent head ultrasound showed his hemorrhages resolving and only mild enlargement of the lateral ventricles. That was good. But they also showed the results of his long battle with the brain bleeding. He was diagnosed with *Encephalomalacia*, a condition the neurologists described as a "localized softening of the brain substance." It added to the already tenuous state of his brain's ability to function normally. Whether that would be reversible or not would be told more by time than by tests. Anne was just glad that he was alive. She could hold his warm, breathing body in her arms. Nothing else mattered.

If there was a silver lining in all of this, it was that the blood debris that had been accumulating in his left ventricle had essentially disappeared. Like Wyatt, Timmy had been a candidate for a diagnosis of hydrocephalus based on earlier ultrasounds, but back then everybody was focused on his heart and bowels. What happened to his brain would be a moot point if he did not survive. Now that he had, whatever brain disorders awaited him in the future, it appeared hydrocephalus would not be one of them.

We had all been nervously awaiting the results of Wyatt's latest head ultrasounds. His hydrocephalus was potentially severe and not as likely to resolve as Timmy's had. Unless he improved Wyatt would need significant medical intervention to avoid acute trauma to his brain. When the HUS came on DOL 40, it found that Wyatt's ventricles were excessively dilated. His brain bleeds, like Timmy's, had left in their wake a witch's brew of blood products and debris in the cerebral spinal fluid (CSF) that filled his ventricular system. That led to blockages in the flow of CSF. For weeks, both Timmy and Wyatt had largely succeeded in flushing the gunk away. And with Timmy's hydrocephalus having settled into a stationary course where it was unlikely to cause further problems, the hope was that Wyatt's would, too. Unfortunately, his most recent HUS was the first telling sign that it wouldn't.

Hydrocephalus in micro-preemies is dangerous and difficult to treat. In a baby whose cranial bones have yet to close and fuse shut, the increased CSF volume begins to expand the circumference of the baby's head and at the same time compress the brain tissue. The situation can become rapidly critical. If the increase in pressure isn't alleviated, vomiting, irritability and convulsions often follow. As unstable as Wyatt's condition was, any serious trauma would jeopardize his very survival. And if Wyatt did survive, epileptic seizures and developmental and intellectual disabilities would be among the likely longer term consequences he would face. In the days immediately following his HUS, Wyatt's skull circumference began growing. His brain was being compressed. The danger was mounting by the hour. Neurology was brought in for a consult. The options were few and none of them good. Anne and Rob had dealt with heart surgeries and bowel surgeries, but the prospect of brain surgery was something they could barely stomach. So much could go wrong.

Anne called us with the news about Wyatt. She was inconsolable. Early the next day, I sent out the morning verses to my wife and daughters. The message was one of hope. We needed it.

> I know it's a dark time as we contemplate the long & difficult days ahead for Wyatt. But I found encouragement this morning in a passage about the faith of Abraham with regard to the promise that God would make him (and his wife Sarah) the parents of a great family...
>
> > *In hope against hope he [Abraham] believed, in order that he might become a father of many nations... And without being weak in faith he contemplated his own body, now as good as dead since he was about a hundred years old, and the deadness of Sarah's womb; yet with respect to the promise of God, he did not waver in unbelief, but grew strong in faith, giving glory to God, and being fully assured that what He promised, He was able also to perform. [Romans 4:18-21]*

I can't say what the promise of God is for Wyatt or his
brother & sisters, but I do commit to each of you to continue
to believe in God's goodness, and that, even in hope against
hope, what He has promised, He is able to perform!

It really was impossible to know what was in store for any
of the babies. So many things had gone awry for them in their
short lives. I wanted to tell Anne that the promise of God for each
of her babies was *life*. Jesus had told His followers as much: His
promise to anyone who came to Him was that they "might have
life, and might have it abundantly." While I clung desperately to
those words I could hardly assure my daughter or even my wife
what it would ultimately mean for Timmy, Edda, Lily or Wyatt.
We only had our hope to sustain us, but in view of Wyatt's growing problem maybe we were hoping for something that had no
reasonable chance of coming to pass. Though loath to admit it, I
had my doubts. I pushed back against them, writing of the faith
and hopes of Abraham in my email as much to me as to my family. But I was wavering, too. Wasn't it hoping for too much that
four babies born so early would all survive?

That afternoon, knowing Anne was struggling, I sent her a
short email. I doubted she'd had the time to read the morning
verses from earlier in the day. What would it matter to her what
Abraham thought about his aging body and the "deadness of
Sarah's womb" anyway? That was thousands of years ago; she
needed hope for the here and now, and hope was running dry. I
knew she needed resilience, too, but she and Rob were learning
that resilience was more than getting up off the matt after taking
a punch to the jaw; it was also about being able to pivot, first one
way and then another. The assaults on their babies' lives were
coming from so many directions at once, rarely with warning,
and without respite. The stress had to be unbearable for Anne
and Rob. My job was to continue to lift my daughter in any way I

could. Whatever doubts I harbored made no difference. Though I could not fight this fight for Anne, I would help her as best I was able until the last round's bell had finally rung.

I quoted from the first verse of Psalm 120 in my email to Anne: *In my trouble I cried to the Lord and He answered me.* And then I told her to do for Wyatt what I hoped I was doing for her: "Be strong for Wyatt. He is a fighter."

The neurologist told Anne and Rob the solution was, in fact, simple. He explained that a ventriculo-peritoneal (V-P) shunt is one of the most common and effective ways to deal with progressive hydro-cephalus. But Wyatt was much too small — and his condition too critical — to undergo the surgical procedure. Wyatt would have to double his weight (to somewhere between four and five pounds) before Neurology would consider him a candidate for the shunt. That could be weeks, maybe even months away. In the interim, something had to be done to alleviate the pressure building inside his brain. Neurology wanted to pursue a conservative course.

First, lumbar punctures would be used to draw CSF from the spinal cord. If these spinal taps were ineffective it could be an indication that Wyatt was afflicted with non-communicating hydrocephalus — the *bad* form — where the normal flow of CSF out of the ventricles is completely obstructed. The spinal taps commenced but were not immediately effective. The doctor told Anne and Rob he would continue trying for another 48 hours, but if the lumbar punctures did not reduce Wyatt's intracranial pressure, he would resort to trans-fontanel taps, drawing CSF directly from Wyatt's brain with a syringe.

There was no change over the next two days. On DOL 43 the neurosurgeon tapped into Wyatt's brain for the first time while the nervous parents stood only feet from their son's isolette. Anne, a doctor who ought to be used to such things, could barely watch. This was not just any patient; this was a baby weighing barely two pounds and this baby was *her* son. It was no easier for Rob, Anne would tell me. Though he wasn't squeamish about the procedure, the idea of a long needle being pushed into the "soft spot" of Wyatt's skull and then pressed down through his son's brain matter until finally reaching the ventricles was almost too much for Rob to bear. His fears surrounding fatherhood were being realized before his eyes. Wyatt was already developing high tone — medical parlance for stiffness in the limbs and major muscles — and that was a significant precursor for cerebral palsy. Hydrocephalus was compressing his brain tissue. Now needles poked through the tiny baby's head were necessary to relieve the increasing volume of CSF. What else would Wyatt have to endure? It was heartbreaking.

The trans-fontanel taps were only a temporary solution, however. Neurology told Anne and Rob it was time to take the next step: surgically implanting a ventricular reservoir. They had first wanted to be sure that Wyatt's hydrocephalus was both "non-communicating" and progressive. Now they would implant a reservoir just beneath the scalp on the top of Wyatt's head. A catheter would be inserted into the brain's ventricular cavity and attached to a port in the reservoir from which excess fluid could then be drawn. Though less invasive than the V-P shunt procedure Wyatt would need later, the placement of a ventricular reservoir was not without risk — it *was* still brain surgery, after all.

Donna and I returned to San Antonio right in the middle of Wyatt's ordeal. While I could only stay for a few days, Donna would remain until Wyatt's brain surgery was done. It was a difficult time for everybody. That was no surprise. But there was one surprise in store for us, and that gave me the hope that there was still light at the end of the tunnel. On Saturday morning before my flight home, Donna and I finally got to hold our grandchildren for the first time.

Edda and Timmy were both awake, their eyes half open, sus-
piciously following the increasing activity around their isolettes.
Lily and Wyatt were sleeping soundly and that saved them from
the intrusion to come. As I sat in a high-backed chair pushed close
to Edda's isolette, a nurse reached in and gently lifted her up and
out. Holding the tiny girl in one hand, she carefully straightened
the tangle of leads, lines and tubes draped around the child with
the other. And then, so quickly it surprised me, she placed Edda
high against my chest and tucked the receiving blanket that
swaddled her between my uplifted arms. I didn't dare breathe.

A few feet away, another nurse was preparing Timmy. Donna
watched apprehensively, her eyes darting from Timmy's nurse to
Edda and me, from the baby she was about to hold to the baby
she was afraid I might drop. And then her eyes went wide as the
nurse carefully lowered Timmy onto her chest. My wife tilted her
head to one side so she could see the baby boy's face resting against
her and then squeezed her eyes shut. She was trying not to cry.

Holding them was something like holding a party balloon.
There was form but no real mass to them, and something so deli-
cate about them that I feared they might pop. "They won't break,
you know," Edda's nurse said, sensing our unease. Then she lifted
Edda's head, pulled the receiving blanket away from her torso
and shoulders, and gently pressed Edda against the bare skin of
my chest, giving me a reassuring smile. She had encouraged me
earlier to unbutton my shirt to allow the baby I'd be holding to
enjoy the benefits of what's known in the NICU as kangaroo care.
Glancing down at Edda, I wondered about the enjoyment part.
Her face was half buried in chest hair.

Timmy's nurse was doing the same for him, pulling open his
blanket so that his shoulders and cheek lay skin-to-skin on the
bared top of Donna's breasts. No doubt Timmy had gotten a better deal than his sister, I thought to myself. He lay motionless for
a moment, his eyes still at half-mast. I could hear his breathing,

raspy and uneven. He reached his right arm up, stretched his little
fingers wide apart and rested them on his grandmother's neck.
Then he fell asleep, his breathing softening so that he sounded
like a kitten purring.

They were still so unimaginably small. Edda's head, which I
held cupped in the palm of my hand, was no bigger than a ten-
nis ball. I looked at her arm and hand, drawn up tight against
her chin, and realized a wedding band the size of Rob's or mine
would still slip easily over her wrist and up the entire length of
her forearm like an oversized bracelet. The bracelet I was wearing,
the *Hope*Resilience*Miracles* cuff that had come from Graham's
Foundation, would have fit like a belt around her waist. Her ears —
one of them was poking out beneath the knit hat she wore — were
hardly as big as my fingernails. And *her* fingernails? They were no
bigger than the dried split peas Donna used when making soup.

Don't imagine they looked like miniature full-term infants,
though. They remained — a month and a half after birth — rather
odd looking and more like tiny old men than pudgy, pink newborns. Their skin was still mostly translucent, their veins and arteries appearing beneath it like the red and blue lines on a roadmap.
All the babies were showing the signs of wear and tear, too. The
backs of each of their hands were mottled purple, the result of
innumerable needle sticks to draw blood for lab workups. Their
cheeks and chins were often red and raw from the tape used to
keep the tubes running into their mouths and noses from being
pulled out of place. And all of the babies — the girls especially —
had grown a light coat of fine, colorless hair that spread from the
tops of their shoulders all the way down their backs and arms.
I remembered reading something about the soft hair that grows
in utero beginning around the sixth month of pregnancy. That
hair is called "lanugo," but if that's what was growing on Anne's
babies, I had no way of knowing. Unfortunately, there was not
much in the way of hair on any of their heads, except for Lily, who

had just enough that her nurse could clip a tiny pink and purple bow to it. They *were* odd looking, but to Donna and me that day, they were also utterly adorable.

"You look like a grandmother," I told my wife.

She smiled. "I'll take that as a compliment."

I looked at Timmy, now sleeping soundly in her arms and then down at Edda, her face still lost in the weeds of my chest hair. I could not tell if her eyes were open.

"Is she asleep?" I whispered to Donna.

She shook her head.

I told her that Timmy was long gone and she nodded knowingly. She looked at the tiny child in her arms and then back at me.

"Babies," she whispered. "We got babies."

DOL 47: Monday, May 24

There was a second reason Donna remained in San Antonio: Anne's maternity leave was ending. She would be returning to the Dermatology Clinic three floors below the Wilford Hall NICU. Rob would be with Timmy, Edda, Lily and Wyatt every day, but we hoped having Donna available, too, might put Anne more at ease. Maybe it would also reduce some of the guilt we knew she would feel for "abandoning" her children during the work day. How much more emotional trauma Anne could take before she snapped was becoming less a question of if as it was of when.

I didn't know it at the time, but the *when* very nearly came that Monday morning. It was Anne's first day back. She'd hardly slept the night before. She was anxious about work, upset and worried about Wyatt's surgery and out of bed every three hours to pump.

It was just an unfortunate coincidence, I suppose. First-time patients at the Derm Clinic are randomly scheduled with whichever doctor is next on the list. When Anne's name was reinserted into the clinical rotation the staff tech started filling her appointment book.

The tech would've had no reason not to schedule the woman who'd requested the next possible appointment as Anne's first patient.

She was a first-time mom, married to an enlisted airman. Her baby was two months old, and a chubby, healthy-looking child. Maybe neither of them had any family within a thousand miles of Lackland Air Force Base to help them when problems with their baby arose. She was afraid the baby was sick. She didn't know what to do. Her baby was crying incessantly, and she'd tried everything she could think of. Nothing seemed to help. And it kept looking worse and worse. She pulled the diaper from around her baby's waist.

"Diaper rash. It was just diaper rash," Anne told me as we sat together in Starbucks on a Saturday morning after I'd returned to San Antonio. Her eyes narrowed. "I wanted to help her. I really wanted to, but I couldn't. I just couldn't do it."

I waited for her to go on.

"I looked at the baby and then the mother. Something started to come over me — I don't know how else to explain what I suddenly felt. I thought that maybe I would lose control. It wasn't that poor girl's fault, but I just wanted to grab her and shake her. Diaper rash? She's in my office because she has a baby suffering from diaper rash? What did *she* know about a baby's suffering? What did she know about anything that could go wrong with her baby? There she sat in my office with her fat, full-term child while just floors above us my four children, my four babies who *together* didn't weigh as much as hers, were in a neonatal intensive care unit fighting for their lives. I mean they were sticking needles in Wyatt's brain and I was supposed to care about her baby's diaper rash?"

Anne dropped her eyes. "I don't remember what I told her. I hope I didn't say anything inappropriate, but I'm not sure. I was about to tell her to get over herself, that babies don't die from diaper rash, but then I realized it would be all I could do not to start screaming at her."

She hesitated before going on. "I knew I was about to cry, and the mom is giving me a funny look. She must have thought I was crazy. I was scared she was right. I didn't know what I was going to do. At some point I just got up, walked out of the exam room and went to Dr. Cowan's office." Emily Cowan was the Dermatology Department Head. She was a physician and full-bird Army Colonel, but she was also a mother and a refuge in the storm Anne was sailing straight into. "I went into Colonel Cowan's office, and I broke down. I told her I couldn't do it. I couldn't bring myself to care about some baby with diaper rash."

I saw how hard it had been for her. She was so filled with guilt for what her children were going through; she felt responsible for all of it. It did not take much effort on her part to convince herself she was a failure as a mother. And then, in the first five minutes of her first day back at work, she was faced with the realization that she was now a failure as a doctor, too.

"It was like any compassion I'd ever had was gone," she said.

I looked straight into Anne's eyes. She was as compassionate a human being as I'd ever known. That was the gift God had given her. Though she would never admit to being gifted like that, it was the way she was most easily able to give to others. That morning she saw that gift slipping away. I think it scared her to death to see such an important part of her drying up and dying.

"All I felt was bitterness, Papa. I don't know why all this is happening to me. And I don't know when everything is going to just fall apart."

Colonel Cowan oversaw her appointment book from then on, making sure there was time every day for Anne to pump, to slip upstairs to see her babies and — when she needed it — time to hide and cry. It helped. She would tell me in an email only a couple weeks later about crying with a patient who she'd been treating but hadn't seen in nearly eight months. The woman was from Germany, the wife of an Army officer who had been stationed there many years before. Her sweet spirit and accent reminded Anne of her mom's Aunt Edda, who'd come to America with her own soldier-husband decades earlier.

Anne's email began with a note about the morning verses I'd been sending. That morning's passage had been from *Romans*, and in it Paul encouraged people to "consider that the sufferings of the present time are not worthy to be compared with the glory that is to be revealed to us." It was hard to know how such an admonition might go over with Anne in light of how her own children had suffered, but I sent it anyway. In return, she wrote:

> Papa — I just wanted to thank you for the verses this week; I've found them particularly comforting... and at a time when I needed it most.
>
> I cried today for the first time with one of my patients... I didn't mean to, but I suppose it was bound to happen at some point. She's the German woman who once gave me a piece of the Berlin wall! She'd asked me about the hospital bracelets I still wear and wanted to make sure I wasn't ill. She was quite surprised when I told her I'd had four babies since she'd last been in to see me in October. She said it was funny to think that I'd been so tiny back then and was just as small now and yet had somehow in the intervening few months produced four lives. She wanted to know how they were doing and I just broke down when I told her about the boys. We had a good cry together and she gave me a big hug; I was really touched that she would show emotion towards me and my babies.
>
> And, yesterday, one of my other nice patients brought me a gift bag with four children's books and a jar of homemade jam. I'll save it for when you come out again in a couple weeks.

DOL 51: Friday, May 28

On the last Friday in May, the beginning of the Memorial Day weekend, the NICU team prepped Wyatt for surgery. When the call came from the OR, Colonel Cowan was able to get another resident to cover for Anne. The nurses were just about to move him from the NICU — his first time outside its walls — to the operating suite. Anne rushed upstairs and grabbed the *Uglydoll* Erin had given Wyatt as a birthday present seven weeks earlier. When she reached his isolette, she stuffed the odd-looking little doll into it, let her hands slide off the clear acrylic sides as it rolled away from her, and called after Wyatt, "I love you!"

While that was happening, Donna sent me a text: *Wyatt going now to OR.* By the time I left my office Wyatt had been intubated and was under general anesthesia. During the half hour it took me to drive to the jobsite where my crew was working, the neurosurgeon had made an incision in Wyatt's scalp and retracted a flap of skin to allow placement of the access reservoir. He then used a procedure called electrocauterization, burning tissue in order to control the bleeding, as he accessed the tough, fibrous tissue layer of the dura mater that protected the brain. Next he directed the reservoir's catheter on a trajectory leading into the right part of Wyatt's lateral ventricle.

In the time it took me to inspect the progress my guys were making, the neurosurgeon had pushed a 25-gauge needle into the top of the newly placed reservoir and slowly withdrew 20cc of discolored cerebrospinal fluid. As he did, Wyatt's fontanel began to soften and sink.

In the late afternoon, Donna would send me her second text of the day: *In recovery now.* By evening Wyatt was back in the NICU with his *Uglydoll* at his side and a thick, white gauze pad covering the top of his head. He would not open his eyes again until morning.

CHAPTER 12

DOL 55 to 84

June, 2010

JUNE FELT LIKE THE best of times and the worst of times for the babies and for us.

Timmy, Edda, Lily and Wyatt had all made it to Memorial Day weekend and by the beginning of the month, their adjusted gestational age was 33 weeks. Had Rob been able to have his way, he would have agreed to let Anne deliver their babies around this point. Each of them might have weighed as much as four pounds. Their brains would have been teeming with billions of developed neurons. More importantly, the babies' lungs would have been almost fully developed. That milestone alone might have staved off so much of the hardship the babies had already endured. One online pregnancy calendar described Week 33 as the point when the final touches were being applied to "your baby masterpiece." It also noted, "Your baby will have an excellent chance of survival outside the womb if you deliver now." For Timmy, Edda, Lily and Wyatt — now eight weeks outside Anne's womb and weighing between 3lbs 3oz (Timmy) and 2lbs 10oz (Edda) —

the odds of survival were much improved. But having lived to see May become June still guaranteed nothing — not for any one of them.

There were many challenges to come. There were still foreboding diagnoses and gloom-filled test results portending exactly what we didn't always know. In the middle of the month, first Edda and then Lily developed inflammation of the connective tissues surrounding the long bones in their arms and legs. For Edda, whose earlier diagnosis of Rickets of Prematurity had raised concerns about her bone growth, this was especially alarming. What the effects on her or Lily would be, no one — as usual — could say for sure.

Head ultrasounds for the boys did little to dispel our worries about the extent of the damage to their brains. Timmy's latest tests confirmed that as a result of the severe nature of his earlier brain bleeds he had suffered significant cerebellar hemisphere damage. No one could say what the consequent fallout from that would be. The HUS results for Wyatt were even scarier: the images showed small holes appearing around his ventricles. That meant a softening of his brain tissue was likely occurring, which in turn would lead to death of the white matter in his brain. Because the area surrounding the ventricles contains nerve fibers that carry messages from the brain to the body's muscles, Wyatt was at risk for motor skill and developmental disabilities, not to mention possible impairment to his hearing and eyesight.

Rob and Anne did their best to remain hopeful through all the uncertainty. Anne decided to focus her attention on what she could see rather than worry about what she couldn't. Edda and Lily's legs *looked* normal to her, and the girls seemed in no particular discomfort. Maybe the problem would resolve itself. Wyatt and Timmy showed little outward signs of what had been happening inside their heads, and from Anne's perspective they *seemed* to be doing better and better. If my daughter was being naïve, if as a medical doctor she should *know* better, what did it matter? She was simply trying to survive along with her babies. She loved them. They were still alive. Nothing else mattered.

But survival was no panacea. We were coming to realize that extreme prematurity was the gift that just wouldn't stop giving. What Anne and Rob and their babies were going through was something akin to a family traversing a minefield together. Every step was either one closer to redemption or to annihilation. There was no way to know what that next step might bring. The only choice was to keep walking forward. There was no escape and no turning back. More than anything, I thought this was why Graham's Foundation preached "Hope, resilience and miracles." This journey began with hope because there was nothing else, was sustained through resilience in spite of heartbreak and was rewarded by the miracle of life itself in the end — even by lives that only came home from the NICU as memories.

Though Timmy and Wyatt had endured the most, the girls weren't spared the "gifts" of extreme prematurity, either. Each of the quads had begun routine eye screenings on DOL 42. By the beginning of the second week of June what had been routine quickly became emergent. The news was the same as ever: good and bad. Timmy's eyes were fine for the time being; Wyatt's were more concerning. For the girls it was much worse. Edda's prognosis was little different than her younger sister's. And Lily was going blind.

The babies had their first screening for Retinopathy of Prematurity (ROP) on May 19th when no concerns for any of them were noted by the ophthalmologist. By DOL 56 all the babies had ROP developing in one or both of their eyes. In two weeks' time Rob and Anne had gone from wondering what color eyes their daughters might someday have to worrying whether Lily and Edda would be able to see at all. At this juncture, the girls both had Stage 2 ROP and were fast approaching a tipping point. The disease advances, sometimes rapidly, in stages from 1, the mildest form of ROP, to Stage 5, where the retina is completely detached resulting in substantial or total loss of vision. For Lily and Edda, the stakes were becoming increasingly high.

ROP was just another one of the confusing acronyms abounding in the *sequelae of prematurity*. There seemed to be no end to them. I tried to brush the thought of Lily and Edda losing their sight away, as though ignoring it might somehow negate the medical possibility. Donna, who was trying to explain it all to me and Cait, accused me of being insensitive. She'd first learned about the condition when she was with Anne in late May.

"Your daughter is devastated by this. Why don't you think about how she feels?"

"I don't know. It's just..."

"Just what?" Donna demanded.

"I guess I just don't believe it."

"You don't believe what? You don't believe the doctors? You don't believe your daughter?"

"You want me to believe this ROP thing is just going to progress on its merry way until both girls are blind?"

"They're going to do laser surgery before it gets to that point. That's probably going to be the only option going forward."

"Laser surgery?" Cait asked. The term startled her.

"That's the only way they can stop the abnormal growth of the blood vessels in their eyes."

Cait looked at her mother for more.

"They'll lose their vision in the parts of their eyes where the laser treatment is done," Donna added.

I was skeptical and frustrated. "What are you talking about? The treatment is to fight blindness with blindness? They're going to destroy their sight to save it?"

Donna looked at me like I was an idiot.

"I'm not going to believe it," I said. "I want to believe God for better than this."

Donna got up to leave the room but turned back and looked at me. "You should call your daughter. She needs you right now."

I looked away, back to the TV screen.

I didn't call Anne that night; I couldn't bring myself to.

Turns out, not calling Anne was about the smartest thing I could have done. It wouldn't be until much later that I would understand that the most frightening thing about Retinopathy of Prematurity is how quickly it advances and how devastating the damage to the eye can be if not effectively treated in time. I probably would have ended up slowing Anne and Rob's decision.

No doubt that from the moment Rob learned that ROP was a threat to the babies he was digging into every journal article and reviewing every blog post he could find about the condition. He would bug the ophthalmologist, the NICU doctors and the nursing staff for every tidbit he could get. He would try desperately to leave no stone unturned. And in short order, he would come to understand the crux of the issue: that like so many of the maladies his children had already encountered, ROP is yet another disease caused by not getting the right amount of oxygen to the right place at the right time.

Running the risk of total blindness was not a wager Rob was willing to make, and he knew the window of opportunity for effective surgical treatment would be quickly closing. Before I had even come close to terms with the ROP diagnosis — and before I finally called Anne — she and Rob had already signed the surgical consent form for Lily. They would soon do the same for Edda, and eventually for Wyatt.

On a Sunday night in mid-June the babies' ophthalmologist arrived in the Wilford Hall NICU. I would meet him in subsequent weeks. He was the kindest, gentlest man and perhaps of all the physicians who worked with Anne and Rob's babies, the most compassionate. Maybe he *had* to be. He knew that the ROP screenings he performed again and again were agonizing for the babies. He knew that what he observed in those screenings often meant giving a baby's parents gut-wrenching news. And he knew that in many cases, the only good he could do was to save what he could by destroying what he could not.

Lily's prognosis went downhill rapidly. Her ROP was aggressive and the blood vessels on her irises were becoming engorged. Her pupils were having difficulty moving. She needed immediate treatment to avoid scar tissue formation and the risk of retinal detachment. The ophthalmologist performed a procedure called "peripheral retinal ablation" on both her eyes, using a laser to stop the abnormal blood vessel growth. By doing so he saved Lily's central vision. But he also eliminated virtually all of her peripheral vision.

Five days later, Edda had a similar procedure on her right eye. The trauma of the surgery put her into serious respiratory distress; she required additional oxygen support for days after. Before the month was out, the doctor would use the laser on her left eye, too. He didn't think her loss of sight would be as significant as her sister's, but only time would tell what the extent of the vision impairment was for each of them.

Wyatt was the last of the three to have eye surgery. He had an even more difficult time than Edda. Post-surgery, he had to be re-intubated because oxygen saturation levels in his blood decreased dangerously. At the same time his oxygen requirements kept increasing. The risk was that his need for ever richer concentrations of oxygen meant he was getting closer and closer to a whole new set of problems resulting from oxygen toxicity. Ultimately, it would take another course of steroids to bring Wyatt's lung function back to normal.

I'd written my last email update in early June. In it, I mentioned how I'd begun to think of Anne and Rob and their babies as crossing a minefield together. After Lily's surgery, I read to Donna how I'd concluded it: "And while, once the smoke has cleared, no one can say what the outcome will be or what the long term implications of this trauma will have on each of the babies, we rejoice, for in the eyes of these little guys we have seen the love and goodness of God."

Had I actually written that? Where once I'd boldly exclaimed I was seeing the love of God in my grandchildren's eyes, now those words hung hollow and cold. They had been prescient in a way I could have never imagined. And whereas my hopes had been sustained to this point by believing that Anne and Rob might shepherd all their little ones across a metaphorical minefield alive, the harsh realization was sinking in that if they did, none of their children would survive the ordeal whole. They were losing their babies piece by piece: Timmy's motor skills were likely so eroded by the damage to his cerebellum and brain stem that walking would be a nearly impossible feat for him. Wyatt might never breathe without supplemental oxygen. His hydrocephalus was a likely precursor to cerebral palsy. He might not walk, either, and frankly we knew things could get worse. And now, Edda and Lily had lost much of their eyesight. The picture in my head of two nearly blind girls trying to push the wheelchairs in which their limp brothers sat was too sad for words.

"I signed that email, 'God is good,'" I reminded myself as much as my wife.

"Yes, you did."

"Are we still holding onto that?" I asked.

Donna finished the row she was knitting and set what she was working on in her lap. "We still have Anne, don't we?"

I nodded.

"And at last count, we still had four grandbabies."

I agreed that we did.

"Then that's enough 'good' for me for right now." There was no bitterness or anything in her voice to suggest that she was being facetious.

"I wanted to believe God for more."

"Lily could have gone blind," Donna said.

"And you're okay with that?"

"No."

"Then what now?"

"What are you always telling me?"

I shrugged.

"Put one foot in front of the other. One step at a time."

I knew then where she was going, so I finished the thought for her: "We walk by faith not by sight."

"Now more than ever," she said and went back to her knitting.

Timmy was crying so hard he could barely make a sound. Though each of the babies had been screened for ROP before, this was the first time Anne had witnessed the procedure. She came up to the NICU after a long day in the Derm Clinic. It was early evening, and Rob had left the babies earlier to go home for the night. A nurse was putting drops in Timmy's eyes to dilate his pupils when Anne arrived. After a few minutes, the nurse administered a topical anesthesia. The eye doctor was coming!

Anne had been warned it was a ghastly exam, but she knew it was a necessary evil. The babies hated it; seeing the procedure performed would turn any parent's stomach. It brought Anne to tears. The ophthalmologist worked quickly and carefully, but because Wilford Hall was a teaching hospital, he had a fellow with him to reexamine Timmy's eyes and that made the procedure seem endless. Being a resident physician herself, Anne could hardly complain, but as a mom she struggled with each passing second her baby writhed in agony while the doctors completed their observations. Timmy's heart rate was above 200 bpm; it continued

to climb until it was approaching 230. Just as the nurse was about
to intervene, the doctor nudged the fellow aside, carefully released
the speculum holding Timmy's eye wide open and put his hand
gently on the baby's torso, patting him lightly.

Timmy's chest was heaving up and down as he gasped for
air. His face was beet red, and tears were pouring from his eyes.
His mouth was stretched wide and his tongue rolled back, but
he made no sound. The nurse lifted him and placed him in his
mother's arms.

"Wow! That was brutal enough just to watch," Anne said to
the nurse. "I can't imagine how horrible it is for him."

"I can tell you, it's not just him; no baby tolerates it," the nurse
replied.

"He was so upset that he couldn't even get a cry out."

The nurse kept looking at the baby boy now settled against
his mother's breast, but said nothing.

"Is it like this with the girls, too — I mean, so upset that they
can't cry out loud, that they can hardly make a noise at all?" Anne
asked.

The nurse thought about that for a moment, and probably
sensing Anne's apprehension, answered the question somewhat
obliquely. "Edda — now that child can make some noise!"

Anne smiled. "You've heard Edda's shrieks?" she asked,
forgetting for the time being about Timmy's silent cry. "We call
that her *War Cry*. Amazing how so much noise can come from
someone so small."

"Oh, and she *really* lets the eye doctors know it, too."

But this was only a brief diversion. Anne asked again if Timmy
was always this upset during the exams, so upset he couldn't even
make a sound. The nurse said that she honestly didn't know — this
was her first time on duty with Timmy when the ophthalmologist
had come to call. But she also said she would talk with Timmy's

day nurse when the shifts changed again. That nurse might know something more.

The something *more* turned out to be something *bad*.

For Anne and Rob, I know it was like another limb lost, another piece of one of their babies gone. Timmy's silent cry during the ROP screening was not because he was so upset he couldn't make a sound. We would soon learn that he'd lost the ability to make much of any sound at all. Anne's question led to a consult with the ear, nose and throat specialists. They performed a flexible laryngoscopy, sliding a thin fiber-optic camera into Timmy's airway so they could observe his throat and voice box. His response to being scoped was little different from his reaction to the ophthalmologist's exam. A "very quiet cry despite forceful effort" was how the ENT doctors noted it in their report. They also observed paralysis of Timmy's left vocal cord.

The likely culprit was the PDA ligation he had undergone when he was only nine days old. The laryngeal nerve (which controls the left vocal cord) is so close to the surgical site that a surgeon performing a PDA might not even be aware he has touched the nerve, and even the slightest contact can result in irreversible damage. Blaming the surgeon who performed Timmy's PDA would accomplish nothing; the surgery he performed had *saved* his life. What was done was done. The paralysis meant that since one side of Timmy's vocal cords could no longer move, the flow of air between the two cords would be compromised. Anne wanted to know if her son would be able to talk. The consensus was that he would. Timmy would likely have a hoarse, raspy voice, but a voice nevertheless.

A more immediate concern was that Timmy might not be able to safely swallow food or liquids. Babies with vocal cord paralysis can easily aspirate when they vomit and the consequences can be fatal. Complicating this was the fact that micro-preemies often suffer severe reflux disease. The NICU team scheduled a consult with Speech Therapy to begin an immediate evaluation to assess the risks of feeding Timmy. His sisters were already beginning their first nipple feeds. We would have to wait to see whether it would be safe for Timmy to do the same. Only time and tests would tell. He might do fine. Or — as sometimes happens in the most severe cases — he might have to be fed through a tube for the rest of his life.

Anne did her best to keep her chin up, juggling her work in the Derm Clinic with the incessant pumping she continued to do day and night and squeezing NICU visits in whenever she could. She tried to balance the "down" of Timmy's vocal cord paralysis and the concerns she had about his ability to swallow with the "ups" that were like lights in the darkness. One such light was Lily's first feeding, which she described in an email.

> Lily drank from a bottle for the first time today. The very first drop of milk in her mouth made her make a hideous face… like she thought it was gross. But by the end of her teeny bottle, she seemed to really enjoy it. Mechanically, it was quite hard for her to get through the couple of teaspoons… you could actually watch her struggle to put together a sequence of 'sucking, swallowing and breathing'. Next time you eat, take note of all the steps you have to take to get the food into your tummy… Wow, we take a lot for granted! We'll probably try feeding her again on Monday when her favorite nurse, Sheila, is back on.
>
> I miss you a lot, Dad, and can't wait to see you.
>
> Con mucho amor,
> Ana y Timmy, Edda, Lily y Wyatt

That Anne signed her email "with much love" in Spanish (a greeting she and I often used in easier times) told me she was feeling a little better; that she signed it with her name and each of her children's names hinted that her hopes for them were being renewed. Maybe all the babies really were going to pull through, even if some would be worse for wear than others. While none of us knew what the next day might bring, I think we all were beginning to let our hopes cautiously rise. In little more than a week, Donna and I would be returning to San Antonio to see the babies' progress for ourselves. And we would finally have a baby shower for Anne.

In spite of the eye surgeries for Lily, Edda and Wyatt, the discovery of Timmy's paralyzed vocal cord and the continuous tapping of the reservoir to reduce the CSF volumes in Wyatt's head, June really was a good month for the babies. Overcoming one hardship after another, their cumulative resilience was rekindling all our hopes. By the end of the month, with each of the babies gaining weight almost daily, the NICU docs began to talk for the first time about prospective discharge dates. We were beside ourselves with joyful anticipation.

On June 19th, the 73rd day of their lives, the quads had reached an adjusted gestational age of 35 weeks. Had they still been in utero, they would have been in position for delivery. Their lungs would be ready to start working. Had they been singletons, they would have weighed around five pounds by this point, and the rest of their time in the womb would be spent packing on weight (mostly fat) to the tune of 8 to 12 ounces per week. Even for one baby, movement inside the womb would be increasingly restricted; had Timmy, Edda, Lily and Wyatt all still been crammed inside, I think Anne would have simply exploded. Most importantly, the puzzle that represents a baby's complex systems would be nearing completion. Having missed so much, it was amazing Anne's babies had been making do outside of their mother's womb for more than 10 weeks.

Whatever their losses, whatever difficulties their futures might hold because of their early birth, none of us could deny that the babies were absolute miracles to behold. And by late June, the biggest miracle of all was how big they were getting and how baby-like they were becoming.

Lily remained the biggest; her cheeks and chin so chubby that you just wanted to pinch them, her puckered lips so cute that they invited kisses. Even her palms and fingers seemed pudgy — her father's wedding band that had once slipped so easily to her shoulder could now not even get past Lily's hands. Her skin was creamy pink, not the translucent, mottled shroud of red that had once hung on her like a wrinkled suit. She was tipping the scales at 4lb 6oz. It occurred to me that Lily, now nearly the same gestational age Anne had been when she was born, was almost the exact weight her mom had been then. Edda remained much smaller than Lily and her brothers, but at three and a half pounds she was close to tripling her original birth weight. Timmy and Wyatt each weighed around four pounds and were growing quickly. While it had taken the babies the first month of their lives to gain (and maintain) seven ounces, they were now gaining that much or more every week.

With the babies breathing more easily, Anne and Rob had more and more opportunities to hold and touch their children. They were changing diapers, giving baths and dressing them. The babies wore clothes much of the time, something that had been impractical when they were younger because of the web of tubes and lines that had entangled their tiny bodies, and the outfits were always colorful and cheery. They each had their own special colors: Lily always wore purple and *only* purple; Edda, pink and occasionally yellow (which brought out the strawberry blonde hair that she had suddenly sprouted); Timmy wore brown and sometimes blue; and Wyatt was always dressed in blue or green.

The girls were living in open cribs that were luxuriant by comparison to the isolettes, and the nurses frequently let Lily and Edda co-bed for hours at a time. They seemed to enjoy each other's company, as though being near something else so small was both a revelation and reminder that their world might not be such a threatening place after all. Timmy was sometimes placed in the open crib between his sisters, and while they seemed more suspect of him, he beamed with delight every time he was with the girls.

Timmy, we decided, was the happiest baby *ever*, and with all he'd gone through he deserved to be. He seemed to have an endless supply of energy and an insatiable exuberance about everything. Wyatt was another story. The last born, the smallest at birth, and beset by one problem after another, he was the baby people seemed instinctively drawn toward, the underdog everyone cheered for. And he was charming, with a disarming smile and a beauty we suspected would melt women in the years to come. But he had an angry streak in him that was as fierce as it was unnerving. It didn't take much to make Wyatt mad, and it usually took an awful lot to calm him again. But if it was an angry temperament that had kept him clinging to life the last two months then I said rage on, Wyatt, rage on!

The babies weren't the only ones growing during their stay in the NICU. We were all being stretched by the experience. Donna did a better job dealing with the pain than the rest of us. It's not that she didn't have doubt or despair, but every day the babies survived seemed to make my wife stronger, as though whatever it was that kept the babies' hearts beating was giving her new strength, too. Having been given the gift of grandchildren, it appeared Donna had at the same time received the gift of childlike faith, a faith she would hold in safekeeping for the babies until the day they were old enough to claim it for themselves. I envied that.

It was harder for my daughter and her husband. I sometimes wondered whether Anne and Rob would survive at all. They were both physically and emotionally exhausted. So much had changed so quickly in their lives that some days they were simply in shock. Only nine months earlier they'd agreed that if hormone therapy was what was required to help get Anne pregnant then they would give it a shot. In doing so they had walked into a proverbial tunnel toward a hopeful light, but had found themselves in the path of an onrushing train. They each had to deal with unavoidable guilt and the feeling they should have done things differently. No doubt they asked themselves if they should have known better or weighed the risks more carefully. They might have reconsidered adoption while giving Anne more time to ovulate naturally. Were they wrong *not* to have considered reducing the number of babies Anne was carrying? Shouldn't they have pressed harder for the option of visiting the Phoenix clinic? How could they be sure they'd made the right decisions for their babies and for each other? By late June, Anne and Rob had certainly changed — maybe even grown through their experience, but that was little more than a glib concession to the adage *what doesn't kill you makes you stronger.*

It's difficult to say how the NICU ordeal was affecting me. Maybe it wasn't so much growth at all, but a slow shifting, more like the shedding of a snake's skin, a peeling away of the old and the discovery of something both familiar and new in its place. We were all being stretched by the babies' journey — the rapid pace of events, the myriad changes, the never knowing, the accumulating tension pulling us ever thinner, and in many ways we all coped alone. For me, the instinctive recoil from the pain gave way over time to surrender. I began to slowly yield, to give in to a process that was exposing me to my core, revealing my own helplessness in the face of what was happening in our lives. In that condition, as unsteady as I was unsure, the discovery of something that I already knew, but that was also wholly new to me, became possible. What I found — not quite through realization or by revelation, but rather through the crucible of circumstances the babies' NICU journey was — was a glimpse of the most humbling sight. I saw the love of God for me.

I was startled by how quickly and how deeply the roots of love for the babies had been sunk in me. By late June, I realized I loved them in a way I had never quite been able to love my own children. It was the same *kind* of love I had for my daughters, bound from the get-go by the burdens of parental responsibility and the weight of my own pride, but set free. Free from the fear of failure. Free from apprehensions of the future. I was free to love them without restraint. There seemed nothing I wouldn't do for them; nothing I would be unwilling to give. Wasn't that feeling the essence of the Christian love I knew? I thought that such a love rising within me for *them* was surely a reflection of God's own love for *me*. And it was. But seeing His love for me through these babies' lives let me perceive it anew, and seeing it again as though for the first time, I saw that I had only been getting half the story.

I don't know exactly when it happened, only that it did. It wasn't miraculous. I didn't see God walking in the corridors of Wilford Hall, just Timmy, Edda, Lily and Wyatt resting peacefully in their cribs one afternoon. Looking down at them I saw for the first time what God must have always seen in me. And what I saw was *nothing*. These tiny lives lying helpless in the NICU possessed nothing; prostrated, they could offer nothing; their only hopes were those given to them by others. Pitiable as they were pathetic at birth, their condition desperate as it was wretched, they could no more conceive of what they needed than they could ask for it. The wonderful paradox was although there was nothing the babies could do to make me love them there was at the same time nothing they could do to make me stop. Realizing that truth revealed another: I could never love the babies in the way I did except that God had loved me like that first. As surely as His eyes were on Timmy, Edda, Lily and Wyatt, they had also always been on me. He saw my life no differently than I did theirs: lying helpless before Him I possessed nothing to gain His love, prostrating myself I could not ever merit it, forlorn of hope I could not even conceive of the possibility that He loved me.

But He did. He had to. He could not help Himself.

Deep inside me, I suspect I've known as much all along. I've always believed God's love is buried somewhere in each of us; try though we might, we cannot separate ourselves from it. But it took Timmy, Edda, Lily and Wyatt to help me find the truth, for me to actually see it, to take hold of it and — more importantly — let it take hold of me. Knowing you are loved, truly loved, changes us. It changed me then and there. As the end of the babies' first spring became the beginning of their first summer, I knew — no matter what the future might yet bring — that I had already gained so much more from them than I could ever possibly give in return.

Caitlin flew with Donna and me to San Antonio for Anne's baby shower. But for her, job #1 was to get to the NICU as soon as she could. It was her first time seeing her nieces and nephews since those surreal first days of their lives. "They're so big!" she exclaimed, and when her chance finally came to hold the babies she looked like she didn't know whether to laugh or cry. Cry she did, though, when Anne placed Timmy in her arms. She had been no less affected by the emotional roller coaster than the rest of us. She, too, had cautiously let her hopes rise and then had seen them dashed. But through resilience and sheer will she'd managed to summon hope even when it seemed none could possibly be left.

She knew it had been worth it now. You could see it in her eyes as she cradled the still so very small boy. One of Timmy's arms slipped free and dangled from the blanket swaddling him, his tiny hand and fingers draped lazily upon Cait's wrist. On that wrist, she wore the same bracelet that we'd each been wearing for weeks with its engraving of *Hope*Resilience*Miracles*. Its message was a poignant reminder of all that little Timmy had been through. Having returned to Texas to find each of the babies alive — when for endless weeks away from them Cait didn't know whom among them she would ever see again — she realized her hopes had not been in vain. She was holding a miracle in her arms. The NICU nurses would have to pry that baby boy away from her if she had anything to say about it.

There were more tears that weekend, but also smiles and more joy than any of us had felt in a long time. On Saturday we gathered at the home of Anne's fellow Derm resident, Tim, who with his wife Ami hosted a much belated baby shower for Anne. It was a wonderful celebration, festive and fun, with balloons and ribbons, cake and sweets, and four framed black and white photographs prominently perched on the mantle above the fireplace in their family room. A close-up picture of each baby had been placed in an ebony frame, each image with a name spelled in tall, white letters beneath it: TIMOTHY, EDDA, LILY, WYATT.

The babies were all asleep in the pictures. Timmy with his face burrowed deep into the crook of his arm; Edda's head propped on the palm of one hand, the fingers of the other resting lightly on her cheek; Lily's forearms drawn up snugly around her chest and her lips parted, giving just the hint of a smile; and Wyatt flat on his back, sleeping so soundly he seemed lost in his dreams. Captured by the camera, each of their faces appears pudgy to the point of being nearly plump, their forearms and fingers almost fat, and except for the nasal cannulas and feeding tubes taped to their cheeks and chins, they might have been *regular* newborns. But the photographs did more than transform the babies; they also seemed to transport each of them for a few magical hours that Saturday afternoon from the confinement of the NICU to the company of the friends and family who so desperately longed for them.

We celebrated Father's Day that weekend, too. It was Rob's first, and Donna marked the special occasion by cooking so much food for her son-in-law I thought there might be enough leftovers to last till his second. On Sunday morning, we went to church together for the first time in no one knew how long. And of course we trekked to the hospital to see the babies as frequently as we could. Suddenly, we were allowing ourselves the luxury of indulging in the kind of questions we had for too long been afraid to even ask. Questions like: "How much longer until they leave the NICU?" and "Who's going to be the first to go home?"

There was one more positive that came out of that trip. Donna described it briefly when we sent out an email update shortly after returning home.

> "Big Tim" was able to feed Timmy his first bottle on Monday. There was real concern about Timmy's ability to swallow because of his vocal cord paralysis. Everyone gathered around as Tim placed the teeny-little bottle into Timmy's mouth — he sucked away with no sputtering or coughing at all!! His voice is really affected (you need to watch for him to cry rather than expecting to hear him!) but we're hoping the vocal cord that is still intact will get stronger over time and help to compensate...

There was a reply in my inbox the following morning from Lisa, the office manager of a construction company with whom my business worked. She'd been distributing our email updates throughout the office and to their field personnel since the babies' birth and was responding for them all when she wrote, "We wish you all the best as your roller coaster ride begins to journey through the lower hills and hopefully to level ground soon."

Maybe, I thought, ground level was coming into sight. There were rumblings that Edda and Lily might be able to come home by their original due date in late July. Timmy would soon be scheduled for another bowel surgery and — if everything went okay — to have his ostomy bag removed. If his GI tract could manage after that, he might be following his sisters home. We knew that Wyatt still had a long road ahead. Fluid was being removed via the reservoir in his head almost daily. That would likely continue until he was old enough to have a V-P shunt implanted. No one was talking about a time frame for him leaving the NICU. But after so much had gone so wrong, things seemed to be smoothing out. As I reread Lisa's reply I was more hopeful than ever that she was right about the roller coaster ride coming to its end.

CHAPTER 13

DOL 85 to 107
Three weeks in July

B<small>Y THE BEGINNING OF</small> J<small>ULY</small> we all thought Wyatt was turning a corner, finally reaching the top of a wall he had been so desperately climbing. Though still in a world of hurt, he was more stable than ever. But that changed suddenly. When the news reached us it was as unexpected as it was devastating. The memories from that time are chilling…

I remember the tablecloth. It was pistachio green. I can see the cream linen napkin, too, crisply folded beside my place setting. The neatly arranged silver flatware still untouched. Steaming black coffee in the white china cup in front of me.

"Don't make such a big deal of it, Dad," says Erin. "Get yourself something to eat. The buffet is great."

She's seated on my right, Donna to my left. They are both spreading cream cheese on freshly toasted bagels. I am fuming about having wasted 20 minutes at the hotel's front desk debating the room bill when I wanted to be enjoying breakfast with my wife and daughter.

Erin's phone rings. She reaches into her purse, looks at her phone, and lifts it to her ear. She does not even bother to say hello. "I'm having breakfast with Mom and Dad, Anne. I'll call you later."

But Anne talks right over her sister.

I lift my coffee to my lips and sip. It's still hot. My eyes meet Erin's for a second. She turns away, looking down at her plate. I tell myself it's nothing. Just a conversation. They *are* identical twins; they have talked to each other first thing in the morning since they began babbling in their cribs.

For a long time Erin says nothing. Then she's shaking her head, saying, "No! It's not your fault. How can you say that?"

Silence follows. I can't hear Anne's voice at all.

"No, you're not," Erin says.

More silence. Donna puts her knife down, cream cheese still on the blade.

"Don't say that!" Erin is agitated now. "You're not a bad mom. That doesn't make you a bad mother."

Donna's eyes are fixed on Erin.

"I'm going to go up to the room. I'll call you back in five minutes." She reaches for her purse. I can tell she does not know how to say what she must.

"Anne thinks she's a terrible mother?" I ask, knowing full well that's not all that's going on.

"She slept in this morning. It's her first day off since she returned to work. She forgot to put her cell phone by the bed —"

"Good for her," I interject.

"When she checked her phone this morning she saw that the NICU had been trying to reach her all night." She stops there.

Donna's face is ashen; she knows something is seriously wrong. And she knows in her intuitive way that it is Wyatt. When she asks Erin to explain, I hear only one word.

"Meningitis."

Less than a day earlier, Donna and I are waiting. Erin is hard to spot at first. She is mixed in the horde of people riding the long escalator that carries the mass up from the Metro buried deep under Washington, D.C. It is a hot summer evening, the first day of July, a Thursday, and for Erin the beginning of a long Fourth of July weekend. Donna and I are in town to celebrate our 31st wedding anniversary. We haven't seen our eldest daughter since her twin sister's babies were born. Erin is joining us for a night of wine and pasta in a bistro just off DuPont Circle. And then, because we don't want her to have to ride the subway back to her apartment in Bethesda at a late hour, she will spend the night with us at our hotel a few blocks from the Metro station.

She is radiant when I finally catch sight of her at the top of the escalator, and she beams when I hand her the bouquet of red and pink carnations I bought from a street vendor. She gives Donna and me a kiss and the smile on her face just plain lifts me. I draw her closer, hug her and when we release I tell her how much I've missed her, how much I love her.

We turn to head toward the hotel, and as we do I stop momentarily and point out the inscription cut into the apron of the Metro station's concrete concourse where it circumscribes the escalators rising from below. The words are Walt Whitman's. Erin is beginning the fourth and final year of her residency; she has worked long hours in the wards and clinics at Walter Reed; she has seen our soldiers returned in pieces from their tours in Afghanistan and Iraq and knows something about the pain and loss they endure.

Thus in silence in dreams' projections,
Returning, resuming, I thread my way through the hospitals;
The hurt and wounded I pacify with soothing hand,
I sit by the restless all dark night —
Some are so young, some suffer so much —
I recall the experiences sweet and sad.

"The poem reminds me of you," I tell her, and after I've read it aloud, I pull her close once more and tell her how proud she has made her mom and me.

Everything has changed the next morning. Erin's expression is one I hardly recognize. When I push open the door to our hotel room she is sitting on the edge of the bed talking with Anne. Her expression is void of emotion. She is all business now. It's clear she has abandoned the notion that she should be debating good mothering with Anne. They are both physicians. They both understand the cold calculus doctors have to employ. What either of them feels is of little consequence; nothing matters besides what's *out there*, the disease and its pathology. Erin's questions are quick and direct. She nods knowingly at her sister's responses. She does not acknowledge me when I walk into the room; as she continues talking with her sister, she still does not. Her eyes are focused on the wall across from her. She's deep in thought. It is not until she puts her phone down that she looks at her mother and me. But her expression is mostly blank. She says something about a bacterial infection, that it is swift moving, about ventriculitis being likely. Something about antibiotics and not knowing if they will work in time. There is a long silence then; none of us know what to say. Finally, I reach my hand out and pull her up from the end of the bed. I take her hand and Donna's, and I say that maybe we ought to pray. I don't remember what I prayed except I knew we were asking God for a miracle.

Before we leave the hotel, Donna sends a quick email. The subject line reads: "Urgent Prayer Request." In it she briefly explains that Wyatt has developed meningitis. The little guy is really sick, she writes, and we all could use your prayers. That's it; she doesn't have to say anything else. The first responses come from my family. They get right to the point. My sister, Mary, sends just this: "Praying and sent to others who will pray. Keep me posted." Bill expresses his thoughts in less than two lines: "God promised us grace, and through grace, strength. God knows you need it and I remind him."

Donna and I drive home in silence. There is nothing to say. The rest of the holiday weekend is like a slow torture. I recall that the days and nights seemed like they would never end. I don't remember who I talk to when. What difference does it make? I begin thinking the less I know the better. What I do learn is frightening enough. In the days following Father's Day, Rob began to notice small amounts of fluid accumulating around the reservoir on top of Wyatt's head. He knows it wasn't there previously, suspects it shouldn't be there now. He points it out to Chris, the Neonatology fellow he had gotten to know so well in recent weeks. Chris shares Rob's concern with Neurology, but the neurosurgeon does not seem fazed by the observation. He says something about a positive pressure system that will not allow anything into Wyatt's head; the reservoir is only for pulling fluid *out*. Rob is wary; he fears that if fluid is oozing out then couldn't something also get *in*? The neurosurgeon says no.

But as days pass, more and more cerebrospinal fluid is accumulating in Wyatt's reservoir. The captured CSF is no longer clear but cloudy. Subsequent taps produce fluid that shows a tinge of pink and then yellow. It is sent to the lab. When they learn the results, the NICU team spends the early morning hours of July 2nd trying repeatedly to reach Anne and Rob. But they are both sound asleep, exhausted. They do not realize Rob's cell phone battery has died, that Anne mistakenly left hers in the kitchen the night before. They only know they need to contact the parents. Their youngest son has meningitis and is close to death.

The clock is ticking for Wyatt, but for me it has stopped. Donna and I have nothing to do but wait for the phone call we hope will not come. Yet we are desperate to hear from Anne. When she does finally call she is completely spent. The sound of her voice is crushing. I know she is reaching the end of her rope and there is nothing I can do for her. The news is bad. Wyatt was irritable for hours and then began vomiting. Now he has become totally listless, barely alive. The staff suspects he will begin having seizures soon. She does not say what will happen then.

When I hand the phone to my wife, I cannot make out much of anything between her and Anne. They talk for a long time, and in the last few minutes I see that Donna is crying. After she hangs up, I ask if Anne is going to be okay.

Donna sighs. "She asked me to forgive her for being a bad mother."

I say there is no point in Anne blaming herself.

"She said she thinks that she wants Wyatt to die, that she can't take seeing him suffer any more," Donna blurts out.

I feel tears in my eyes.

"She said he's so young and has already been through so much. She wants the suffering to stop. She wants it to stop now…"

"What about him?"

"They are pretty sure that the infection will be complicated by ventriculitis if he lives. They will have to remove the reservoir until the infection clears. That's more brain surgery. And until they can operate again they will have to go back to tapping straight into his brain with a syringe to relieve the pressure."

She explains that inflammation of the ventricles will cause more severe brain damage… that nobody can say how additional surgeries will affect him… that going back to sticking needles into his brain would be anything but good for Wyatt.

I struggle to digest it all but one thing is completely clear. Poor little Wyatt is being tortured — and for what? If he even lives, the trauma will leave his brain in shambles.

"Annie asked me what kind of life I thought Wyatt would have if he did survive."

I waited for Donna to continue.

"I said the hardest thing for any mom is seeing her child suffer. I told her I didn't know how it would go for Wyatt. No one can know."

"And?"

"When I said that, she started sobbing."

Now Donna is fighting to hold back her own tears. "That's when she asked me if I thought she was a bad mother because she wanted her child to die."

"It's Dave Smith, Tim."

I picked up the phone only to find I couldn't speak.

"Tim, is that you? Are you there? Tim, are you okay?"

It's a full minute before I can talk, and in the silence I realize that no, I am not all right. I am about to ask a man I met only weeks earlier to stand in for me on what will likely be the hardest day of my daughter's life. I also realize that it is no coincidence that this man is now in my life and Anne's. And it is no small consolation that I know he will do what I'm about to ask of him faithfully and without hesitation.

Dave is the pastor of a small community church not far from where Anne and Rob live. I found his church when I realized that we were going to need *serious* support from a local "body of Christ" in San Antonio. That's what I was searching for when I came across the website for Northwest Community Church. It prominently featured on its homepage a passage from Paul's Letter to the Romans: "But God demonstrates His own love toward us, in that while we were yet sinners, Christ died for us." That very same morning I had sent the exact scripture to my wife and daughters. Coincidence or affirmation, it was reason enough to introduce myself to Dave. It didn't take long for me to come to trust him as a brother. Now I will ask him to be more than that. "I didn't think you'd get back to me so quick, with tomorrow being Sunday and all," I say, my voice still weak.

"Hey, we're here for you," he says in a reassuring voice.

Though 1,800 miles separate us, I can see him in my mind's eye. He is not a big man, but in that moment his heart seems to me as big as all of Texas. When he asks, "What do you need me to do?" that's all I need to hear.

He already knows the dire situation Wyatt is in; Anne has emailed him with enough of the details. I tell Dave that my daughter and her husband are not sure where to turn or what to do. Though they'd gone through something like this with Timmy, it was easier to hold onto hope for him. Maybe then we were all just blithely naïve. But Wyatt has been through so much for so long that their hope for him is spent. They are walking in the shadow of the valley of death now. They are scared. Things have spiraled out of control.

I tell Dave that Donna and I are ready to go to San Antonio right now, but Anne isn't sure she wants us to fly out just yet. Rob's folks and his older sister and her baby were already planning a visit sometime in the coming week. They don't want the chaos of too many people. Maybe they don't know what they want. My heart is breaking for them.

Dave says the church is already praying. He has been unable to reach Anne, but as soon as he can he will arrange to visit her and Rob and Wyatt. They will pray together.

I tell him I am grateful. But that is not what I need from him.

"When Wyatt dies —" my voice catches and it is almost impossible to continue.

Dave waits patiently while I struggle to string the words together.

"If we lose Wyatt, my daughter is going to need her dad. Right away. I'll be on the next plane but... I don't want her to be alone when he goes. You be there for me, brother. I need you to be there for my daughter. I need you to be there for me."

I am crying when I ask him to be the dad she will need until I can get there.

I remember the tiger lilies, their fiery red and gold petals, and the wild flowers lining the country roads around our home that June. By the first week of July they're fading fast. The tips of the lilies' once green lance-shaped leaves are brown and beginning to wilt, and the plants' long, sturdy stems are already starting their slow bend back toward the dirt from which they sprang. This is how it is, I know; I remember the prophet Isaiah's words: *For all flesh is as grass, and all the glory of man as the flower of grass. The grass withers, and the flower thereof falls away.* The lilies are a harbinger. Winter will come. For the most beautiful things, it comes too soon.

I roll my bike slowly forward until I can no longer balance it, unclip from its pedals and slide off the saddle to let my feet touch the road. The bridge's deck is narrow with barely enough room for one car to pass, and as I consider this, it occurs to me that I have never stopped here before, though I have ridden over it a hundred times. This is the bridge where — once it is crossed — the hills of the Devereux Road ride begin. But I have not come to test myself against the climbs. I have come to ask for something. I'm here to ask for Wyatt's life back.

Downstream from where I stand, towering sycamore trees arch toward the sky from either side of the river, their long, thick branches reaching over the water to form an entwining canopy of leaves and limbs. It is beautiful, the kind of image that makes me want to stop and take a picture, would make me want to paint it if I could. I tell myself I should have stopped here before, and promise myself I will stop here again. But I turn from the sycamores, the lily-laden banks and the gurgling river that runs between them. I turn because the water downstream is part of the past, already come and gone. If I am going to ask for a miracle, if I am going to ask to have Wyatt back, then I will do it facing the future. I know what is downstream, and what is there we can never have again.

There is not much to see upstream. I see why now, on so many rides across this bridge, I have never bothered to venture more than a glance in this direction. It is an entangled mess of reeds and prickers, of swamp willows and mounds of rotting brush lying in muddy heaps around gaunt trunks, with scraps of garbage and waste marooned within it, all washed up away from the banks by the river's frequent flooding. There are afternoon flecks of sunlight reflecting off the surface of the water, but in less than 50 yards the glitter recedes and the river is gone, bending sharply to the north, lost in the surrounding wood. But I continue looking, straining to see, as if there might yet be something hidden from sight, something coming from just around the river's bend. There is still time, isn't there? There can still be hope.

I want him back. That is my prayer, my petition.

Lord God, let Wyatt Lee live.

You can give him back to us.

As the Fourth of July weekend came to an end Wyatt was hanging by barely a thread. His medical chart read like a train wreck. The complications from the infection were manifold. It had caused sepsis that created havoc in his tiny body. His heart rate and respiratory rates began increasing while his oxygen saturation levels plummeted. The little boy's lips began smacking and his shoulders shuddering. He was started on phenobarbital to sedate him and to help control his seizing.

Late on Sunday night, Wyatt was re-intubated in preparation for surgery. As critical as his condition was the operation was unavoidable: he needed to have the source of his infection removed. Early the next day, after being administered anesthesia, the still so very small baby boy was wheeled out of the NICU into a waiting OR. A knit teddy bear Donna had made months before lay in his isolette beside his head. Anne had placed it there.

Less than 30 minutes later a neurosurgeon began to make an incision in Wyatt's head, reopening the same spot he had cut into only weeks before. He carried the incision down until the ventricular reservoir appeared. He carefully lifted the device up and out — this was the location where the meningitis infection originated — and as he did, straw-colored cerebrospinal fluid oozed from Wyatt's brain. The CSF was collected and sent to the lab for interpretation. The incision was then sutured closed. The surgeon's post-op notes dryly recorded that "the child tolerated the procedure well."

How much more Wyatt could tolerate, however, no one would say.

In the hours following the surgery, Wyatt's respiratory function became so distressed that he had to be put back onto the high-frequency oscillating vent that had kept him breathing in the very first, difficult weeks of his life. He remained under sedation and was having frequent brain taps to draw out the ever-accumulating CSF. Ongoing head ultrasounds showed an evolving hemorrhage. A CT scan revealed that Wyatt had also suffered a stroke. His torso and limbs were swelling as extra fluid accumulated in his tissues. To make matters worse, his Broviac catheter that provided IV access for his necessary medications was leaking. A blood clot had formed at the site of the catheter's entry, and an expanding mass of tissue was forming around his right clavicle. The device had to be removed and a new avenue for catheterization found.

It was DOL 89. Wyatt was nearly three months old. I knew no one gave him much chance to live any longer, and even if he did he would have to face another brain surgery to have the reservoir re-implanted. Anne and Rob's hopes for their son were near gone. Donna held onto little more than they. I didn't know what to think.

DOL 92: Thursday, July 8

Time continued to crawl for all of us. We were waiting for the inevitable. If it did not come today, it would tomorrow or the day after. The little good news there was came via the lab results — Wyatt's CSF cultures showed the infection abating and then, finally, gone. Another plus was that a neonatologist had been able to get a peripheral arterial catheter into Wyatt to replace the failed Broviac catheter. But despite the help of the HFOV and the fact that the meningitis had subsided, Wyatt was slowly dying. His oxygen saturation levels were too low. As a last straw, the neonatologists ordered inhaled nitric oxide therapy to supplement their effort to avert outright respiratory failure. There were often multiple caregivers at Wyatt's bedside; he was never left alone. Everyone was doing everything they could. I don't think anyone expected him to make it.

But Wyatt Lee hung on.

He would have to clear at least one more hurdle to have any hope of surviving. Images from the head ultrasounds performed after the reservoir's removal showed Wyatt's right lateral ventricle still increasing in size, as well as a prominent hemorrhage within the left lateral ventricle appearing. Despite the recent onset of meningitis, ventriculitis and the associated complications, Wyatt had severe hydrocephalus that predated all of that and it was not going away. To prevent further brain damage, he would need the device re-implanted, sooner rather than later. It would further stress a baby already stretched beyond the breaking point. We were all waiting for the balloon to burst. Would this surgery finally do it? The trauma of another operation would probably kill him; without it he wouldn't survive for long. Anne and Rob were counseled by the neurosurgeon on the surgical plan for the re-implantation of the reservoir, the expected results and the complications. They claimed to understand the risks and benefits. They signed the consent form.

Anne would later tell me how in the hours before the earlier surgery to remove the reservoir, she had spent time with Wyatt, talking to him. She had placed his teddy bear next to him. He opened his eyes then; for a brief moment it seemed he had heard her voice. He fixed his gaze on his mother. She told him he would be okay, that she would be there waiting for him when he came back to the NICU. But her little guy had not opened his eyes since, and he did not open his eyes again when she talked to him before the surgery to put the reservoir back into his brain. He would not have heard her anyway. Anne was whispering so quietly she barely made a sound. She told him she was sorry he had suffered so much. She told him she was sorry *she* had made him suffer like this. "It's okay if you can't fight any more," she told her son. "You don't need to hang on any longer if you're doing it for me. It's okay to just let go."

Wyatt's consent form was not the only one Anne and Rob signed that week. They also signed another one for Timmy. He needed his bowels reopened.

His laparotomy had not been unexpected, the date having been set by the same pediatric surgeon who had already operated on him twice, but falling as it did in the midst of Wyatt's struggle with meningitis, Timmy's surgery felt like a blow below the belt. For Anne and Rob, it had to be almost unbearable. One operation on top of another when each of their boys had already gone through so much. It was unfair. But when I talked to Anne the evening after Timmy's surgery, she was oddly laconic about the whole ordeal. He did fine, she told me; they reconnected his bowel and removed the ileostomy bag without any problem. They also repaired a hernia. Oh, and while they were at it, she said, they circumcised him, too. "Is that all?" I asked, half-joking. He did okay, she repeated. She said she had given him his *Uglydoll* to take into the OR to keep him company — as if that would be all he would need — and then added, "You know Timmy. He's basically indestructible."

Anne told me she thought that would be the end of it. Once Timmy recovered from the surgery and was removed from the ventilator they could turn all their attention back to Wyatt. They knew Timmy would not be allowed to eat for a few days and then only gradually weaned back onto a full feeding schedule, but if that was going to be the extent of his problems they'd gladly take it. Timmy might finally have finished running his own personal gauntlet. Though she had long since given up taking anything for granted with her babies, Anne told me she thought this could be his last major obstacle. How I hoped she was right.

I felt like a defendant waiting for a jury to return its verdict. There was little to do besides wait. Donna found some solace talking with friends, but as for me, I was fine with isolation. I talked to my older brothers, and those conversations were poignant enough. John called only a short time after Timmy was out of surgery and just a day before Wyatt was scheduled for his next one.

"How's the little guy — who is it now? With so many babies, I can't keep track, you know."

I couldn't blame my brother for being unable to keep pace with the rapid churning of events in my grandchildren's lives.

"It's both of the boys, I guess." I told him that Timmy's operation had been a *trifecta* — abdominal surgery, hernia, circumcision — but we thought he would recover without a hitch. I tried to be upbeat about Wyatt, telling John that lab results showed he had cleared the meningitis infection, but when my brother suggested that must mean the worst was behind him, I couldn't hide my worries. "He's not doing well — not at all," I said.

There was a long pause. I could hear background noise through John's phone as his pickup rolled along some highway somewhere; he had called on his way home from work. He cleared his throat and said, "I mean, you think the little guy's gonna make it, right... probably?"

I told him the last few days had been downright miserable for Wyatt. "They're sticking a needle into his brain every day; tubes stuck in him everywhere; a machine breathing for him; always pokin' and proddin' him. It's so hard on him."

There was another long pause before he said, "So now what?"

"They're going back into his brain, another surgery." I added that maybe that was a positive sign, suggesting that they wouldn't bother if they didn't think he still had a fighting chance, but I confessed I really didn't know for sure. "Anne only tells me so much. I don't push her."

"Is she okay?"

Again I had to say I didn't know. I didn't know if one day she wouldn't just come totally undone.

"What about Donna?"

She was hanging in there, I said, but it was frustrating being unable to do much of anything to help. "That's the hardest thing, you know — Anne can't do anything to help her children, and we can't do anything to help Anne."

"I don't know how you guys are doing this," he said. "I mean I can't even imagine."

I was dumbstruck. My brother who had not very long ago lost his own son was telling me that he didn't know how *we* were getting through our ordeal.

"I mean it," he said.

"I'm going to tell you how hard *my* life is?" I was not mocking him; I just couldn't equate what his family had gone through with what we were. They had lost so much.

"It was different for us," he said. "It happened and then it was over. We dealt with the aftermath. But this stuff, it just doesn't stop."

I agreed with that. It did seem like it never would and that we couldn't find a way out of it. Things might not get better ever. I told him it was just too difficult to look down the road — especially for the boys.

He sighed and said, "My son had a good life. He really did," and then added, "If you believe all the stuff that's in the Bible then he's in a better place now, anyway. Who knows? Even if it's not true, he's still at rest."

I sat with the phone in my hand for a long time after my brother hung up, just looking at it. I'd ended the conversation by saying Wyatt needed a miracle, but even before the words left my lips I was uneasy. Where had the miracle been for my brother? Why hadn't his son been saved? Maybe I was asking for too much. Maybe the only miracle coming for Wyatt was that he, too, would finally find his rest.

There was no easy way for my brother, Bill, to share what was on his heart.

He had no way of knowing yet how severely harmed Wyatt's brain was, but he seemed to sense the inevitable. A CT scan showed the extensive damage his brain had endured as a result of his bout with ventriculitis. There was dead brain matter everywhere. Not only had the area around Wyatt's ventricles been severely harmed, but there was also significant damage to his frontal lobe. This is the part of the brain that helps a person feel and understand emotion and humor; interact with and relate to others; and recognize and make complex choices in a social context. Language and the creative thinking required to solve complicated problems are seated here. Personality emanates from this area of the brain. Even many of our physical movements are controlled via the frontal lobe. The breadth of loss was staggering. For Anne and Rob, it meant their worst fears coming true: they were losing so much of who their son might have been.

When Bill called, what he had to say, he warned, would not be easy. He told me about a friend of his, Clark, from his college days. They'd had a great time together, living the dream, two young men in a trendy city on the West Coast, all that the world had to offer still lying before them. They graduated and went their separate ways, but over the years were never more than a phone call away. They both started careers, married and decided to raise families. Their wives gave them each a son. And for Clark and his wife, that was where the dream died.

That son was born with severe hydrocephalus. They did not think he would survive long. When he did, they could scarcely imagine that a life could be so tortured, so filled with pain and hardship. For Clark and his wife, life was forever changed. For their son, it was impossible to say what his life really *was*. The damage to his brain was devastating; the physical and cognitive impairments that followed debilitating. Convulsions, seizures and incontinence, deformity and defect — the list was harrowing. It was agonizing even to hear.

"If it comes to it," Bill said, "Annie is going to come to you to ask what they should do."

It took a moment before I understood.

"I don't know the protocol, how they decide," he continued, "or when the doctors feel like there's just no more reason to continue."

"I'm hoping we don't go there again," I told him.

"Again?" I'd never recounted to Bill how the NICU staff had asked Anne and Rob to let them know when they were ready to let Timmy die.

I explained the circumstances briefly to my brother and then said that while Timmy's situation had been acute Wyatt's problems just went on and on. "I think if Wyatt was a cat he'd have just about used up all his lives by now. I don't know what keeps him going."

"You can tell them to stop, can't you?" Bill asked.

"I don't know."

"If the question comes — she's going to look to you, you know."

"I know. But the hard part is I don't know what Anne wants anymore," I said.

"I'm sure she doesn't, either."

"Nobody should have to go through this kind of stuff. How do you choose when there are no good choices?"

"You pray. I know you are."

I told him that I was hoping for a miracle, and he told me he was praying, too, but he wasn't asking for that. "I don't pray for outcomes because I don't know what the right outcome is. I pray for people when I pray. I'm praying for your daughter."

"She and Rob are so tired, so worn down. I'm afraid she's ready to give up on Wyatt."

"It wouldn't be giving up."

"You don't think so?"

"No," he said.

I told him I did not want Anne to have to face that kind of decision again. I worried none of us were strong enough now to make the same choice for Wyatt that she'd made for his brother.

But she didn't have to.

Maybe that was the miracle I was looking for. Maybe Wyatt had been so sick that asking his parents if they wanted to withdraw care was deemed an unnecessary formality. The NICU team would do everything they could for the boy, but in the end he would certainly die. There was no point in making things more painful than need be.

July 9th was DOL 93 for Anne and Rob's babies. That morning, as Wyatt was being rolled from Wilford Hall's NICU into a nearby operating suite, Donna and I were clinging to the hope that he would live to see DOL 94. It was a Friday, and with more than 72 hours elapsed since his last positive CSF culture, the neonatologists agreed with Neurology that it was the right time for re-implantation of Wyatt's ventricular reservoir. If they were going to go ahead with the procedure, the thinking was the sooner the better. I remember the exact date because July 9th is also my brother Mike's birthday. I wanted to call my brother to wish him a happy one. And more than that, I wanted to call him for a fresh boost of faith.

The phone rang so long I was sure it would go to voicemail. When he finally answered I said, "Sleeping in on your birthday, Mike?"

"Not quite, brother. I was on another call and got off as soon as I saw it was you."

I wasted no time wishing him a happy birthday, telling him how much I appreciated him as an older brother. When I asked if he had made any special plans I could hear him hesitate. I should have expected as much. I'd warned him that the next time he'd hear from me could be when I was calling to tell him that my grandson had not made it. He got right to the point.

"How are my little peeps?" He'd been referring to the babies like that since they were days old.

I told him Timmy was doing better by the hour since his surgery, that he was already off his ventilator and they would be starting to give him simple feeds before too long.

"Praise God," he said, and then paused before asking, "And what about Wiley?"

It made me smile that in the midst of a crisis my brother would still call my grandson by the nickname he'd given Wyatt shortly after birth.

"They're wheeling him into surgery right about now." Before I could tell him anything more he cut me off.

"Let's pray, Tim."

I don't know why some prayers are answered while others seem to go unheard. If there was a formula for success someone would have copyrighted it long ago. Mike favors the "make no bones about it" approach. Say what you have to say; be firm about it. That morning, with Wyatt's life hanging in the balance, Mike made his case. I remember he asked that the God who gives life, who gives the *abundant* life promised through Jesus, not take the life already given to Wyatt. But he did not leave it at that; he made it exactly clear what he wanted. "Lord God," he continued, "not only do we claim that abundant life for Wyatt, but we stand against evil, against the thief who comes only to steal, and kill and destroy. In Jesus' name, we tell the thief to be gone; we tell him to take his dirty hands off this baby boy. We want Wiley back. We want him back now."

We were standing together in the driveway in front of our barn when Donna's phone rang. It was now nearly 12 hours since Wyatt had been taken from the NICU into surgery. We had heard by late morning that the surgery had gone well, but nothing since.

Though it was a relief knowing the surgery was over, it was just as likely Wyatt would die in the immediate aftermath of the operation as during the procedure. The rest of the day had gone by slowly, the late morning and long afternoon hours almost interminable for my wife and me. We were trying to enjoy the evening, watching the sun make its exit from the western sky with drinks in our hands. We were hoping no news meant good news.

"It's Annie!" Donna said. Before she could lift the phone to her ear, I put my hand around hers, pulling it away from her.

"It's Papa, honey. How are you doing?" I started to walk up the driveway toward the setting sun, the distance between Donna and me growing with each step. I did not want my wife to be the first to hear what our daughter might have to say. I thought I was prepared for anything. I was wrong.

When Anne told me the news, I started crying, causing Donna to come running to my side, her face already steeled against the hurt of what was to come while her eyes began to well with tears. I pushed her away. Anne was crying, too. She could barely get the words out, but what she said I will never forget.

"You tell your mom," I said. "You tell her yourself." And I handed the phone to Donna without saying a word.

Inside the house, I sent a brief email to my brothers and sisters. I knew they had been praying for Wyatt throughout the day. I wanted to let them know before anyone else: "Wyatt doing OK after surgery, still on vent; long hill to climb yet." And then the stunner: "Tonight he opened his eyes!" When Anne told me Wyatt had opened his eyes it was like a weight lifting from my shoulders. Our miracle had come. I told Anne through my sobs that I was sure of one thing: I believed her son would live. When I hit "send," I did so without sharing what Anne had said to me before I gave the phone to her mother. "I don't get it, Papa. He just doesn't want to give up."

DOL 96: Monday, July 12

But there were more storm clouds. Always more. While Wyatt's improving condition was remarkable — by the end of the weekend he was beginning to breathe well enough on his own that he was weaned from the mechanical ventilators that had kept him alive for the last eight days — trouble returned to knock on Timmy's door.

I never got the facts straight. Anne at this point was shutting down, as if her mind refused to engage any longer with what was happening around her. What she did know was that what happened to Timmy came close to costing him his life. Again.

When Anne called her mom that evening she was so distraught she could hardly speak. Even my levelheaded wife was too upset to make sense of what had happened. After putting the phone down Donna practically howled. "I don't know what else can go wrong for these poor babies!"

I couldn't understand what she tried to recount to me. Something about someone doing something wrong. She thought it was a nurse, but wasn't sure if that's what Anne had said. There was a resident there, and an x-ray tech, too. "There were just too many things going on at one time!" Donna was so exasperated that I didn't know if she was going to throw something or just sit down and cry.

"What happened?"

"A drain got dislodged, came loose. It backed up."

"What drain?"

"Timmy's drain! Who do you think we're talking about?"

"I thought they took his drains out. Isn't that what they operated on him for last week?"

"Yes. No! I mean, yes, they removed his ostomy bag, but there's still some drain somewhere to help him while his bowel heals from the surgery."

"Okay," I said, still not getting it.

"No, it's not okay! The thing came loose — somebody was moving Timmy, rolling him over or picking him up or something — the drain backed up and spilled into his belly."

"How's that happen?"

"I don't know. What difference does it make? Anne said he vomited, that there was fecal matter in it. She thinks he aspirated it."

"And?"

"If it got into his respiratory tract it will cause an infection. She's afraid he'll get septic."

I knew sepsis spelled big trouble.

"If that boy dies from an infection because of some..." My wife couldn't finish her thought. She just dropped her head and started to cry.

Fortunately, after a tense 48 hours of monitoring Timmy for signs of infection, nothing materialized. The incident did, however, throw his growth curve for a loop. He could not return to full feeds until the NICU doctors were confident the potential ill effects of the drain debacle were behind him. The poor guy spent days living on a glucose IV and sucking frantically on a pacifier that did nothing for his hungry tummy. He would lose weight, dropping almost four ounces in the week immediately following, and it would be two full weeks before he would gain it back.

Timmy's weight loss put any talk of him getting out of the NICU and going home on hold. In fact, because all of the babies had problems with eating or breathing or both, I wondered how any of them would ever escape the hospital. We couldn't get anyone in the NICU to even hazard a guess when Timmy, Edda or Lily might at last be set free. There were still too many variables, so much about their futures that remained unpredictable. And for Wyatt, whose eventual need for V-P shunt surgery meant he would certainly be the last of Anne's babies out of intensive care, going home was not even on the radar. It was more than frustrating.

Frustration is one thing, but the fact that Wyatt had survived was truly a wonder. He should have died. Throughout that first week of July as the meningitis and ventriculitis progressed, the NICU staff kept a tireless vigil over the baby boy, but no one held out much hope that Wyatt could possibly beat his infection.

The word *miracle* literally means "wonders," and the wonder of a miracle arises from the fact that its cause is unknowable. It is an extraordinary event, something outside of the natural realm. We were given Wyatt back. No one expected that. No one could say why he had been given another chance at life. But as worries about survival were gradually replaced by concerns for Wyatt's recovery, we were all left to wonder what *life* actually remained for the child. How does one even begin to define what a "life worth living" is, anyway? It would be one kind of miracle for Wyatt to survive; it would be a wonder of a whole other kind if he survived to live a life that wasn't in many respects *already* dead. And if that was the case, then we were still waiting to see the miracle unfold.

I would ponder that, wondering just what kind of miracle we had received when God gave Wyatt back to us. I thought about the miracles of Jesus, the signs and wonders He'd performed. And I would pray. I would stop every time I crossed the Brandywine on the Devereux Road bridge, pull my bike to rest against its old iron trusses and offer my prayer, first of thanks and then supplication. The miracle, I knew, had begun here. Wyatt's life was still *upstream*, still in front of him. But unlike the wedding feast where Jesus had turned water into wine, this miracle was far from finished. Wyatt's miracle would be of a different sort — a slow unfolding, a retrieving, really — of what once should have been his and, I prayed, would be his again one day. His miracle, it occurred to me, might be more like Lazarus'. There, the story goes, a dead man was raised when Jesus called him out from his tomb. But that's only half of the story.

By the middle of July I was confident enough of Wyatt's survival that I sent an email update to our friends and family. For many, this would be the first they'd heard about Wyatt since we told them of his meningitis two weeks before. It was also my attempt to put into words how I thought the second part of the story of Lazarus might apply to Wyatt and to us.

> Hey All — I have to admit, the week following Wyatt's diagnosis of meningitis was one of the hardest times our family has ever been through. It was obviously hardest for Anne & Rob and, especially, Wyatt. The last couple days, things have stabilized, but the long term still remains very much in question...
>
> All through this time, I said that we were looking for a miracle, and I believe Wyatt's survival is certainly that. By

last weekend, in the hours after his surgery to put another reservoir in Wyatt's head, we just didn't know that he would make it back. Anne had even told Wyatt that it was OK if he couldn't fight anymore, that he didn't need to hang on any longer for her, that it would be OK if he just let go...

I'm happy to say that Wyatt didn't let go. By the end of the weekend he was able to breathe on his own, open his eyes, and spend some time in his mom's arms. In my book, that was a miracle by any measure.

But Wyatt faces some real challenges ahead. Surviving the meningitis was only the beginning. We now know from CT scans of his brain that there has been considerable damage to his frontal lobe. I'm no neurologist, but the impact of that kind of injury on a person is devastating. The developmental challenges, the disabilities for him are harrowing if we look very far down that road. For Anne & Rob it is just so discouraging...

Donna has been great, however, to point out that little Wyatt has been such a fighter his whole life. Whatever abilities or capacities he may have lost in the course of the trials he has endured, he has never lost that tenacity, that drive to hang on. That's who Wyatt is and that part of him gives us all hope and the courage to hang in there with him.

Over this time, I have thought a lot about miracles. In John's gospel, the story is told that when Jesus came to visit Martha and her sister, Mary, he had come because their brother was sick. But He had come too late — Lazarus was already dead! And though Jesus told them that their brother would rise again, when He came to where they had laid Lazarus, Jesus was so troubled and moved, that He wept...

Our family came to a similar place last week as we saw Wyatt slipping away. I know I wept. But like Martha and Mary, we were given our loved one back. What strikes me most now about the account of Jesus raising Lazarus from the dead is that when He called to Lazarus, *"Come forth!"* Lazarus did so, but he *"was bound hand and foot with wrappings; and his face was wrapped around with a cloth."* I think that must have been a terrifying sight — this mummy walking blindly out from a tomb — why hadn't Jesus just come and healed Lazarus while he was still sick? Why this? But Jesus turned to Martha and Mary and the others there and said, *"Unbind him, and let him go."*

There is a lesson in that for our family, I think. It will now be our job to unwrap, unbind and let Wyatt go. What will we find as we do? We are both fearful and hopeful. How far Wyatt will go is hard to say, but as we work together to unbind him we trust that God's grace will be there for us all. So much of this miracle still lies ahead...

Maybe I was only grasping at straws, struggling to come to terms with the fact that when Wyatt and his brother and sisters did come home, none of them would be coming home whole. Lazarus had been raised from the dead, but the Bible records nothing more about him other than to say he was seen the following day "reclining at the table" with Jesus, in his sister Martha's house. When he was unbound and set free from his wrappings was he also set completely free from the after-effects of the sickness that had killed him? Nobody knows. We only know that his family continued to care for him.

So what about miracles? Anne was so shaken by the events of the first two weeks of July she didn't even try to explain what happened to her son except to shrug her shoulders and say with a funny, perplexing grin, "That's just Wyatt being Wyatt!" Rob was never comfortable with the idea that his children were going through some kind of manifestation of the miraculous. He would later tell me that Anne's pregnancy, the premature delivery of their babies and the traumas that filled the first scary months of life were, to him, something cumulatively more akin to a kind of "black swan event" — a rare, unexpected event yielding an impact that explodes beyond the boundaries of the norm. To Rob, Wyatt's survival was implausible, but not impossible; statistics always include room for anomaly. For me, whether Wyatt was an outlier or a miracle wasn't the point. I knew that by the middle of that summer that God *was* a "rewarder of those who seek Him" and I would soon be holding the reward in my arms.

When Donna and I flew back to Texas on July 22nd we could hardly wait to get to the hospital to see Wyatt and his siblings. An early morning flight out of Philadelphia had us in San Antonio by midday. We rented a car, rushed to Lackland Air Force Base without stopping to eat lunch, showed the guard at the Main Gate the 30-day guest pass Anne had given us and headed toward the parking lots surrounding Wilford Hall. When we finally found a space it was so far from the hospital's entrance that we were both dripping with sweat when we reached the air-conditioned lobby. But no matter, we practically ran down the long corridor with its wall of pictures and memorabilia, stopping only to wash our hands at the sink just outside the double doors that led into the NICU. Anne was three floors below, seeing patients. Rob said he would meet us at the NICU, but in our rush we had beaten him there.

I saw Timmy first as I walked toward the corner dominated by the babies whose cribs still identified them as Spillane 'A', Spillane 'B' and so on. He was sound asleep in an open crib, swaddled in a white receiving blanket speckled with blue dots so that only his head and the tops of his shoulders were visible.

In a larger double crib where the girls lay, Lily was also asleep, her purple pacifier having fallen from her lips to rest in a spot just under her chin. Edda was awake. She was staring intently at the white ceiling tiles, one arm alternately reaching up and then slowly down, her fingers and thumb spreading first apart and then closed, as if keeping time. She continued gesticulating with quiet concentration, completely unfazed by the two new visitors standing nearby. Deciding it probably best not to disturb her, I stepped away and looked toward the back of the room, where the isolette in which Wyatt was still regularly confined was set. A nurse stood to one side, leaning over so I couldn't quite see the baby beneath her. She was untangling wires and tubes with one hand while gently unraveling a receiving blanket with the other. I could hear Wyatt's protesting grunts, but he did not cry. When I took another couple steps closer, the nurse turned to face me. She was holding her little charge in her arms. She smiled, recognizing Donna and me.

"He's been a little irritable this morning," she said.

"I guess he's entitled to be," I replied.

The nurse took a step toward a rocking chair to the side of the empty isolette. But as she was about to sit she stopped and asked, "How about it Grandpa? You can hold him if you want."

I was startled by the offer, not sure that holding a baby who had been so sick was a good idea, but before I could say anything I felt Donna's hand against the small of my back. "Sit down," she said. "Hold your grandson."

His head, even now after three and a half months, seemed so fragile and small resting in the palm of my hand. There was a large bump on top, a reddish semicircular scar around it. Beneath the flap of skin, sticking down into his brain, I knew, was the new reservoir. I knew he needed it to survive. I also knew it was what had nearly killed him.

"Your hands are shaking!" Donna scolded.

I didn't answer, did not even look up. My trembling grip seemed to suit Wyatt just fine. He had fallen fast asleep. He was wearing a blue and white striped top with short sleeves. A large brown baseball glove was sewn onto the front of it; a bright white baseball rested in the center of the mitt. I watched him breathe, slow and heavy, and as he did the ball and glove on his chest rose and fell.

When I lifted my eyes up from the boy in my arms it was to turn and watch the monitor to my side. I didn't care what the numbers were saying; that they were there told me all I needed to know. He was alive.

On the ceiling, in the center of the room, a sign read, "Quiet Please." I grinned. Looking back down at Wyatt, there was nothing I could possibly say.

This was not my reward.

This was a gift.

CHAPTER 14
DOL 108 to 198
Coming home

W<small>YATT ALONE WAS MORE THAN</small> enough proof for the existence
of miracles. In fact, once home I sent out another update, along
with a photograph of Wyatt. "I'm attaching the picture," I wrote,
"so you can see for yourself what a bona fide miracle looks like!"
The photo was taken the afternoon I'd first held him, right after
the nurse had pried him from my arms and put him back into
his isolette. The picture captured Wyatt in a moment of pure
contentment. He is wrapped in a cheery emerald green blanket
with only the top of his ball glove shirt peeking out. And though
he is sound asleep, he has one arm raised up over his head, the
other out to his side, and an impish grin that seems to say, "So,
what do you think of me now?"

The picture touched a lot of people. Bob Griffiths, whose construction company I'd been doing business with for nearly 20 years,
admitted that every time he got an email update he'd cringed.
You just never knew what to expect, he'd said. But now, seeing the
smile on Wyatt's face, Bob also saw the light at the end of a tunnel.

336

"I look forward to these now," he wrote. "Thanks for keeping us in the loop! God bless all of you, and let everyone know that we are pulling for them." Likewise, my brother Mike expressed his relief, writing, "Standing in the gap with you and the rest for our little quads, and for Anne and Rob, is a great calling and privilege." My youngest sister, Laura, simply said, "Oh, Tim, how great is our God? It's hard to see Wyatt's picture through my tears…"

But Wyatt was not the only miracle in this family.

On July 24th, Timmy, Edda and Lily joined their younger brother in celebrating their birthday. Or rather what might have been their birthday had they been carried full term. By the time they reached the "corrected gestational age" of 40 weeks, they had been out of Anne's womb for 108 days. Any *one* of the babies now weighed more than the four of them combined when they were born in early April. Lily was still biggest at 6lb 12oz. Wyatt was again the smallest of the bunch, weighing in at a pound lighter. Edda had a growth spurt in the middle of July, surpassing Timmy (who remained on a restricted diet), and she was tipping the scales at a tad over six pounds.

Now instead of wondering which of the babies had the best chance of survival, we began betting on the order in which the babies would come home. I went all-in on Timmy, figuring the rest would follow in order of their birth. Understandably, no one was willing to wager on Wyatt — we knew just getting him home at all would be like winning the Powerball. Everyone else divided their chips between the two girls.

By the end of July we thought the babies' sojourn in the NICU was almost over, the minefield crossed, the roller coaster ride finally coming to an end. But any lofty thoughts of the future, we would discover, were still premature. There were bumps in the road ahead. There always were.

We had to hold on to hope. Sometimes it was all that was carrying us forward.

Only days after returning home from San Antonio, Donna was on the phone with Anne, who'd called while my wife and I sat on the screened porch enjoying a few minutes together before dinner. Donna was desperately trying to console our daughter. But it was not going well. They had been talking about Wyatt, about another surgery. The conversation seemed to have shifted to Timmy, though. When Donna set the phone on her lap she said nothing.

"No problems with Lily and Edda?" I prompted, knowing they had not been the topic of conversation.

"Wyatt's going to have to have another surgery. They're having problems draining his reservoir. It keeps getting clogged." She said Wyatt was getting increasingly irritable. The NICU docs didn't want him going back into respiratory distress. They were consulting with Neurology to determine when to go ahead with the V-P shunting procedure.

"So soon?"

"He's big enough now. And pretty stable. They don't want to miss a window of opportunity."

She sat quietly for a few minutes, staring straight ahead and then, taking a deep breath, she continued. The bad news was Timmy's. In order for Timmy to be released from the NICU they had to do an MRI of his brain, she explained. "They did the scan yesterday."

"They actually said something about Timmy going home?"

"They do the scan to determine what services a baby will require after being released from the hospital. Anne knew Timmy would have some issues because of his brain hemorrhages."

"And?" I asked impatiently.

Donna started to describe the extent of the damage to his brain as if she were simply going down a checklist, but her voice broke, and she choked on her sobs when she tried to continue. It didn't matter. I'd heard enough. I didn't want to hear anymore.

I rose early the next morning and booked a flight back to San Antonio. I told Donna I would do whatever I could to help Anne get through it.

DOL 119: Wednesday, August 4

I was doing my best not to reach over the counter and start choking the guy.

"I don't see any email, sir. We don't seem to have any record of it. Maybe you could have her — did you say she was your daughter? Have her call us, and then we'll see if we can't do something."

I swallowed deliberately, looking down at my hands grasping the edge of the counter separating the young airman from me. He couldn't have been more than 20, with acne all over his face and big, black plastic glasses. I decided that strangling the youngster inside the security post might get me shot, but a little intimidation couldn't hurt.

"Listen to me, soldier," I said looking straight into his eyes. "My daughter is a captain. She's a doctor. But right now her son — *my* grandson* — is in that hospital behind you, and they're operating on his brain. You do what you have to in order to get me in there. Get me a pass and get me in there now!" I pushed the 30-day guest pass into his chest. "The damn thing just expired yesterday!"

When I got to the NICU, they had just brought Wyatt back from the operating room. Rob glanced up from the isolette for a brief moment to tell me that Anne was in the bathroom, and then turned back to his son. Wyatt looked awful. Intubated and with clear plastic surgical wrappings covering the top of his head, his face was bright red and swollen, his whole body puffy and his bare torso mottled red and purple. His legs were stiff, his arms taut by his sides; his eyes closed so tight that it seemed like he was trying to ensure he'd never have to open them again. A nurse and two respiratory techs were at the side of the isolette, rearranging him, trying to position his little body just so, trying to make his breathing a little easier. One of Wyatt's lungs had collapsed during the V-P shunt surgery. I wondered how many times a baby can be brought to the brink like this. When would Wyatt just decide not to come back?

"Papa!"

Anne practically leapt into my arms. She apologized for not being there when I arrived and then thanked me for coming on such short notice. "You didn't have to."

I smiled at her and gave her a kiss. Then I noticed Rob was gone. I looked around to find him and saw he was talking to Timmy's nurse and a doctor I didn't recognize. Rob was nodding, his hands on his hips and his back toward me. The doctor handed him a clipboard and a pen. I started to ask Anne what was happening, but then Rob was calling to his wife from across the room, as quietly as he could, but loud enough so that she could hear him. "I'm going with Timmy. You and your dad stay with Wyatt."

Anne nodded, and then turned back to Wyatt's isolette. She took two steps toward it, found a space between a nurse and a tech and bent her face close to the clear acrylic side. I heard her coo to her son. "It's okay, Wyatt," she said. "You're okay, little buddy. You're home now."

They were never going to leave, I thought; this *was* their home.

I stood, arms folded, staring out the NICU windows, looking across the broad Texas horizon. To the west I could see the curving outlines of the SeaWorld theme park rides that corkscrewed through gravity-defying twists and loops. Rising in the east, the tall buildings of the San Antonio skyline emerged from the surrounding pan-flat landscape like an island volcano. And above the horizon, a massive C-5 Galaxy cargo jet crept ever closer, inching downward toward the Lackland AFB landing strip below.

Behind me, Wyatt lay unmoving in his isolette. The respiratory techs were gone, only one nurse sat close by his side. She peered up occasionally at the monitors, looked at the watch on her wrist, and jotted notes onto a chart set on the small desk in front of her. Anne had stayed with Wyatt until she felt he was settled and then had asked me if I didn't mind staying with him until she came back. She had come from the Derm Clinic in the morning when she'd been notified her son was going into surgery and felt obliged to get back to address the chaos she'd left in her wake. Timmy was still gone; Rob was with him. They were somewhere down in the bowels of the hospital, Anne said, doing some kind of evaluation that had to be done down in Radiology. Timmy had been having a difficult time swallowing — chest x-rays a few days earlier showed his right lung collapsed, maybe due to aspirating his feeds.

The words of comfort she spoke to Wyatt rattled in my head. *You're home now.* One hundred nineteen days in neonatal intensive care. Wilford Hall *was* their home. Looking through the bank of windows lining the NICU wall was like looking out from a gold-fish bowl. Out there — that's where I wanted my grandchildren to be, and I wanted to be there with them. That's where life was being lived. I could practically picture the moms with their babies snuggled into car seats driving on Highway 90 below. There were dads and their toddlers strolling hand in hand along the river walk in downtown San Antonio. There were families gathered at SeaWorld, kids on rides screaming with delight while parents watched with bated breath. And there, coming out of the sky, were children now fully grown, young men and women bringing a giant aircraft back safely to base. Why was it so hard for some and not others, I asked myself. Did it have to be so hard just to come home and start growing up?

I knew Anne was worried sick for her boys. Even if they survived the NICU, there did not seem to be much of a future for either of them. The report from Timmy's MRI had read more like an autopsy. It was filled with ominous phrases like *severe right cerebellar encephalomalacia* and *no evidence of myelination within the subthalamic nuclei or posterior limb of the internal capsules.* Parts of his brain had suffered extensive volume loss; other areas were described as being "remarkably thin." Large portions of his brain were for all intents and purposes gone. There was no prognosis for recovery. What was lost could never be replaced. Though no one said it at the time, with such brain stem trauma it was a miracle Timmy had even survived. The day before, after watching Timmy — his arms reaching, hands grabbing, legs kicking happily — I'd cornered a senior neonatologist and suggested that Timmy's brain could hardly be so damaged seeing how full of get-up-and-go he appeared. The doctor looked down at the joyous little baby boy bouncing in an infant seat set on the NICU floor. He'd slid his hands into the pockets of his white coat before saying anything. "Purposeless motion," he'd finally said, "is not the same thing as motion with purpose."

Things were not very encouraging for Wyatt, either.

He was recovering from his surgery, but his overall condition was concerning. It had taken less than 48 hours to get him off the ventilator he'd been on since the V-P shunt surgery, and actually he'd handled that chore *himself* in the middle of the night, grabbing onto the endotracheal tube that ran down his throat, ripping it up and out and then fighting the nurses and respiratory techs who struggled three times to re-intubate him before finally giving up. But Wyatt remained extremely irritable and his head circumference was not decreasing. Something was wrong.

I joked about Wyatt's ventilator antics with the neurosurgeon who came the following morning to do a post-op. But when I asked about Wyatt's head circumference, which was, in fact, *increasing*, he admitted that they were concerned about fluid retention and the possibility the shunt was not working as it should. He didn't make a big deal of it, though. "Basic plumbing" was how he described what the surgery entailed, adding, "Sometimes the pipes get clogged."

Plumbing wasn't the problem, however.

Later that day, while I was holding Wyatt, a different doctor and a tech brought a mobile ultrasound machine and set it next to us. When I realized they intended to use it on Wyatt, I started to put him back into his isolette. They stopped me, suggesting that since he was quiet, they would just as soon do their exam while he rested against my shoulder. They said it shouldn't take long; they were only trying to verify something. But as time ticked by I could tell something wasn't right. The doctor kept looking at the display, then at the tech and then back at the image on the screen. After a few more minutes of obvious frustration, the doctor took the probe himself and began slowly moving it over Wyatt's head. Either he did not like what he saw or he couldn't locate what it was he was looking for. I was becoming uneasy; Wyatt was beginning to fuss.

"Can you tell me about your grandson?" the doctor finally said. "Where did the neurosurgeon say he was going to put the shunt?"

DOL 122: Saturday, August 7

It was supposed to be a distraction. But the midday heat was brutal, the sun scorching and I did not bring enough water. "If this trail doesn't lead us out of here soon, I think they're going to find us dead," I said, pushing the single water bottle we had toward Anne.

"That might not be such a bad thing, Papa." She said it with a half-smile, but I still worried she really meant it. She took only a small sip before she pressed the bottle back into my palm. "You get the last drop. You need it more than me."

"Your babies need you more than they'll ever need me," I protested, but she was already starting up the trail.

"I don't know what those babies need," she said without looking back.

It was mid-morning when we'd arrived at the bulbous, pink granite outcroppings of Enchanted Rock State Park. The full heat of day had yet to set in. I'd looked at the park map and chosen a trail that did a loop around the southwestern edges of the massive rock formation, waiting while Anne sat in the car to pump. After she placed her milk in the cooler I pulled our lone water bottle out and pointed my daughter in the direction we were headed.

"The stone is so beautiful," she said, running her palm across the smooth face of a boulder alongside the trail.

"The brochure says it's basically one giant rock. A 'batholith,' I think — just a big chunk of granite gradually being uncovered by erosion." We both turned when we heard the hootin' and hollerin' of young boys. They were coming over the top of a mound of granite not far from us, their father scrambling to keep pace. "Every boy's dream," I said, "a giant playground of rock."

Anne watched as they charged away and out of sight. "Do you think we can bring the babies here someday?" she asked wistfully.

"We could bring them in strollers, sure," I said. The loop trail we'd followed thus far was wide with hard-packed gravel.

"What about Timmy and Wyatt?"

"I don't see why not," I said, but wondered. It was barely conceivable they'd be able to run and jump around on these rocks one day.

"I want them to be able to have some kind of life, Papa. I just want them to be happy. If they're in wheelchairs, we can still bring them, right?"

"We'll bring them no matter what," I said. "I promise."

In another couple hours we finally emerged from the trail we were following. We were dying for something to drink, but we'd survived. After leaving the park, we stopped to buy summer peaches and cold drinks in nearby Fredericksburg. Anne said

Rob loved fresh peaches, and she wanted to surprise him with a basket. Ten minutes after leaving the peach stand Anne was fast asleep. I took her large cup from her loosening grip and set it in the console. Her hand fell into her lap. We would be back in San Antonio in an hour or so. She needed all the rest she could get.

As I drove, I thought about the massive formation of pink granite we'd hiked around now far behind us. It was an amazing sight, the dome of solid rock pushing up out of the Texas plain and into the broad blanket of sky above. I turned to look again at Anne, grateful that she was able to sleep. I wanted to help her so badly, help her in any way I could, but I didn't know what my daughter needed.

Though so much had changed since, the reason for our hiking together was little different than it had been in January. Still early in her pregnancy, Anne had been overcome by the fear that she would not be able to carry her babies long enough to give them a chance at a healthy life. Then, I'd hoped to help ease the anxiety that seemed to be closing around her like a vise. Now I was trying to use any excuse to get her away from the worries of another day in the NICU. Then, in the cool, crisp weather of winter, I'd encouraged her to draw close to God as the Psalmist wrote: "When my heart is overwhelmed / Lead me to the rock that is higher than I." Now her fears had come true in a way neither of us could have imagined, and it was as if the heat that had bedeviled us on the day's hike was also sapping her hopes for the future. I'd tried to help her find a rock to hold onto back in the winter. Now I was struggling, too, not knowing how to get her to the top of the thing. Maybe it was just a toe hold she needed, even if it was only enough to get one step higher. Maybe I could still help her find that.

DOL 124: Monday, August 9

I sat by myself in San Antonio's airport. I'd already called Donna to tell her the first leg of my flight home looked like it would be getting off the ground on schedule. She would keep an eye on the connecting flight, she'd said, and meet me at the Philadelphia airport. She had stayed behind this time, and there was a lot to do both at home and work. We were already planning to drive out to San Antonio in less than a month so we could bring some things for an extended stay. I'd recently signed a lease at a new apartment complex a half mile from Anne and Rob's. Donna knew, sooner or later, the babies would be coming home and when they did our daughter would need all the help she could get. She also knew the last thing any man wanted was his mother-in-law living in his house for weeks at a time. I felt less sure about the babies' imminent homecoming — possibly because I'd almost killed Lily the morning before!

Anne and Rob had gone out for breakfast. It was my idea — a rare opportunity for the two of them to be alone and enjoy each other's company. After all, how much trouble could I cause while they were away?

I was in the NICU when Jay, the nurse watching over both the girls, asked me if I wanted to feed Lily the remainder of her bottle. He had already gotten her started and she was sucking well; her oxygen levels were holding steady. Havoc was reigning elsewhere in the NICU. Timmy was upset about something; his heart rate was pushing well above 220 bpm. Wyatt was having difficulty breathing; he had episodic panting and his respiratory rate was above 150. Warning lights were flashing on monitors in every direction; alarm buzzers went off incessantly. Edda was so bothered by the chaos that she pitched in with her ear-piercing war cry. Jay was scrambling from crib to crib, working in tandem with Rebecca, the boys' nurse. I tried to act unfazed by it all, hoping the little girl in my arms would follow suit.

She did, too. She was staring up at the ceiling, her pudgy cheeks drawing in and out as she sucked, a continuous stream of air bubbles rising in the little bottle I held. And then she burped. Or was it a cough? I wasn't certain. The air bubbles ceased forming in the bottle; a drop of milk slid out from the corner of Lily's mouth. I pulled the nipple from between her lips and sat her upright in my lap. She continued staring ahead, her eyeballs crossing slightly, just as they had from the first day she'd opened them. For a brief moment, I thought she turned her eyes to look at me. But they'd rolled back in her head. "Lily?" I said to her softly. "Are you okay, Lily?" Then her eyes closed and her head fell forward, her chin coming to rest against her chest. "Jay?"

But he was busy with Wyatt, and I couldn't get his attention. I looked at Lily's monitor, but couldn't be sure what, if anything, it was telling me. Rebecca was on the other side of Timmy's crib, and I couldn't make eye contact with her. Lily just sat there, plump, pink and warm. Maybe she had only fallen asleep.

"Jay?"

But he was still preoccupied and I didn't want to seem foolish for making a fuss about nothing. I took a minute more with Lily, gently rubbing her upper back, tapping softly between her shoulder blades, hoping she would burp. But she didn't. And then she began to discolor right in front of my eyes, turning ash-gray and then blue.

"Jay!" The monitor's alarms sounded. What had I done?

Sitting in the airport, I shuddered at the thought of what I would have done if Jay had not been able to resuscitate Lily. I'd dreaded telling Anne about it later that day — I felt so horrible. It would be more than a week before I could admit to my wife what had happened. I would never include it in an email update; I didn't even tell Erin or Cait about it for the longest time. It was too frightening. All that the babies had already gone through — for something like that to take Lily, I just couldn't imagine it.

While my misadventure in the NICU would do nothing to impede Lily's overall progress, Wyatt's path home had become more convoluted — if that was even possible — than ever. The concerns arising in the days immediately following the shunting procedure grew more ominous. The first report was that there was an "underlying shunt dysfunction." But that wasn't exactly accurate. The catheter that should have been inserted into his left lateral ventricle during the surgery had missed the mark altogether. Instead, the device had been dangerously misplaced, penetrating the frontal lobe of his brain. He would need another surgery to get the shunt properly placed and he would need it soon.

As my plane drew close to Philadelphia, I thought about the young couple and their son who came through the airport terminal just minutes before I boarded my homebound flight. They looked no older than Anne and Rob; I could not easily judge the boy's age. They pushed his wheelchair between them; one hand each on a handle, their other hands pulling carry-on suitcases behind them. It was hard for me to look away. The boy's head was cocked to the side, his arms and hands limp, one lying in his lap and the other against an arm of the chair. A tracheostomy tube ran from his throat to an oxygen tank mounted on the back of the wheelchair. I remembered he had thick, dark curly hair but when I tried to recall the expression on his face, I drew a blank.

I feared it was a glimpse of what the future might look like for Anne and Rob.

Timmy and Wyatt were both still alive; how they had made it this far no one could say. What the future held for either of them, no one *would* say. Anne was upset by the results of Timmy's MRI. She and Rob had resigned themselves to the likelihood that Wyatt's life would be an ongoing struggle. They had come to terms with the fact that Edda and Lily might be legally blind. But they'd thought that somehow Timmy's brain might have escaped the worst. They were not naïve. They knew their oldest child had suffered terribly. Still, they'd told themselves that everything he'd overcome was proof of his strength. The scan of his brain seemed like hard evidence they'd been hoping for too much.

I didn't know how to make any of it better for my daughter. I called Dave Smith when I got home. We prayed together for Timmy, Edda, Lily and Wyatt. I wrote an email to Anne the next morning to tell her as much.

> Pastor Dave prayed with me on the phone yesterday when I called him to tell him about Timmy. "Father, we know you love each of these babies," he prayed. "We know that you love them more than Tim and Donna do, even more than Anne and Rob do."
>
> His words hit me right in my heart; I was taken aback for a moment. As much as we love Timmy, Edda, Lily and Wyatt, they are God's children. They were His before they were yours and they will be His forever. That is a miracle, to be a child of the living God and to be loved by Him. What more could we ask? Our hope has to be fixed on that love. My prayer for you is that you find that love in your own heart and walk on, finding in His love the resilience you need to carry on for one more day.

I don't know if sharing this was any help to Anne. But it helped me finally recognize that it wasn't up to me to make things right. My job was to let Anne know she was loved no matter what. I didn't know what kind of miracles we'd need in the years to come. For now, I hoped putting the focus on love would be enough for us each to survive one day at a time.

August 15 marked DOL 130. The quads' adjusted age was calculated at 3 weeks, 1 day. By this age most babies born full-term would be well adjusted to life outside the womb and adapting to their new home. At the same age, Timmy, Edda, Lily and Wyatt had been adjusting to life outside the womb for more than four months, but knew nothing about home. For them, the roller coaster ride of life in the NICU was one that never stopped.

The babies all weighed over seven pounds; Lily was nearly eight. None of them, however, were doing very well with their feeds. They each took bottles with varying degrees of success, but had it not been for the oral feeding tubes supplementing their caloric intake I think all of them would have starved. Breathing was just as much a challenge. They all had chronic lung disease. Lung tissue scarred by mechanical ventilators was the price of admission into "this breathing world" for most babies born so young, and they were no exception. It would be months, perhaps years, before they'd breathe without difficulty.

"Eat! Breathe!" I scolded them each before leaving the NICU earlier in August. I told them I would be personally embarrassed to have toddlers still living in a hospital nursery. "Have you seen yourselves lately? You're getting fat as ticks and twice the size of any other baby in the NICU. It's well past time you came home!" But they paid me no mind.

Frustrated with the babies' poor eating abilities, the NICU ordered video fluoroscopic swallow tests for Edda, Lily and Timmy. But the tests were largely inconclusive. So much remained uncertain about their futures. There were suggestions that all four would need G-tubes for feeding. Now closing in on 20 weeks in intensive care, the journey Anne's babies were on was becoming a frustrating meander. There seemed to be little forward progress and no clear finish line. I joked with Donna that we might just have to kidnap our grandchildren if we ever wanted to see them outside of the NICU.

Wyatt was hanging in his own limbo. He'd been scheduled for a second V-P shunt surgery, but it was delayed without explanation.

As it turned out, an MRI of Wyatt's brain had led to a debate about what exactly had gone wrong. This led to a heated discussion between Neurology and Neonatology over who exactly should perform the subsequent procedure. The Army did not have any *pediatric* neurosurgeons in San Antonio; I'm not sure they had any anywhere. But there was a very well regarded neurosurgeon at Christus Santa Rosa with a great deal of experience doing these kinds of procedures on small babies. It was finally agreed that she would consult on Wyatt's case. But she wanted her own set of diagnostic tests and that would take time. Wyatt's surgery was moved off the NICU schedule.

For me, the hardest part was wondering what it would ultimately take for any of the babies to finally come home. The end should be near, I kept thinking, maybe right around the next corner. But no matter what I tried telling myself I could not shake my unsettled feeling. It was my wife's unfailing optimism that lent me the hope I sorely needed.

"Can you book tickets to San Antonio for the last week of August?" Donna asked.

"I thought we were driving this time. You said you wanted to bring your clothes and things for the apartment."

"I don't think we have that much time," she said.

"Do you know something that I don't?"

But she didn't have to answer. I could see it; deep down inside her she did. It didn't matter that the NICU hadn't yet set any dates. She knew the babies were coming home.

DOL 138: Monday, August 23

Neonatology won the tug-of-war with Neurology. Once they grudgingly allowed an outside neurologist to consult on Wyatt's case, the neurologists at WHMC relented completely. The babies were separated again, with Wyatt now moved to Christus Santa Rosa to have his V-P shunt surgery performed by the specialist there. Anne and Rob were back to splitting shifts between hospitals. Since Anne was working at Wilford Hall, she could be easily reached in an emergency and be up in the NICU in a matter of minutes. So Rob would spend the days with Wyatt in the downtown hospital. They swapped in the evenings and then met back home for a few hours of much needed sleep.

Wyatt's operation went well. Santa Rosa's pediatric neurosurgeon installed a state-of-the art shunt unavailable in the military hospital and agreed to take charge of his post-op care even after he was transferred back to Wilford Hall. She also agreed to assume oversight of his long-term neurological care, but would not speculate on what damage might have been done to the baby boy's brain by the first, botched procedure.

We hoped Wyatt would be back with his siblings in just a few days, but his recovery was slowed by poor blood gas reports that resulted in his remaining on mechanical ventilation. We all hated it, knowing how uncomfortable it was and that the venting wasn't doing his already damaged lungs any good. But it was necessary. The truth was that the machine was keeping him tethered to the edge of life. The surgery was just plain hard on his little body. Once again, however, Wyatt took matters into his own hands.

"We warned them," Anne told me. "They knew Wyatt had extubated himself before when no one was watching." This time, after 72 hours on the vent, he did it right under their noses.

"You have a feisty little guy there," I told Anne.

"I think Wyatt's decided if he's going to live he's going to do it on his own terms."

He kept improving from that point on. In another couple days, Wyatt came "home" to Wilford Hall, but when his isolette was rolled into the NICU his brother and sisters were gone. They were not home yet, but across the hall, having been moved finally from the Level III to the Level II NICU. We were hoping that in another week or so, if he kept improving, Wyatt would join them.

But by then, Timmy, Edda and Lily would be gone. Really gone.

We scurried around like squirrels collecting nuts for winter. The plan was for Donna and me to fly to San Antonio on Thursday, August 26 and stay for a long weekend to work on getting our new apartment livable, if not exactly furnished. There was still no clear indication from the NICU that anybody was about to come home. But my wife had the feeling that at least one of the babies would soon, and she wanted to make sure she had somewhere to live before then. Even if she was right, we might still have time to drive from Philadelphia to San Antonio with the extra things she would need. She wanted to be sure, however, that no matter what happened, her new "home away from home" was ready.

We took the earliest flight out of Philadelphia we could get, rented a full size SUV at the San Antonio airport and by noon were on our way. First we moved a few wicker pieces from Anne and Rob's sunroom into the new apartment, and then drove across town for an old, overstuffed easy chair and a small table with matching chairs donated by Anne's friends, Tim and Ami. Next we went mattress shopping, and bought linens, kitchenware and knick-knacks at Target. When we finished, it was nearly dark, and we had the makings of a place that reminded me of the first apartment Donna and I ever shared.

When we finally got to Anne's house, she was only just returning from Christus Santa Rosa. Rob was out shopping.

"Shopping at eight o'clock on a Friday night?" I asked.

"We need a car seat."

"Well, sure you do. And I've got a secret for you — you need four of them. You guys haven't bought car seats yet?"

"You know how Rob can be when it comes to buying things."

I did. He hadn't been able to pull the trigger on buying the minivan they needed until just a few weeks earlier. Why buy car seats if you won't have a car to put them in? Sometimes the way my son-in-law went about life drove me half insane. But in the things that really mattered — like loving my daughter and staying strong under circumstances that would immobilize most people — he was a star.

"You need car seats tonight, though?"

"They're doing a car seat test on Timmy as soon as we get one to the NICU."

"More tests?"

"The NICU does one on all their preemies before discharge, to make sure they can sit in it without respiratory or heart rate problems," Anne explained. "It's been recommended by the American Academy of Pediatrics for a while now," she added, making it sound like a *Good Housekeeping Seal* of approval.

"Better safe than sorry," I said, joking that the only car seat test she and her sister had gotten when they were discharged was to make sure they could both fit on their mother's lap. But then I stopped, realizing that I'd missed her point entirely. "What does this mean?"

"Timmy's coming home."

I know I asked when but I don't remember anything Anne said after that. In fact, the following 24 hours were a blur.

What I will never forget is the car pulling into the driveway, Rob nervously rushing to open the minivan's sliding door. I remember Anne lifting the little bundle out of the new car seat and how gingerly she held the baby boy in her arms. Anne smiled. Donna was wiping away tears. I threw open the front door and waved them inside.

We had tied bright blue and white balloons declaring "IT'S A BOY!" and "WELCOME NEW BABY!" to the light fixture by the door, but I don't think Anne ever saw them. I think there could have been a parade out in the street and my daughter would not have taken her eyes off her son. She was still staring into his face when she stepped into the house.

I pulled a camera out of my pocket, but put it back down after taking only a few pictures. I wanted to see this with my own eyes, to drink it all in.

In the single photograph I attached to my next email update, Timmy's eyes are wide open, too, peering curiously at his new surroundings, a quizzical, circumspect expression on his face. No doubt he was thinking *"How* did I get here?"

However he'd done it, he had made it.

It was a few minutes after five o'clock on Saturday, August 28th. He had spent 142 days in the NICU. But Timothy David Schlender had finally made it home.

Our long weekend trip hadn't quite ended the way Donna or I had thought it would. I certainly hadn't expected Timmy would be coming home so suddenly.

"I told you I had a feeling," Donna said.

"Yes, you did."

"Are you going to be all right by yourself back home? I think I'm going to be living in Texas for a while."

"Cait and I will be fine. But what about you?"

"Erin Elizabeth will be here full time starting this week. She's going to be awesome. We'll do fine. It's going to be pretty crazy for a while, but I think we'll manage."

Erin was Pastor Dave's daughter, but we took to calling her Erin Elizabeth to keep from confusing her with our own Erin. She'd just graduated from Abilene Christian University with a degree in Family Studies. She had been looking for a job, and boy, did she find one. Words could scarcely express how blessed we were to have found her. We would need her help desperately in the coming months, but we would really need her now. We'd just learned from the NICU that Timmy wasn't going to be home alone for long.

DOL 146: Tuesday, August 31

I was about to leave Anne and Rob's house and fly home alone. Donna was holding our new grandson in her arms. He had been born a Texan. She was about to become one. Neither of us had any idea how long she'd be living in San Antonio.

"Car seat tests for the girls sometime today?" I asked.

"As soon as Rob gets two more car seats to the hospital," Donna answered.

"If he doesn't buy one for Wyatt this time, just do me a favor and kill him, will you?"

When Rob had gone to buy Timmy's car seat he came home with just one. He muttered something about wanting to be sure it was the right seat. He said he hadn't had enough time to do his research. I thought that if he came home this time with anything less than three car seats, it would be reasonable to shoot the guy and put him out of his misery. Donna laughed.

The girls were expected to be discharged in the next 24 hours. I would be gone by then so I'd asked Anne to do me a small favor.

"Anything, Papa," she'd said.

"Bring Edda in the front door before Lily, that's all." It was only a small technicality. Though the girls were being discharged at the same time, getting Edda home first (if just in order of entry) meant that not only would I have won the baby homecoming pool because no one else had bet on Timmy, I'd also hit it dead-on for getting them all in order: Timmy, Edda, Lily and then, hopefully, Wyatt.

"That was good guesswork," Anne said.

"I knew it all along," I joked. "Just figured they'd come home in the order they were born."

Of course, Wyatt was still waiting, with no guarantees. Getting him home, even weeks or months from now, was going to be a struggle. As I backed the rented SUV out of the driveway and turned toward the airport, I thought about the odds I'd calculated long months before. It had been more than 130 to 1 against them all coming home from the NICU. The odds of winning one of those mega lotteries are a lot steeper. So what?

We were living a miracle.

We really were.

Less than 48 hours after Edda and Lily were released from the hospital, Wyatt's prospective discharge from the Wilford Hall NICU was becoming a hot topic. No one was suggesting he go home. Instead, a debate arose over whether he should be returned to Christus Santa Rosa and this time, whether he should be admitted there for good. He needed surgery. Again. Another brain surgery. More than that, though, I thought that what Wyatt needed was an advocate. He needed someone willing to stand up on his behalf and say, "Enough is enough!"

She had already done as much for Timmy, Edda and Lily.

Christine Wyeth was a staff neonatologist at WHMC and a major in the US Army. A short, sturdy woman with military bearing and a stern expression that was at times belied by a disarming smile, Dr. Wyeth was only a few years older than Anne. She was a mother, too, and having given birth to a very premature baby herself she knew too well what Anne had faced. More than that, though, to me she seemed like a guardian angel sent to watch over my daughter and her four babies.

She was not afraid to make the tough calls. She had come to Anne in that first week of April to let her know that she was rapidly reaching the point where she could no longer do the babies in her womb any further good. She told Anne the hard news straight-up: by continuing to carry her babies, she could only do them harm. Who can say how Anne might have responded had the news come from someone else? But coming as it did, not just from a doctor, but a mother, too, and from a woman who had endured a similar ordeal herself, had made all the difference in the world. If it hadn't been Dr. Wyeth who intervened then, we might have lost them all.

She was there at delivery, too, and then with the babies in those very first minutes when life was at its most tenuous. Her hand-scribbled notes on the medical reports attest to the hectic pace of events that afternoon as one baby after another was taken from Anne's open belly and rushed to the NICU. She was there in the ensuing hours when first one baby then another had to be resuscitated due to the respiratory trauma and cardiac arrests that were all but unavoidable for babies so small and so premature.

She was the one who came to Anne's bedside to update the new parents, assuring them things had gone as well as anyone could have hoped. Four babies, all alive, she told them, and each with a fighting chance. She would follow the course of each of the babies throughout the coming months, providing direct care and personally monitoring their ups and downs. When she was not on call in the NICU, she made sure Anne knew she was never far away. And though it seems odd to suggest as much, in retrospect I'm glad she *wasn't* there in mid-April when the senior neonatologists gathered us all into the conference room to say that Timmy had little hope for survival. She wasn't there when they told Anne and Rob that they didn't need to let him suffer any longer. Had Dr. Wyeth been the one to say, "You need to let us know when you think your son has had enough," I don't want to know what might have come of Anne and Rob's resolve to let Timmy keep fighting on.

When the late summer doldrums came, and Timmy and his sisters were mired in the bog of feeding issues and breathing problems, when their progress toward discharge from the NICU seemed to have stalled, she was the one who finally said, "Enough!" She said they should go home. She would be their advocate.

As a neonatologist, she knew what they had come through. Between them, the babies had spent more than 18 months hospitalized in intensive care. Their medical charts were littered with diagnoses ranging from anemia and apnea to bacteremia and septicemia. They collectively had endured surgical procedures for everything from patent ductus arteriosus to retrolental fibroplasia, from necrotizing enterocolitis and intestinal perforation to ventriculitis and hydrocephalus. She knew that Timmy had nearly died at least twice, that Lily might well have succumbed to sepsis and that, even by late August, an echocardiogram showed that Edda's PDA was still open. She knew personally that a micro-preemie's journey through the NICU was like walking a minefield for a child and a roller coaster ride for parents. She knew professionally that some babies made it through without much trouble, but others needed more help, more luck and outright miracles to finally get home. And she knew some never made it out of the NICU at all.

She didn't need anyone to remind her that Timmy, Edda and Lily, once home, might slip into a complex medical condition better known by its dreaded colloquialism "failure to thrive." *They might not eat.* "Then we'll bring them back for G-tubes," she said. *Their respiratory problems could escalate.* "We'll readmit them if needed," she countered. *They all have special needs and there are four of them.* "But they each have only one mother," she was quick to point out, "and they all have a special need for her."

She knew that better than anyone. Her own experience taught her what very premature babies gained from being home and in the care of their parents. If it was a risk to let a baby leave the NICU too soon, she also knew there was so much that could never be reproduced in a hospital; all the medical technology in the world couldn't pretend to provide what a loving family could.

I'd begun to think of what Dr. Wyeth and her colleagues in the NICU had done in preparing the babies for their homecoming more in terms of art than science. While in Italy with Donna for our 30th anniversary — only months before Anne would conceive — I was struck not by the wonderful and ubiquitous frescoes so much as by their scarcely seen red ochre *sinopia* underdrawings. Where the color-laden *intonaco* layer of plaster had fallen away from aging frescoes, the vitality of the artist's hand, hidden for centuries beneath the pigmented finish coat, was revealed anew in the sinopia. The underlying sketches are rare, little noticed and perhaps even less appreciated. But it's there that the artistic vision originates. The etchings of a sinopia seemed to me a fitting analogy for babies making their way through the NICU.

The work of creation in the mother's womb is begun much like a fresco at its start — fleshy-red lines drawn onto a bland base of wet plaster, one simple stroke followed by another and another until the design is at last complete. Like the explosion of pigment the artist adds to the fresco once the underdrawing is finished, a newborn full term baby is ready to be colored thereafter by the experiences of its life. In that sense, the premature baby — especially babies born as early as Anne's — is like a sinopia interrupted, the composition left nearly unrecognizable. It becomes the task, the *craft* of the neonatologists and the whole NICU team, to ink in the missing lines, to finish sketching the primitive design of the not yet ready-to-be born child. And it is not until they have finished their work that the creative act is able to be returned again to the hands of parents.

This is what the Wilford Hall NICU had so carefully done for Anne and Rob's babies. And it was Dr. Wyeth who saw that it was time for WHMC to let them go. First Timmy and then his sisters. Their underdrawings were finally complete; the NICU had done all they could. Only mom and dad could finish the fresco now; only Anne and Rob could bring forth the rest of their stories. It would be up to them to bring color to their children's world.

Christine Wyeth could not do quite as much for Wyatt, but her greatest gift to him was to secure him a one way ticket out of Wilford Hall. She could not send him home with his brother and sisters; he was still too sick. What she could do was see that he got the best care possible in the immediate future. He would need it, and as a neonatologist, she knew they owed him as much.

While Neonatology was responsible for the babies in their care, they were themselves dependent upon a slew of medical specialists who provided the acute and critical care they could not. These relationships were sometimes fraught with challenges growing out of ignorance, ego or both. We'd seen this firsthand when the head of Wilford Hall's OB-GYN department went on his tirade about Anne and Rob considering having her prenatal care transferred elsewhere. Bureaucracy could turn the careful and complimentary intertwining of medical relationships into an entangling snare.

We'd seen it again when Neonatology butted heads with Cardiology over where to deal with Edda's PDA. Cardiology admitted they didn't have pediatric heart surgeons trained to operate on babies so tiny. But military regulations required them to keep as much of their care in-house as possible. Neonatology pushed for surgery. Cardiology pushed back saying they could manage her care without the procedure. When Edda was eventually discharged from the NICU, Cardiology's own disposition report, referring to a recent echocardiogram, read in part, "Impression: small to moderate restrictive patent ductus arteriosus; subjectively slightly larger... Needs to f/u with Cardio in 6 months, sooner if pulmonary problems develop suggesting volume overload." It goes without saying, Dr. Wyeth and the rest of Neonatology would have been more at ease sending Edda home with the full knowledge that her PDA had been conclusively addressed.

A similar situation had arisen between the NICU docs and Neurology over Wyatt's care. Hydrocephalus was not uncommon among very premature neonates; post-hemorrhagic hydrocephalus complicated by ventriculitis was. Trans-fontanel taps and implanted reservoirs were routine in the care of babies born with congenital hydrocephalus. But Wyatt's PHH was not congenital; it was the direct result of extreme intraventricular hemorrhaging, and the IVH itself a result of an infection Wyatt had gotten in the NICU. Neurology was directing the chorus of events that led from spinal tap to daily trans-fontanel taps to implantation of the reservoir in Wyatt's brain. They continued to be in charge after the removal of the reservoir once it was discovered to be the route of the infection that led to meningitis and finally ventriculitis. While the re-implantation of a new reservoir was also under Neurology's direction, Neonatology was at the same time ultimately responsible for Wyatt. And they knew things were not going well for the child in their care.

There had been discussion as to whether the first V-P shunt surgery, which everybody agreed Wyatt needed, should be the responsibility of Wilford Hall's Neurology department. It was outside their domain in the same way that PDA ligation was outside of Cardiology's when it came to very premature babies. Only the neurosurgeons did not see it that way. Blame it on ignorance or ego or bureaucracy or all the above, Neurology would not agree to send *their* patient to a specialist at an outside facility. It was a simple shunt surgery, after all, just "basic plumbing." Only in Wyatt's case, they managed to hook the pipes to the wrong fixture.

Still, it would take a fight from Neonatology and an impassioned plea from Dr. Wyeth to get the V-P shunt revision performed by a renowned pediatric neurosurgeon outside the military. But that was a short-lived victory. A head ultrasound done in Wilford

Hall as a routine follow-up to the V-P shunt revision was disheartening. The HUS results were sent to the pediatric neurosurgeon at Christus Santa Rosa. She was alarmed. It was possible, she told Anne and Rob, that the new shunt was malfunctioning or that blood product debris and proteins were accumulating in Wyatt's cerebrospinal fluids, clogging access to the drainage catheter. Or maybe the single shunt might not be adequate by itself. An additional V-P shunt placed in another location — another full-blown brain surgery — would be necessary if this was found to be the case. Decisions needed to be made quickly. So much had happened in these past few months, but little had changed for Wyatt. His life was still in jeopardy.

The Neurology Department at Wilford Hall now all but washed their hands of the boy. If Wyatt was not their full responsibility then they would do almost nothing for him. They argued that was the only viable policy. The responsibility for his care fell squarely on the shoulders of Neonatology. He was *their* patient now — having fought for the transfer of Wyatt's neurologic care to an outside specialist they had painted themselves into a corner. Without the full cooperation of the Neurology Department, they could not get Wyatt the care he needed when he needed it at WHMC. So Dr. Wyeth and her colleagues agreed to give him up. It was in Wyatt's best interest to have his total care transferred out of Wilford Hall.

Early on the morning of September 2nd, Wyatt was prepped for medical transport, placed in an ambulance and taken downtown to Christus Santa Rosa. From her office in the Derm Clinic three floors below the NICU, Anne felt a strange and cold loneliness. All her children were now gone; she could no longer run upstairs at the drop of a hat and be there for them when they needed her. The NICU staff might have felt something similar.

Three and a half months earlier they had parted with Timmy in much the same fashion. They did not know then if the tiny baby boy would ever come back to them. Now, saying good-bye to Wyatt, a baby into whom they had poured their very hearts and souls, a baby who had come back to them from all but dead, the Wilford Hall team knew they would never see him again. If Wyatt survived and recovered, it would be from the Christus Santa Rosa NICU that he would be finally sent home. If not, they would hear of his passing before long. They would know, too, that they had done all they could for him. Difficult as that was, transferring him was the right thing to do. Dr. Wyeth had seen to that; that's what guardian angels do.

The last thing she did for Wyatt was sign his transfer papers. Wyatt was 148 days old. She no doubt knew that at birth nearly four and a half months earlier he had been the tiniest of the quadruplets, the least likely to survive. She would not be the one sending him home, but under her care he had gained 117 ounces. Every one of them, I knew, represented a hard-won victory.

Wyatt would live for 50 days in the NICU at Christus Santa Rosa.

A week after he was admitted, he had a second shunt placed into his brain. The procedure went well, but the news from the neurosurgeon in its aftermath was not good. Wyatt appeared to be retaining fluid in the frontal lobe of his brain. It could mean another round of surgery, but she was willing to wait. She would see how he did over the next month before going ahead with another procedure.

Wyatt was alone now, still in the minefield, a step away from sudden catastrophe. Anne and Rob were left on the roller coaster. Only it was worse now. With three babies at home each with mounting needs of their own, their lives were close to coming apart at the seams. They could never make the time to visit Wyatt together. They could hardly make the time to meet with the neo-natologists, neurologist and other specialists clamoring for their attention. And they had no idea what to do. Wyatt was stuck on a merry-go-round and they could not get him off.

Donna was exhausted, too. She had been going night and day for five weeks. None of the babies were eating well, and she was spending hour after hour feeding Edda, one drop of milk at a time, pinching and prodding the baby girl to keep her awake, to keep her eating *something*. For a "break," she flew home from San Antonio and got in a car with me, turned around and drove straight back to Texas. We were finally bringing a car and the few extra things she needed for the apartment in San Antonio. It was the trip we had originally planned to do back in late August until Timmy unexpectedly came home.

Two days after we returned, Wyatt endured yet another round of anesthesia, intubation and a machine doing the work of breathing for him as he struggled through recovery. It was not a brain surgery, however, but rather the insertion of a feeding tube directly into his belly so the NICU nurses could feed him without a fight. He was always pulling the feeding tubes out of his nose and mouth, and he was more determined than they. He was also nearly impossible to nipple feed any longer. His deteriorating condition had left him so irritable that just holding him was a chore. As stubborn as the boy could be, without the G-tube he probably would have succeeded in starving himself to death.

He did not recover well from the surgery that placed a feeding port in his belly. He was so exhausted that he did not even bother to extubate himself when no one was watching and seemed entirely uninterested in the happenings around him. When he wasn't fussing or fighting with anyone who tried to touch him, he spent most of his time lying flat on his back staring at the ceiling tiles. The G-tube surgery felt like a setback. But there was also something suddenly *possible* as a result. It was conceivable that Wyatt might actually come home.

Though his recovery was slow, the G-tube helped not only with Wyatt's nutrition, but also his breathing. Only a week after his feeding tube surgery, the respiratory specialists started weaning him off of oxygen. For the first time in his life, he had nothing taped to his face, stuck up his nose or run down his throat. He was still an irritable little cuss, though. And nobody seemed to know how to help him.

"Sometimes I think his head is just killing him," Anne said.

"Is that what the neurologists think?" I asked. We were in the NICU together the evening before I was scheduled to fly back home. I wanted to see Wyatt one more time with my daughter.

"They don't come out and say as much. Babies can't tell them what they're feeling, right? But all the pressure that builds up in his head — how could it not?"

Wyatt was particularly irritable that night. Anne was holding him against her shoulder while she rocked him in a chair. But it wasn't helping. She switched him from one shoulder to the other as she struggled to console him. "You want him?" she said, only half joking.

I told her I did. "What's the worst that can happen? He'll cry louder and they'll throw us all out of the NICU for making too much noise?"

Anne laughed, then got up and traded places with me. When I was situated in the rocking chair, she placed her son in my arms. He wailed.

"You don't have to — let me," said Anne.

But I ignored her and after another minute, I cleared my throat and started to sing softly into his ear. Wyatt suddenly threw his head back, fixed his eyes on mine and stopped crying.

"He likes it when you sing, Papa."

"He's maybe the only person on earth who does." I could scarcely carry a tune, but since his bout with meningitis I would often sing to Wyatt. For some reason it seemed to settle him. Don't ask me why. In another few minutes he was asleep. His nurse saw him dozing and came to help us put him back into his crib.

"We should go," Anne said. "You have a long day tomorrow."

"And yours are short and easy?"

She gave me a hug.

"Annie?"

"Papa?"

"He needs to go home."

She looked at her son now lying peacefully in his crib, but said nothing in response.

"He's dying here," I said.

Anne lifted her head as if to say something, but then looked back down at her son.

"He can be fed now. He's breathing so much better."

"They don't know what they're going to do about his head," she finally said.

"When they figure it out you'll bring him back," I told her. "He needs to go home."

"What if he dies at home?"

"What if he dies here? I don't want him dying in some sterile hospital. If he's going to die let him at least be with his brother and sisters."

Anne started crying. I told her I was sorry, that I didn't mean to upset her. But she shook her head. "I think you're right," she said, wiping her nose on her sleeve. "Maybe the only thing that will help him is coming home."

We stopped at the nurses' station to sign some forms before leaving. There was always something to sign, some consent to be given. Wyatt's nurse looked up at me from behind the counter. "What was that song you were singing?" she asked.

I hadn't realized she'd heard me singing to Wyatt.

"The words — what were they?"

"Just some old Pentecostal hymn from way back when," I told her. I could feel myself blushing.

"I want to write them down," she said. "I like that song."

I said I wasn't going to embarrass myself trying to sing to her, "but the words go like this..."

> *He's my bread when I'm hungry*
> *He's my water when I'm thirsty*
> *He's my shelter in the time of storm.*
> *He's the lily of the valley, the bright and morning star,*
> *He's Jesus, He's Jesus and He's still around.*

I don't know if I stirred the pot or if Anne listened to what I'd said. I don't even know if she told anybody else. The decisions about Wyatt's care went so much deeper than I could possibly know. But someone at Christus Santa Rosa must have been thinking along those lines.

Less than a week after I flew home to Philadelphia I got a call from Donna. She filled me in on how Timmy, Edda and Lily were doing. Things were crazy, she said. And they were going to get worse before they got better. I told her to keep her chin up and to hang in there; being negative wasn't going to help.

"I'm not being negative," she replied. "In fact we're all pretty giddy right now — scared, too — but giddy."

When I asked her to explain she said she would put Anne on the phone.

"He's coming home, Papa. Wyatt's coming home."

On Saturday, the 24th day of October, 2010, at 6:24 in the evening, I sent out the last — and longest — email update chronicling the babies' NICU journey:

Family & friends — Good news from Texas. Yesterday afternoon, Wyatt Lee Schlender finally came home. For the first time since the womb, he is now close enough to touch his brother and sisters. In fact, yesterday was the first time Wyatt had actually even seen his sisters. Anne told me when they drove him home he just sat and stared out the window with a big smile on his face — not surprising when you consider he'd been staring at hospital ceiling tiles for the first 198 days of his life.

That Wyatt is alive today — and finally home — is a testament to the grace of God and to this little guy's own stubborn will to live. Wyatt's last surgery was only a little more than a week ago; it was to have a gastric tube inserted in his belly for feeding purposes. What the longer term prognosis for him due to the hydrocephalus is, well, that's hard to gauge. What we are certain of, however, is that this little guy is a fighter and tenacious, and as a family, we are buoyed by the faithfulness of our Lord who has seen not just him, but each of Anne & Rob's babies through an amazing journey. We have been so blessed, so humbled to have witnessed so closely the hand of God in these little lives.

Human "hands" have done so very much, also, and the dedication, skill and concern shown by so many doctors, nurses and technicians has been overwhelming. The NICUs in which the babies spent the first scary days of their lives and then the subsequent months as they slowly grew before finally coming home are incredible places; they possess such an unfathomable combination of medical technology and plain old-fashioned loving care that it just melts the heart and boggles the mind. We will be forever grateful for the selfless services rendered to our babies there.

Just as necessary (and just as appreciated) through this journey have been all your hands which tirelessly reached out to support us in so many ways, that were raised to God so faithfully in prayer, and that sent out to us the good thoughts and wishes that carried us through the darkest times. I know that while my family was often hard pressed to see beyond our own needs over the course of the last half year, that hardship and loss touched some of your lives: A young friend's mother died just weeks after she proudly watched him graduate from medical school; a cousin's husband died after an unexpected illness; a friend in business lost his wife when her cancer suddenly returned. To these who continued to care about us in spite of grief and pain, Donna and I are especially grateful. And to all who have stood with us, we say thanks — how useless words seem now when trying to express how much our lives have been touched by your vigilance, your concern, your love.

I have been wearing a bracelet on my wrist from almost the first days after Timmy, Edda, Lily and Wyatt were born. I got it from a father whose son died after 45 days in the NICU. His son's name was Graham. He and his twin sister, Reece, were born — like Anne & Rob's babies — way too young for this world. In his honor, Graham's parents, and their daughter who turns four years old this Thanksgiving, started a foundation to help parents of micro-preemies. The bracelet is just a small part of the outreach offered by "Graham's Foundation" but there is real strength to be found in the three words engraved on the band: "Hope, resilience and miracles." Those words became a framework for getting through such a harrowing time and for this grandfather of micro-preemies, they helped me stay strong (mostly) for the babies' mother, my daughter Anne. We learned to always keep hope in the face of difficult times; when it seemed we could not, we learned that if we

remained resilient, hope would return even stronger. And
we learned that when hope seems vanquished, when there
is just no more strength to get back up after you've been
knocked down one time too many, that — in spite of what a
cynical world may say — there are still miracles to be had.
We know — we have four of them.

I flew back to San Antonio the first week of November to see
it for myself. I cannot tell you the joy I felt walking into Anne's
house. The place was a disaster. Words can scarcely describe the
mayhem of having four babies under one roof. It was chaos. Utter
and complete, wonderful chaos.

After I'd put Wyatt down, after I'd held Timmy, Edda and then
Lily, I walked toward the fireplace in Anne and Rob's living room.
Four pictures were lined in a row atop the mantle, one of each of
their babies — the same framed, black and white photographs that
had been set on Tim and Ami's mantle during Anne's baby shower.
I looked at the tiny faces in each photograph and could not help but
smile. Even then, in the middle of their journey through the NICU,
they had been beautiful. Anne had carefully arranged the pictures,
the babies placed in their birth order from left to right, Timmy first
and Wyatt the last. I pushed the old pair of glasses I'd been wearing
up the bridge of my nose and squinted to see more clearly. Raising
my right arm I slid the cuff bracelet with the blue balloons from my
wrist and set it on the mantle next to Wyatt's photograph, turning
it so the inscription could be easily read: *Hope*Resilience*Miracles*. I
thought of baby Graham as I did, of what his mom and dad must
have endured, and said a quick prayer of thanks. Not every baby
made it home. But I knew now, more than ever, that whether they
did or not, every one of them was a miracle.

Even in south central Texas, summer eventually ends. That evening, while Anne and Rob and Donna and Erin Elizabeth were

feeding the babies — and they were *always* feeding them — I went outside. The heat of summer had taken its toll on the flowerbeds. They were a mess, once again overgrown and choked with weeds. Now that it was cooler I'd told Anne I would spend some time in them, cleaning the beds out, getting things ready for winter.

The first handful of weeds I pulled from the mulch brought something unexpected up with them. It was the pair of glasses I'd lost, my favorite pair, the ones that disappeared while working in the yard with Donna in the spring, doing what little we could to help at the time. I remembered that April day like it was yesterday. Only the morning before, Timmy had had emergency surgery to repair a bowel perforation. Hours later the NICU docs had told Anne and Rob that perhaps it was time to let the boy go.

We had come so close to losing so much.

I went back in the house, carefully washed the glasses and put them on. They had a zillion tiny scratches on them. Anne was sitting in the living room, still wearing the tan t-shirt, camouflage pants and boots that were part of the Army uniform she wore at the Derm Clinic. Timmy was on her lap. She was working a burp out of him. Donna was on the couch, a cloth diaper draped over the shoulder of a scrub top she'd borrowed from Anne. Each of the babies had such problems with reflux that it was practically impossible keeping your clothes clean. Edda was tucked into the crook of Donna's arm. She was holding a bottle to the little girl's lips. Edda, however, had given up on the task at hand. She was fast asleep. Erin Elizabeth was on the couch, too, with Lily swaddled in a purple print receiving blanket. A half full bottle was set on the table beside them.

From where I was standing I could see Rob in the nursery. He was bent over a crib, reaching his hands down through the web of wires and tubes that were connected to Wyatt. An IV pole held the drip bag and pump that fed Wyatt through his G-tube. From an adjacent room I could hear the low hum of the motor that provided the supplemental oxygen he needed. In fact, all the babies still needed oxygen at various intervals. They all wore pulse oximeters, too, to monitor their O2 saturation levels. All four babies had made it home all right, but the trappings of the NICU had followed them.

"I found my glasses out in the garden," I announced as I walked into the room.

"Are you kidding? That's great, Papa."

"Where were they?" Donna asked.

"Under some mulch out front."

"We must have dug through the gardens looking for them for half an hour," she replied.

Erin Elizabeth smiled though she hadn't a clue what we were talking about.

"I lost my glasses months ago while we were working in the flowerbeds outside," I started to explain. "The babies were only a couple weeks old."

"That was such an awful few days!" Donna winced.

I stepped toward Anne, bent down and lifted Timmy gently from her grasp. I pulled him close, looked at the boy now half asleep and softly said, "Did you know they thought maybe we should trade you in for a Christmas tree ornament? We'd only have a plaster casting of your hands and feet for a keepsake. I think I prefer having you around in person."

Timmy gave me no mind.

I motioned to Erin Elizabeth who stood up and brought Lily closer. I asked her to put the baby in my other arm.

"Are you sure?"

I nodded, and when she did I began to coo quietly to the girl, "Lily Joy — Lily Joyful." But her eyes were heavy, too, and in another minute she was asleep in my arms beside her brother.

It was almost exactly 30 years since I'd held Anne and Erin like that for the first time. Looking now at Timmy and Lily, the memory of holding their mom and their Aunt Erin brought tears to my eyes. I reached awkwardly toward my glasses to reposition them, trying at the same time to keep the two babies upright in my arms.

Anne quickly got up to take one of the babies and when she did she gently swiped her finger across one of the lenses. "Can you even see out of those things?" she asked.

I told her that I certainly could. I could see just fine.

EPILOGUE

"Like a shepherd He will tend His flock,
In His arms He will gather the lambs and carry them in
His bosom; He will gently lead the nursing ewes."
Isaiah 40:11

Chester County, Pennsylvania
Late summer 2013

I CAN SEE THE OLD ASH TREE from my office window. It has already lost most of its leaves, the long, gray limbs left naked under the August sun. There are fewer branches every year; each winter's passing takes a toll. Still, the old tree retains its dignity, standing tall above an oxbow in the stream that meanders through our backyard. I have no notion how old, only that when we bought the land nearly 30 years ago the tree already seemed on its last legs. Back then I'd told Donna that if the ancient ash lived a bit longer, we'd hang swings from it so Erin, Anne and Cait could while away their summers beneath it. Though the ropes that held those swings have long since rotted, the tree never loosened its grip on the rusted eyehooks I screwed into her long ago. Bright new steel chains hang from them now. And sitting in the swings below, two sisters sway lazily back and forth.

Edda and Lily are three and a half. I've watched them from the window for much of the past hour. They have been all over the backyard with Donna in tow. She's trying to manage a photo shoot of our granddaughters with a professional photographer hired to capture some of summer's waning magic in an album for Anne. Edda and Lily know Mommy is on a "big Army trip" and she won't come home until it's cold again. They know she left in an airplane, and when they see one from time to time high above our house they point and say, "Mommy come home!" But her homecoming is still months away. Thinking of Anne I open and read once more an email that came from her early this morning.

Bagram Airfield, Afghanistan —

Life is the usual up-and-down over here. Today I saw a little 2 year old boy who probably only weighed 15lbs. He had blisters all over his body and inside his mouth — he was so malnourished. The father brought him hoping for the "great American skin doc" to make him better... but truly, there is nothing that can be done with this condition. His whole back was an open, weeping blister. He will probably die in a few years from starvation or infection. I gave them lots of bandage supplies and some PediaSure and wanted to cry. He reminded me of my kiddos when they were in the NICU... you could see through his tummy to his little blood vessels and he had little spindly arms and legs just like Timmy once had.

I told the dad that his job was just to love his little boy for as long as God allowed. The mother sews all of the clothes for him in soft cotton so they don't hurt him as much. He was in a cute handmade button-down pajama top and pants with pirates and boats all over it and with little pockets Mom added yesterday so that when he made his trip here, the soldiers could stuff candy and bubble-gum into them...

A few nights ago, there was an 'insider attack' at an outlying FOB (forward operating base) far from here. A number of troops got injured and have been coming through the hospital here...

It's hard to make sense of any of it. Sometimes I feel like I can make a huge difference and other times I feel like I'm a waste of space. Nonetheless, I wouldn't change my experiences — I'm learning a lot about a different culture and doing my best to engender hope in the people that I meet... I may not be able to cure or solve anything, but bringing a small bit of hope? Maybe at least I can do that.

I miss you guys so much and miss my kiddos and seeing all their progress. Thanks for taking extraordinary care of them in my absence.

I look back outside at Edda and Lily. It is like watching our daughters growing up all over again. I shake my head at how the years slip so quickly by. I know that we are living a miracle through the lives of our grandchildren, but having them in our lives now has also shown me how blessed I've been all along. The twins and Caitlin, no longer the little girls who once filled our lives with equal parts joy and angst, continue to blossom as women and forge their way in this world. I cannot help but smile. They make their mom and me unabashedly proud.

I'd never been prouder of Caitlin. "You're sure you want to do this?" I asked.

Cait nodded.

"You know you can come back anytime. If things don't work out," I paused and then said, "You know I'll keep the light on for you, right?"

"I'm more worried about you, Papa. You're going to be all by yourself when I'm gone."

"I still have Clady," I told her. Clady was the lone pet left. After years of dogs and cats, horses and goats, ducks and chickens, Donna and I had seen our population of pets whittled down to one Irish Setter. And with Donna still living full time in Texas and for the foreseeable future, it was going to be just me and Clady on the home front for a while.

"I'm going to miss her, too," Cait said, bending down and hugging the dog she loved more than any pet we'd ever had.

"You'll find yourself a tall cowboy with a paint horse in Texas and forget all about silly dogs," I said playfully. But her eyes teared up, so I grabbed her by the arm and gave her a tug. "Get in the truck," I said, and pointing more or less to the west added, "We gotta get on the road."

Caitlin had made up her mind. She wanted to help however she could, and with four one-year-old babies at home, Anne and Rob needed all the help they could get. She was leaving behind a long-term boyfriend who she'd finally given up on and a good job that would not be easy to replace. She was leaving the only home she'd ever known and going to San Antonio, a place she knew nothing about.

"Let's do it," she said. And with that I nosed my pickup and the U-Haul trailer it was towing out of the driveway. We drove the 1,800 miles in a day and a half. We pulled up outside Anne and Rob's house at midnight. Donna was waiting up for us.

"Can I see the babies?" Cait asked as soon as she stepped out of the truck. "Oh my gosh, I've missed them so much!"

When Cait moved to San Antonio in the late spring of 2011, Erin was finishing her residency at Walter Reed. After graduation she was stationed at Fort Bragg, NC. She rented a condo on the outskirts of Fayetteville — an Army town if there ever was one. It was still known as *Fayette-nam* because of the tens of thousands of G.I.s who had deployed to Vietnam from the base outside town. We knew it would likely be where Erin would leave for her first combat deployment, too.

Arriving at Womack Army Medical Center, Erin found herself atop the Dermatology Department's deployment list. She was a new active duty physician and so that came as little surprise. The only question was how soon she would go. Never one to let come what may, she chose to take matters into her own hands. She volunteered. She would fill the dermatology spot at Bagram Airfield, Afghanistan, and she would deploy in a few short months. But there was something she wanted to do first.

Her boyfriend Andy had graduated from his residency, too, completing an oral and maxillofacial surgical program at Bethesda Naval Hospital. Living only miles apart during that time, their relationship had grown to where they were thinking about marriage. The ending of their residencies, however, put more than 200 miles between them. Andy was stationed at the Norfolk Naval Station in Virginia and attached to the aircraft carrier USS Eisenhower. The "Ike" was slated for deployment to the Arabian Sea later the following summer. It looked like he would be gone before Erin returned from Afghanistan. Being on bases four hours apart was one thing, but being separated by eight time zones was something else. They decided to marry before either of them left.

There was no time to plan a gala wedding. In fact, there wasn't much time to plan anything at all. For now, the local Justice of the Peace would do. In a scene straight out of a Coen Brothers' movie, I walked my oldest daughter, a bouquet of flowers in her hand, through the metal detectors at the Cumberland County Detention Center and into the chambers of the Justice of the Peace. She and Andy exchanged vows. Donna and I and Andy's mom and dad were there as witnesses. Afterward, we went out to dinner together in Fayetteville and then we said good-bye.

I would not see Erin again until she sent us a picture from Afghanistan. In the photo she is standing outside barracks made of only painted plywood and galvanized sheet metal roofing. It is winter, and she is wearing a moss green fleece jacket with baggy camouflaged pants tucked into her boots. She has a 9mm pistol holstered on her hip. Looking at the picture I realized that my daughter was not just an Army doctor; she was a soldier, too.

Erin never blinked when duty called. She went, as so many before her had done; as so many still continue to do. Seeing her in Afghanistan, the full weight of what every soldier pledges to do finally struck me. She would die for me if it came to that. As a father I couldn't have been prouder. Back home, Donna and I did our best not to be afraid.

Anne's turn came in the early summer of 2013 and drove home for us what so many military families have learned: the deployments never seem to stop. Andy had been shipped out on the "Ike" before Erin returned from Afghanistan. By the time Andy's carrier group returned to Norfolk, Anne was already in Bagram filling the same post her sister had nearly a year and a half before. Her official title was "Army Major (Dr.) Anne Spillane, Operation Enduring Freedom Theater dermatology consultant in Afghanistan." Important as that sounded, her status did little to diminish the fact that she was thousands of miles from home, all but completely removed from the lives of Rob and Timmy, Edda, Lily and Wyatt.

We joked with Anne before she left that she was the one getting the better end of the deal. Rob would be stuck with their kiddos and the various challenges they continued to face as toddlers. After three years of visits from physical, speech and occupational therapists too numerous to count; who knows how many nurse's aides fussing with feeding pumps and tubes; a half dozen or so different nannies scurrying throughout their home at different times; after countless appointments with specialists, emergency room trips at all hours of the day and night, and at least six additional major surgeries, it appeared Anne and Rob were running a health care facility instead of raising a family. Going to Afghanistan might actually feel like a vacation. Staying home, everyone knew, would be no picnic.

Watching Edda and Lily play outside with Donna — the photographer still angling every which way to capture that perfect picture — I am seeing something the camera can never quite catch. The girls are beautiful. Adorable. Little angels. I'll admit my bias, but they are all that and more in my eyes. And why shouldn't they be? They have come through so much. They are both over 30 pounds now, more than *20 times* what they each weighed at birth. We came so close to never knowing them. They are miracles by any measure.

The photo shoot finishes and I come outside to sit on the wooden bridge that crosses our little stream. This is the bridge's fifth iteration — flooding waters have taken it away enough times over the years that I had vowed not to rebuild it again. But I am not so sure about that now. Edda and Lily run to join me, calling, "Papa! Papa!" They have brought sticks, and when they sit beside me they launch them into the water below. "Like little boats — watch them go!" I tell them as the twigs bounce with the current until they disappear downstream.

They are wearing cotton sun dresses with embroidered flowers that the photographer has brought for the shoot. Lily's dress is white; it sets off the creamy olive tone of her skin, the rich chocolate of her hair and the deep brown of her eyes. Her hair is even curlier than Anne's was as a little girl, with the tight ringlets long enough now that they brush against the tops of her shoulders. She is beautiful in the same way that her Aunt Cait is, and in time she will break men's hearts, too. To me she is a Spillane through and through.

Edda's look is not so familiar. Maybe Rob's sisters looked like her when they were young, but Edda and Lily are so dissimilar it seems impossible they are even related. In the azure sundress she is wearing Edda's skin appears so fair it is nearly pallid. Her eyes are piercing, though — a bright blue that seems almost white. Her hair is luminous blonde; the wisps of it so fine it scarcely manages to hold the loose curls that Donna (and a lot of mousse) had tried to fashion for the photographs.

Edda is the bossy one, too, the leader of the pack. She still employs the war cry she honed in the NICU when she does not get her way. Despite their differences, I have little doubt that Edda and Lily will always be sisters in a way that goes deeper than blood. They have come together through something so harrowing I still find the experience nearly inconceivable. I can't help but wonder if they remember their long months together in the NICU, the hours they spent co-bedding in a tiny crib, the glances they stole of each other while one rested on Anne's breast and the other on Rob's. Taken from their mother's womb far before their time, I wonder if the experience didn't also meld them in a way they might never have otherwise. Looking at them each with their legs dangling from the bridge, I know they are a gift. They have brought me fulfillment I never dreamed of.

All is not unicorns and castles in the clouds for Donna and me, however. Taking care of two three-year-olds full time is a lot of work. We are both tired. We now know there's a good reason God made it so people have their children when they're young.

Donna and I had told Anne before she deployed that we would help Rob with their kids. We would keep the girls with us if she wanted. Raising girls? We already had that down. Or we would rotate her children, taking one of the boys with one of the girls and switching them from time to time. We figured we could manage that. But I balked at taking the two boys together. "I don't think your mom and I can survive that," I'd told Anne before adding, "Caring for your sons is exhausting. They're just too much for us to handle."

And that is the amazing thing about Timmy and Wyatt today: more than just a handful, they *are* terrors. How my mom raised five boys who were separated in age by only seven years I'll never know. Granted, I was a contributor to the mayhem, but I don't think I ever knew just how rambunctious little boys can be. And Timmy and Wyatt can be more riotous than I would have ever imagined.

The wonder of it is: who would have thought it possible?

In the first few months after his discharge from the Christus Santa Rosa NICU, Wyatt returned to the hospital first for a shunt revision, then twice more for procedures to implant two additional shunts in his ventricles. The pediatric neurosurgeon thought the need for a fourth shunt was also likely. If Wyatt didn't have brain surgery once every month or so, it seemed, we'd all start to suspect something was *really* wrong with him.

Besides dealing with aggressive hydrocephalus, Wyatt was also diagnosed with cerebral palsy after leaving the NICU. The news was more than disheartening for Anne and Rob; it was maddening. Their little guy had already endured so much. Would there be no end to it? But Wyatt soldiered on. His lungs were gaining strength by the day, and he was gradually weaned from supplemental oxygen. He insisted on being included in whatever his brother and sisters were doing. Though he remained as feisty and prone to angry outbursts as he was when he was in the NICU — a temperament that no doubt served him well — ironically, he was also the quietest of the babies. Wyatt could sit in a swing for hours and hardly move. "He's a keen observer," I told Anne once when she'd wondered aloud what he might be thinking. "He's watching the other three. He'll let them figure things out first and he'll learn from their mistakes."

And that's exactly how he got me into trouble.

A month before their first birthday Edda and Lily were able to sit up by themselves. It was a big developmental milestone for the girls, but it would be a huge one for the boys. The babies were all blessed to have Heather, a fabulous and gifted physical therapist, to work with them, but Wyatt was her special project. "He's been watching his sisters sit for a month," Heather said of Wyatt, "and now that Timmy's almost sitting, he's going to want to, as well." To help Wyatt build core strength and balance she started him doing an exercise she called bench-sitting.

I flew out in late April to join Donna and Cait for the babies' dedication ceremony at Dave Smith's church. When we gathered together in Anne and Rob's living room the evening before, the four babies playing on the floor at our feet, Rob couldn't wait to show me the progress Heather had been making with Wyatt. He grabbed the little bench she used and picked his son up. "Watch this!" he said excitedly and placed Wyatt square in the seat in front of me. For a moment the tiny boy sat upright in the thing, his eyes focused straight ahead. "Keep a watch on him," Rob cautioned as he sat down in an easy chair several feet away before proudly adding, "He's getting really good at this."

And then the doorbell rang. I lifted my eyes for a second to look toward the door and as I did Wyatt turned, too. The next sound was an awful thud as his head hit an IV pole's hard plastic foot. In the instant of silence that followed I could hear the collective gasp of everyone in the room, and in the next Wyatt's gut wrenching shrieks filling the air.

I think Rob wanted to eviscerate me. He might very well have if his son weren't so resilient. In ten minutes Wyatt was all smiles.

"The boys are pretty much indestructible," Anne said.

"He might have a black eye when we bring him to church tomorrow," Donna pointed out.

"Child Protection Services is going to hear about this," Cait said impishly.

"Grandparent abuse," I agreed.

"Maybe a good knock on the head is exactly what he needs," Anne suggested. "It's not like there's much more that can go wrong for him up there," she said, tapping his forehead before kissing him above his eye.

Though I appreciated the sentiment, I didn't give Anne's notion much thought. The funny thing is, maybe she *was* right. Wyatt hasn't had brain surgery since.

Who knows what the brain is really capable of, anyway? If a knock on the head was a help to Wyatt, maybe Timmy's brain could just figure a way to rewire itself. From the time he first came home from the NICU it seemed as if it had begun doing exactly that.

Timmy was the first of the babies to grab (*and* hold and hit and throw) his toys; the first one to clap his hands; the first to play peek-a-boo, lifting his hands to his face, covering his eyes, then dropping them into his lap with a smile when we asked, "Where's Timmy?" He began to sit up by himself only weeks after his sisters. But there would be bumps in the road, too.

Though ecstatic Timmy was able to sit, Heather noticed he had significant problems with balance. She told Anne and Rob not to worry, but by September she could not hide her own growing concerns. The babies were by that time nearly a year and a half old. Edda had been crawling since the beginning of summer; Lily followed her lead within a week and by Labor Day, Wyatt was off to the races, too. But Timmy's progress had reached a plateau. He wasn't crawling. Our hopes that he would walk someday were fading. "There's a wonderful neurologist downtown," Heather told Anne and Rob. "He's awesome with children and has been in practice for years. I don't think there's much the man hasn't seen." She arranged for Timmy to see him.

Donna described the doctor as tall and dapper with a kind face and outgoing demeanor. "He came into the room with a beaming smile," she recalled, "stretched out his hand and announced that he was Dr. Rodriquez here to meet Mr. Timothy Schlender! He barely took his eyes off Timmy while he got the full patient history from us, everything about Anne's pregnancy, asked about the other babies — wanted to know all about them, too — and without missing a beat conducted a thorough physical exam of his little patient. He was amazing. I think Timmy was mesmerized by him."

Dr. Rodriquez left the room after Anne gave him a CD of the brain scan done on Timmy prior to his discharge from Wilford Hall. "Five, maybe ten minutes — he wasn't gone long," Donna continued. "When he came back he went directly to Timmy and sat in front of him on one of those little stools doctors use. He lifted Timmy's hands with his own and just stared at him; didn't say anything. He finally swung around to face Anne and Rob and said he wasn't sure he'd ever met anyone quite like their son. He said something about how the brain hemorrhages he'd suffered were profound, how they involved the brain stem, and how severe the secondary complications were. He stopped then and turned toward Timmy and smiled. 'Frankly, I'm not sure what to say. Babies don't survive the kind of injuries to the brain your son has. Who am I to put any limits on what he might do in the future?'"

In Rob's words, after the visit to Dr. Rodriquez, it was "Game on!" for Timmy. No one confused the neurologist's assessment of Timmy with unbridled optimism for his future, but it did help to set some clear goals for Heather, Anne and Rob. In his office on that first visit Dr. Rodriquez noted Timmy's *central tone* was clearly below average. He did not think the boy would walk until he was four or five, perhaps not at all. Verbalization would be a significant challenge. It was probable that his mental status would be below average. Timmy might never be *educable* he told Anne and Rob. But he also reiterated that given the progress their son had made in light of his injury, it was really premature to generate *any* assumptions about what Timmy would or would not do. He invited them to come and see him again in six months.

The following spring they did. With mom and dad in tow, Timmy walked into the doctor's office, pointed to the toy in his left hand and said, "Big truck!"

Dr. Rodriquez just looked at the little boy in front of him. And then he dropped his head and began to cry.

We will return to Enchanted Rock State Park someday, and when we do we will bring the children back with us to the bulbous pink outcroppings of granite as I promised Anne we would. It will be a sight to behold. Wonderful, glorious and sheer bedlam. Timmy will run up the trail first, his long legs trying to carry him faster than his balance will allow. He will fall finally, winded and laughing. Edda, in hot pursuit, will try to jump over him but to no avail. Knock kneed and stubby, hers legs are hardly a hurdler's. She will end up on top of Timmy. Lily will wonder where Edda went. Having lost sight of her sister who an instant before was only a step in front of her, in the next she will trip and join the chaos of limbs on the ground. It will be up to Wyatt to rescue them. But there is no hope of that. Catching his brother and sisters at last, Wyatt will roar with pleasure. He will spread his arms wide, smile with delight and then let the full weight of his barrel-chested torso collapse on top of them. And they will all laugh.

We will eat fresh summer peaches in Fredericksburg after we've left the park. Timmy, Edda, Lily and Wyatt will sleep in the car as we drive. Before long, Anne will fall silent, too, and as she does I will gently pull the large, cool drink from her loosening grip and let her hand slide into her lap. Though we will be back in San Antonio in an hour the journey bringing us here has been so much longer. Looking at her face as she sleeps, I will wish I could have spared my daughter so much of the pain. But that has never really been my job. Instead, I will give thanks quietly and recall again the Psalmist's prayer:

When my heart is overwhelmed
Lead me to the rock that is higher than I.

Come what may, I will never lose sight of the miracles. Timmy, Edda, Lily and Wyatt make sure of that. Though each of their lives remains an unfolding miracle, the journey forward is a hard one. Consequently, resilience still rules the day and it will have to for a long, long time. Surviving the NICU did not diminish the challenges Anne and Rob's children face going forward. They are all developmentally delayed in almost every measureable way. They lack the physical coordination and dexterity, the language and social skills that most of their peers have attained so easily, but really — who *are* their peers? And if it's taken longer to potty train their children than yours, is that really the end of the world?

Each of the quads has chronic lung disease and asthma. They've all struggled with severe eating disorders. The list could go on and on, but in spite of the hardships, we continue to cling to hope. Over the last three years Donna and I have become close friends of Nick and Jenn Hall, the founders of Graham's Foundation. They had every reason to give up hope after losing their son. They chose to be resilient instead. And because of their decision to do so, the measure of Graham's life — all 45 days of it — continues to grow. The legacy of a little boy who never left the NICU now reaches across this country. Like us, so many families of premature babies facing a fearful future are now finding hope renewed because of him. That is a miracle, too.

It is a poignant moment, bittersweet yet triumphant. We've been trying to get a picture of Anne with her kiddos before she deploys but it has been impossible. The day before, we'd piled into the minivan to drive to an appointment at a portrait studio only to discover the photographer was overbooked. Disappointed but undaunted, we decided that we'd try to take pictures ourselves back home. That proved mostly futile. Getting four three-years-olds to sit still together, face the camera and smile is like — the Irish have a phrase for it: "minding mice at a crossroads." If Timmy was looking in one direction, Wyatt was trying to scramble away in the other. If Edda didn't have her hand in her mouth, she had her fingers in Lily's ears. And that was with Anne and Rob wrestling *together* to corral their children. Frustrated, we gave up without even trying for a picture of Anne alone with her four children.

Hope springs eternal, however. With quadruplets, it has to, and there is one last chance to get the photograph we want.

The day Anne leaves for her deployment to Afghanistan, it is beautiful outside. She and Rob have decided to drive to the airport alone. Anne is afraid bringing her kiddos will be too emotional for everybody. So she will say good-bye to them in the front yard, jump into her Mini Cooper with her husband and try to save her tears for later.

Waiting outside, Timmy and Wyatt are in blue shorts, tees and sneakers. We have promised to take them to the park to play after Mommy is gone. But the girls have insisted on dressing up. They are in floral print dresses and bright sweaters. Edda has a pink bow in her hair and Lily red barrettes. We have given the children little American flags to wave when Mommy's leaves.

Anne is wearing her camouflaged Army combat uniform when she comes outside. She stops at the edge of the front stoop just beneath an American flag. The kids rush to her, laughing and shouting, "Mommy!" I am angling for a picture and motion to Anne. She lifts Lily up in her arms to hug her and as she does a low flying jet crosses the sky above. The unexpected distraction momentarily freezes them, and in that instant, with Lily and Edda raising their little flags skyward, Timmy holding his fist forward and Anne and Wyatt still looking at the camera, I have the picture we'd all been hoping to get.

Though Donna and I will hold back tears when we look at the photo in the coming months, we'll also smile as we recognize the triumph that it captures. The picture *is* the miracle. We have our daughter, and Anne and Rob have their children. It is no small irony either that Anne's separation from her kiddos gives us pause to truly appreciate how far they've all come.

Timmy, Edda, Lily and Wyatt were taken from the security of their mother's womb — four before their time — long before they had much chance to survive. But more than just survive, they have thrived. Prematurity deprived Anne of giving her babies so much. What she was able to give them, though, I know now they will never lose. I see it plain as day in the picture. About to be separated from their mother again, they each cling to the gift she has given them. They possess the hope to carry on whatever may come. That has made all the difference in the world.

I have gained something, too. During a time in my life when my own faith was waning, my family and I were brought through circumstances I would not wish on anyone. But neither would I trade them for the world. I have learned never to let go of hope. I have been witness to the kind of resilience that until Timmy, Edda, Lily and Wyatt came along I never believed was possible. Through them I have been given faith back again. And because of that I received the greatest gift of all. I have found the miracle of love renewed.

AUTHOR BIOGRAPHY

Tim and his wife live in Chester County, PA and are the parents of three daughters. They became grandparents when their daughter, Anne delivered quadruplets in April, 2010. A graduate of Colorado College (1979) with a degree in English Literature, Tim returned to school to earn his Masters of Public Health from Drexel University in 2005. He has worked in residential construction for more than three decades but is now focusing full-time on his writing. He currently serves on the executive board of Graham's Foundation, an organization for parents and families going through the journey of prematurity.

ACKNOWLEDGMENTS

Writing *Four Before Their Time* has been a collaborative effort and I am deeply grateful to the many people who have helped me. Katie Hays and Danielle Dubois Barney were early readers and their feedback was invaluable. My nephew, Jordan Spillane was an endless source of encouragement as I struggled with my doubts about the project. Sally Reece provided some much-needed polish to the nearly finished manuscript. And throughout, my editor Christa Terry patiently guided me through revision after revision and rewrite after rewrite until we finally had the story we wanted.

Recognition of a different sort is due the many doctors, nurses, specialists, technicians and support staffs of the NICUs where Timmy, Edda, Lily and Wyatt spent the first months of their lives. The critical care nurseries at Wilford Hall (now located at Brooke Army Medical Center) and Christus Santa Rosa are extraordinary facilities. The dedicated, compassionate service of the teams who work in them is a wonder to behold. These people deserve boundless praise and unbridled appreciation for all they do. They are true heroes.

Finally, this story is about family and I have been blessed with a wonderful one. They are a gift and I am forever grateful to my savior, Jesus, for them. Thanks to my daughter Anne and her husband Rob for being willing to share their difficult journey with others. Your grace in the face of such hardship has been truly astounding. I will always be grateful to Anne's sisters, Erin and Cait for being so selfless over the course of the last few years. Through good times and bad, through the many months when it must have seemed I hadn't time for either of you, both of you remained steadfast and always there for me. And to my wife, Donna — well, what can I say but that you have filled my world with love. Your strength under pressure never ceases to amaze me. I am humbled having you and our daughters in my life.

CPSIA information can be obtained at www.ICGtesting.com
Printed in the USA
BVOW05s2216280814

364589BV00002B/14/P

9 780990 352303